owing,

TEMPORARY WORKS

their role in construction

TEMPORARY WORKS

their role in construction

J. R. ILLINGWORTH, BSc, FCIOB

TI Thomas Telford, London, 1987

Published by Thomas Telford Ltd, Thomas Telford House, 1 Heron Quay, London E14 9XF

First published 1987

British Library Cataloguing in Publication Data
Illingworth, J. R.
    Temporary works: their role in construction
    1. Temporary structures (Building)
    I. Title
    624.1   TH5280

ISBN: 0 7277 0393 5

Set by Santype International Limited, Salisbury, Wiltshire.
Printed and bound in Great Britain by Redwood Burn Ltd, Trowbridge, Wiltshire

Acknowledgements

The author wishes to express his grateful thanks to the following for permission to use material from their publications and literature: the Controller of Her Majesty's Stationery Office and the Health and Safety Executive for the terms of reference of the Bragg Committee (in chapter 9); the British Standards Institution for extracts from BS 5975 : 1982 (in chapter 9) (complete copies can be obtained from BSI at Linford Wood, Milton Keynes, MK14 6LE); British Rail; BSP International Foundations Ltd; Building Employers Confederation; Liebherr–Great Britain Ltd; Lilley Construction Ltd; London Regional Transport; National Association of Scaffolding Contractors; D. Neal; Stent Foundations Ltd.

The author also wishes to express his gratitude to the following organisations and individuals for permission to publish photographs, diagrams and tables as individually acknowledged in the text: ACE Machinery Ltd; Benford Ltd; British Insulated Callenders Cables; British Rail, Eastern Region; BSP International Foundations Ltd; Building Advisory Service and Building Employers Confederation; Cementation Piling and Foundations Ltd; Coles Cranes Ltd; Department of the Environment and Transport, Eastern Region; Howard Doris Ltd; Freeman Fox Ltd; GKN Kwikform Ltd and Jayville Engineering Ltd; A. J. Goldsmith; Sir William Halcrow & Partners; Highland Fabricators; John Howard and Co. Ltd; ICI Agricultural Division; ICI Petrochemicals; Donald I. Innes; Kwikform Ltd; John Laing Construction Ltd; Liebherr–Great Britain Ltd; Lilley Construction Ltd; Sir Robert McAlpine & Sons Ltd; Mechplant Ltd; J. Mustajew; Rapid Metal Developments Ltd; RDL–Graham Joint Venture; Scaffolding (Great Britain) Ltd; Scaffolding (Great Britain) Ltd, distributors of Krings Linings; Scanform, Denmark; F. W. Schwing GmbH through their UK distributors Burlington Engineers Ltd; G. W. Sparrow and Sons Ltd; Stelmo Ltd; Stent Foundations Ltd; Successors to Acrow Engineers Ltd; Swift Plant Hire; Tarmac Construction, National Contracts; Trollope and Colls Ltd; S. Wernick and Sons Ltd; Wickham Engineering Ltd; George Wimpey plc; Wimpey Laboratories Ltd.

Preface

Ask anyone in the construction industry what is meant by temporary works and the chances are that the answer given will be something like, 'Oh! formwork and falsework; holding up excavations—that sort of thing.' On further enquiry, mention may be made of crane tracks and static bases. It is highly unlikely that any mention will be made of scaffolding—yet scaffolding is the most commonly used item of temporary works in the construction field. So common, in fact, that it tends to be taken for granted and is often not seen as temporary works at all.

Whether or not the above statements are true, many people in the construction industry remain woefully ignorant about the scope of temporary works, the important role they play in the construction process and the significance of their cost as a component of the overall cost of a project. Those who design have traditionally regarded temporary works as no concern of theirs, and all the present forms of contract in use reflect this view. It is only in recent years that temporary works have been recognised, in some quarters at least, as an important part of construction: making a significant contribution to the speed and efficiency of construction, as well as the quality of the finished product.

It has been my view for many years that temporary works deserve a better standing. As the structures being built have become more complex, so the temporary works needed for their realisation have needed greater skill from those responsible for their design and execution. At the same time, advances in permanent works design have often only been possible if new ideas in temporary works could provide solutions to their erection. Or, indeed, temporary and permanent works could be combined into a single design–erect entity.

In today's world, therefore, temporary works can be seen as the interface between design and construction. It is also not invalid to assert that, at times, the design of temporary works can be more challenging than that of the permanent works.

In writing this book my objectives have been threefold:

(a) to present temporary works as they deserve—as challenging and worthwhile areas of the construction field—whether in relation to their design or in solving the problems presented by the requirements of the permanent works; at all times emphasising the need to be cost-conscious (*b*) to fill significant gaps in relation to methods and provide ideas and solutions in the less well known areas of temporary works

(*c*) to draw together all the parties involved in the construction process, emphasising the major benefits that can arise from the design–construct team working to achieve the most cost-beneficial result, in overall terms.

To achieve my objectives has involved the assistance of many organisations, companies and individuals. The willingness of such parties to assist has been exceptional and I would like them to know how much I appreciate the trouble they have gone to on my behalf. They are individually acknowledged elsewhere.

If I have been successful in giving temporary works a better status then they have previously enjoyed, and communicated something of the challenge and satisfaction that they have given me over many years, I will feel that the effort has been very worthwhile.

J. R. Illingworth
London 1986

Contents

1 Introduction 1

2 Contractual, legal and code requirements 10

3 Cost and the construction team 19

4 The effect of the site and its boundaries 27

5 Plant-associated temporary works 44

6 Scaffolding 77

7 Support of excavations 103

8 Use of permanent works as temporary support of excavations 137

9 Falsework 165

10 Formwork 195

11 Erection of structural frames 220

12 Miscellaneous temporary works 241

13 The site set-up 260

References and further reading 276

Index 281

1

Introduction

All construction, to a greater or lesser degree, will involve the need for temporary works. While certain items of temporary works receive a good deal of publicity (notably falsework when a spectacular collapse occurs), the wide scope of temporary works is often not realised.

Temporary works can be defined as 'any temporary construction that may be necessary to allow the permanent works to be carried out'. Such temporary works will normally be removed from the site upon completion of their usefulness. There are, however, circumstances where they may be left behind as part of the permanent structure; permanent formwork being a case in point.

From this definition, a moment's thought will recognise that the range of activities included within the definition is very wide. Indeed, they range from quite minor matters to structures of great complexity and large scale, requiring great skill in their design and execution.

One of the simplest activities is the laying of sleepers to provide a temporary crossing of a railway line or pavement, to establish access into a construction site (Fig. 1.1). At the other end of the scale, perhaps the most spectacular example is the design and construction of the flotation collar for a North Sea oil jacket. With this method, the jacket is built on its side, resting on the flotation collar and securely anchored to it. When complete, the jacket is towed out to its resting place supported by the flotation collar. On arrival at the desired location, the whole assembly is made to turn to an upright position by systematic flooding of parts of the structure. At the critical moment, when this operation is under way, the jacket and the flotation collar are made to part company from each other, by explosives. The collar is then towed back to the fabrication yard and used again for the next jacket. Although this method of construction is outmoded today, it is an excellent example of a highly sophisticated type of temporary works. The need for the integration of the design of such a structure with the structure that it will have to carry is all too apparent. The sheer scale of the collar is well illustrated in Fig. 1.2. The length is some 200 m; the width at the widest end (carrying the base of the jacket) is in the order of 75 m. The anchorage points for the jacket members that will sit on the flotation collar are visible as circular elements sitting on top of the collar. They are shown in detail in Fig. 1.3. The arrangement whereby the split collar is locked on to the jacket unit

Fig. 1.1. Temporary sleeper crossing to railway line to provide access for muck-shifting vehicles

Fig. 1.2. Flotation collar for Forties Field jacket (Highland Fabricators Ltd)

Fig. 1.3. Flotation collar release mechanism (Highland Fabricators Ltd)

Fig. 1.4. Repetitive beam forms for ground beams

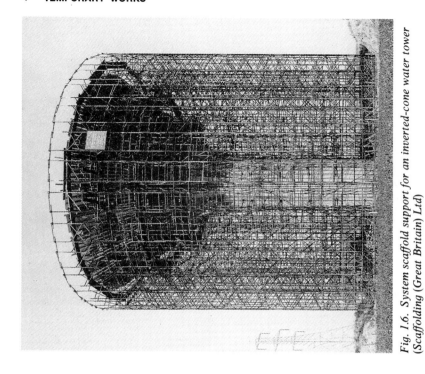

Fig. 1.6. System scaffold support for an inverted-cone water tower (Scaffolding (Great Britain) Ltd)

Fig. 1.5. Major single-sided support for an excavation

Fig. 1.8. Cable spinning on the Humber Bridge (photo Donald I. Innes; consulting engineers Freeman Fox Ltd)

Fig. 1.7. Scaffolding to 28-storey office building; solely for safe working places for installation of services in an external duct, and glazing (George Wimpey plc)

can be seen, together with the arms which hold the collar. On release, the collar sections are blown upwards and outwards, rotating on the shafts at the end of the arms.

Between these extremes come a diverse range of temporary works activities: falsework and formwork; support of excavations; scaffolding; temporary works related to the operation of plant; site access; the provision of site accommodation, and a wide range of specialised items particular to individual circumstances. The list is almost endless. Figure 1.4 illustrates simple repetitive formwork for ground beams, while Fig. 1.5 is indicative of a much more complex situation—a major support of an excavation.

SIGNIFICANCE OF TEMPORARY WORKS

Temporary works represent an area of considerable significance within the construction process as a whole, and they can be a major cost factor in the contract price. For example, in a bridge structure in in situ concrete, with a complex cantilever soffit outside the column line, the falsework and formwork accounted for 62% of the bridge cost. Admittedly, the falsework was 14 m high and only one use existed, but the case serves to make the point that temporary works can be the major cost item on some occasions. Figure 1.6 makes the point about the cost of temporary works in relation to a water tower. Clearly the scaffolding is a major component. In human terms, temporary works play a major part in ensuring that the final result is achieved safely. Indeed, many temporary works are only there to provide a safe place of work (Fig. 1.7).

As construction technology advances, in some fields of design it becomes necessary to integrate the temporary works with the design of the permanent works. In other words, the realisation of the permanent works design can only be achieved if there is a temporary works method that can make it possible. For example, the construction of a long span suspension bridge can only happen in practice because a technique exists that enables the catenary cables to be spun in place (Fig. 1.8). The spinning gear, temporary walkways and link access bridges are all sophisticated examples of aerial temporary works. The falsework to the approach viaduct makes an interesting comparison (Fig. 1.9).

There is a growing use of integrated design–construct situations. At present these are mainly confined to bridge construction and in the major support of excavations. Examples are given in later chapters.

From the above, three conclusions can be drawn in relation to the role played by temporary works:

(a) They represent the interface between design and construction.
(b) They are a key factor in achieving the desired result safely and with the best cost benefit to the client.
(c) Their design and method solution are often more challenging than that for the permanent works. Alternatively, the permanent works design must be carried out recognising the method of construction that will be adopted.

Fig. 1.9. Humber Bridge: falsework to approach viaduct using PAL system support (now known as Triframe supporting deck) (Scaffolding (Great Britain) Ltd)

INTERFACE BETWEEN DESIGN AND CONSTRUCTION

Today, design has become highly sophisticated, using all the marvels of the micro-chip. In the teaching of such design this is especially so, yet how often is any real consideration given to whether the result is buildable? Or, if buildable, is it the most cost-effective solution overall? For example, if the design is always aiming at reducing the material content to save money and weight, are such savings creating additional cost elsewhere? And do these additional costs add up to more than the savings in materials? If the answer is yes, the overall result will be more expensive and the material savings pointless. Such examples frequently arise where savings in material content create excessive cost in the temporary works.

A number of current construction methods lend themselves to the integration of temporary works with the permanent works. Such techniques as diaphragm walling, contiguous bored piles and secant piling lend themselves to a dual role; first acting as temporary support and eventually becoming part of the permanent structure. In this way considerable savings in temporary works cost can be made. For such savings to be effective, close co-operation between the designer and the contractor's temporary works engineer is necessary. Alternatively, the designer needs to have the necessary experience in the temporary works field to appreciate the savings possible if his design is capable of a dual role. The above examples and others are dealt with in detail in later chapters.

CHALLENGING DESIGN

At first sight it may seem presumptuous to claim that the design of temporary works is more challenging than that for permanent works. It certainly is not always so, of course, but many instances arise where the statement is undoubtedly true. The design of the flotation collar for a North Sea oil jacket, mentioned earlier, requires not only the ability to determine the many stresses involved, but also the capability to ensure the separation of the collar from the jacket while the jacket is tilting and sinking.

In falsework for in situ concrete structures, the designer must recognise and allow for the fact that the loads on the falsework will be varying as the pour proceeds; even to the extent of moment changes, span by span. Post-tensioned, in situ structures will provide a uniformly distributed load initially, but this will change to a load at each end of the falsework when the tensioning takes place.

In the support of excavations, assumptions concerning earth pressures can rarely be made with absolute certainty. Experience and engineering judgement play an important part in this type of work. Additionally, the designer of the support must assess the implications of his solution on the methods envisaged for erection of the permanent structure. Do they harmonise? Can the support solution be adapted to become part of the permanent work? Will the Engineer agree?

DESIGN FOR SAFE ERECTION

The Engineer is also being forced to take a greater interest in temporary works by the publication of the Health and Safety Executive's Guidance Note GS 28, *Safe erection of structures*.[1] Part 1 requires the designer to consider whether his design is capable of safe erection. Paragraph 6 states: 'Planning for safe erection can, and should, start at the initial design stage with designers taking into account the need for, and the practicability of, safe methods of working during erection.' Part 1 goes on to explore in detail the ways in which the designer can contribute to making the erection of his design a safe operation.

Part 2 of this guidance note deals with site management and procedures. This section is of importance to both the site manager and the temporary works engineer; the site manager in relation to the organisation and control of the work, and the temporary works engineer for the design of such temporary works as may be necessary to achieve safe places of work and any temporary supports that may be needed to maintain the stability of the structure as construction proceeds.

Part 3 of the guidance note covers the requirements for safe working places and access, while part 4 deals with legislation and training.

The chapters that follow examine the whole spectrum of temporary works as they apply to both civil engineering and building works. It should become abundantly clear, as the chapters unfold, that temporary works and the methods of construction are inextricably tied together; this contrasts with the permanent works design, which in many areas is carried out in isolation, without any thought given to the method by which the structure will be constructed. Because of this situation, it tends to be a truism that those who make the best temporary works designers are those who have a wide experience of construction in the field.

EDUCATION AND TRAINING

With the exceptions of the essential integration of design–construct schemes, and situations where permanent works are initially utilised as temporary works, academic and professional bodies have, in the past, tended to neglect the subject of temporary works. It is only recently that more attention has been paid to the subject, and encouragement given to making sure that the student's design is, in fact, capable of being built. It is also becoming recognised that unless a design is practicable from a construction point of view, the resultant quality is likely to suffer, as well as the cost to the client.

Criticism of the teaching bodies and their lack of time spent on temporary works makes no sense if the material from which to teach is lacking. Too many people with the knowledge and experience at the practical end never record their knowledge. One objective of this book is to try to rectify this situation by providing a wide range of practical know-how for the successful and cost-effective realisation of temporary works.

It is to be hoped that the contents will also prove to be of value to those who plan, estimate and design temporary works, as a source of ideas and information, to enable solutions to temporary works problems to be cost-effective as well as providing good quality in the final result.

2

Contractual, legal and code requirements

FORMS OF CONTRACT FOR USE IN THE UK

Three main forms of contract are in use in the UK. These are the Standard Form of Building Contract, prepared by the Joint Contracts Tribunal and known as JCT 80 (the current edition (1980) replaced that of 1977, which was a revision of the 1963 edition); the Institution of Civil Engineers' form of contract for civil engineering works; and form GC/Works/1, General Conditions of Government Contracts for Building and Civil Engineering Works. In all these forms of contract, the responsibility for the temporary works rests with the contractor, and he is required to make all due allowance for them in his tender. It is important, therefore, that the requirements of the contract are properly understood.

Standard Form of Building Contract (JCT 80)

JCT 80 is the usual form of contract for building works, except as noted under GC/Works/1 below. The Joint Contracts Tribunal is responsible for its preparation and revision as necessary. (The JCT comprises the Royal Institute of British Architects, The Building Employers Confederation, The Federation of Associations of Specialists and Sub-Contractors, and the Committee of Associations of Specialist Engineering Contractors.) The contract is often erroneously known as the RIBA form of contract.

Temporary works as such are not mentioned in the contract. The responsibility for them is implied only in clause 2.1, which contains the basic obligation for the contractor to carry out and complete the works in accordance with the contract documents. It is assumed that in carrying out and completing the works, the contractor will provide such plant, equipment and temporary works as may be necessary to achieve that end.

ICE form of contract (5th edition, revised 1979, reprinted 1986)

By contrast, the ICE form of contract has a great deal to say about temporary works. In clause 1 (1) a rather bad definition is given: ' " Temporary Works " means all temporary works of every kind required in or about the construction completion and maintenance of the Works '. More specifically, clause 8 spells out quite clearly the contractor's responsibility for temporary works.

'8. (1) The Contractor shall subject to the provisions of the Contract construct complete and maintain the Works and provide all labour materials Constructional Plant Temporary Works transport to and from and in or about the Site and everything whether of a temporary or permanent nature required in and for such construction completion and maintenance so far as the necessity for providing the same is specified in or reasonably to be inferred from the Contract.

(2) The Contractor shall take full responsibility for the adequacy stability and safety of all site operations and methods of construction provided that the Contractor shall not be responsible for the design or specification of the Permanent Works (except as may be expressly provided in the Contract) or of any Temporary Works designed by the Engineer.'

Where major road works are carried out for the Department of Transport, the Department's conditions of contract modify the ICE form (5th edition) in respect of temporary works by adding a clause 8A. This additional clause requires the contractor to submit to the Engineer a certificate signed by an engineer of suitable qualifications and experience prior to commencing any relevant temporary works. The certificate is to certify that any erection proposals and temporary works details are satisfactory for the purpose for which they are intended. The person signing the certificate must not have been involved with the design or detailing of the temporary works under review.

The above is necessarily only a summary of the contract clauses. For any temporary works on Department of Transport work, the full conditions of contract and the full text of clause 8A need to be consulted, as amendments do occur from time to time.

The way in which individual contractors deal with the question of who is to be responsible for obtaining approval has to be left to the firms in question. What is important is that a system exists to ensure that no doubt arises as to who that person will be. Failure in this respect can cause a good deal of trouble and delay.

In general terms, it is desirable that site managements are made responsible. They are best placed in relation to timescale and ensuring that construction is carried out in accordance with the approved drawings. Where bridges or other structures are subcontracted either for erection or for design and erection, the site management team is still best placed to ensure that all the required procedures have been complied with.

Form GC/Works/1—General Conditions of Government Contracts for Building and Civil Engineering Works

In GC/Works/1, clause 2 (1) states: 'The Contractor shall be deemed to have satisfied himself . . . of the risk of injury or damage to property adjacent to the Site . . . the nature of the materials to be excavated, the conditions in which the Works will have to be carried out . . .'.

Clause 26 (1) is quite clear in stating: 'All things not for incorporation which are on the Site and are provided by or on behalf of the Contractor for the construction of the Works shall stand at the risk and be in the sole charge of the Contractor . . .'. This clause, while not specifically saying so, includes all temporary works as well as the contractor's plant, and clearly puts the onus on the contractor.

In spite of the above two clauses, clause 7, which deals with the powers of the Superintending Officer, has this to say: 'The Contractor shall carry out and complete the execution of the Works to the satisfaction of the SO'. While this is no different from the duties under the other forms of contract, clause 7, in stating the SO's powers to issue instructions etc. includes (7 (1) (m)) 'Any other matter as to which it is necessary or expedient for the SO to issue instructions, directions or explanations'. Experience has shown that this part of clause 7 can be used by the SO, if he considers it expedient, to override a contractor's decision in relation to temporary works. A great deal of confusion can be caused when clause 7 is invoked in this way, as clause 26 still makes the contractor responsible!

Case study

A contractor working under GC/Works/1 presented a scheme for the upholding of a major excavation. The SO disagreed and used his powers to make the contractor use a different method. The contractor, in writing, pointed out that the method proposed was unsuitable for the ground conditions and refused to accept responsibility for the SO's instructions. In the event, the SO's method was installed and some time later failed—resulting in an adjacent building being split from top to bottom. Argument ensued for some six months before the contractor was paid for the repairs to the adjoining property. Even then, it was only an *ex gratia* payment.

FORM OF CONTRACT FOR OVERSEAS CIVIL ENGINEERING WORK

In overseas civil engineering work, the form of contract most commonly used is Conditions of Contract (International) for Works of Civil Engineering Construction (third edition, 1977), prepared by the Fédération Internationale des Ingénieurs-Conseils. This document is more commonly known as the FIDIC contract.

FIDIC form of contract

Temporary works are referred to in a number of clauses. Clause 8 (1) states: 'The Contractor shall . . . provide all labour, . . . materials, Construction Plant and all other things, whether of a temporary or permanent nature, required in and for such execution and maintenance, so far as the necessity for providing the same is specified in or is reasonably to be inferred from the Contract.'

Clause 8 (2) enlarges upon the above: 'The Contractor shall take full responsibility for the adequacy stability and safety of all site operations and methods of construction, provided that the Contractor shall not be responsible, except as may be expressly provided in the Contract, . . . for the design or specification of any Temporary Works prepared by the Engineer.'

Sections 53 to 54 specifically deal with plant, temporary works and materials. Clause 53 (1) states: 'All Construction Plant, Temporary Works and materials provided by the Contractor shall, when brought onto the Site, be deemed to be exclusively intended for the execution of the Works . . .'. Clause 53 (2) states: 'Upon completion of the Works the Contractor shall remove from the Site all the said Construction Plant and Temporary Works remaining thereon . . .'. Clause 53 (3) states: 'The Employer shall not at any time be liable for the loss or damage to any of the said Construction Plant, Temporary Works or materials . . .'.

It is clear from the above that the responsibility for temporary works rests entirely with the contractor, except in so far as any temporary works designed by the Engineer are concerned. As with the ICE form of contract, it specifically recognises that the Engineer may get involved in the design of temporary works. If he does, the responsibility rests with him.

MAIN ACTS AND REGULATIONS

Once the implications of the contract are understood, the same attention needs to be given to all legislation that may have an impact on temporary works. The bulk of the legislation in this respect relates to safe working practices and the safety of operatives. The main legislation related to temporary works is as follows: Health and Safety at Work etc. Act 1974; Control of Pollution Act 1974, sections 60 and 61; and construction regulations—specifically, The Construction (General Provisions) Regulations 1961, The Construction (Working Places) Regulations 1966, The Construction (Lifting Operations) Regulations 1961, The Construction (Health and Welfare) Regulations 1966, and Fire Certificates (Special Premises) Regulations 1976.

Health and Safety at Work etc. Act 1974

The preamble to the Health and Safety at Work etc. Act states that this is 'An Act to make further provision for securing the health, safety and welfare of persons at work, for protecting others against risks to health or safety in connection with the activities of persons at work, for controlling the keeping and use and preventing the unlawful acquisition, possession and use of dangerous substances, and for controlling certain emissions into the atmosphere; to make further provision with respect to the employment medical advisory service; to amend the law relating to building regulations, and the Building (Scotland) Act 1959; and for connected purposes.' This Act is the head legislation in relation to the requirements for safeguarding the health, safety and welfare of all employed persons. Its requirements have to be complied with, whatever the activity involved.

Control of Pollution Act 1974

Section 60 of the Control of Pollution Act deals with the control of noise on construction sites. Under this section, local authorities have power to publish notice of their requirements to avoid nuisance to others. They may specify, first, plant which may or may not be used; secondly, the hours during which the works may be carried out; and thirdly, the level of noise coming from the premises or any specified point on the premises. Clearly this can be of considerable significance if noisy methods of work are contemplated (e.g. the driving of sheet piling). (Today it is usually obligatory to use driving enclosures. The cost of such extra equipment must be allowed for.)

Section 61 covers the way in which prior consent can be negotiated.

The importance of this Act in relation to methods adopted or proposed for, in particular, the support of excavations will be only too apparent.

Construction regulations

In view of the special hazards inherent in the construction process, specific regulations have to be complied with. These regulations are applicable equally to works of civil engineering construction and to building operations. Anyone involved in temporary works must be familiar with their contents and must act upon them in appropriate circumstances. While the following is a summary of their content, more detail in respect of these regulations will be given as the need arises in the chapters that follow.

The Construction (General Provisions) Regulations 1961

In the Construction (General Provisions) Regulations the part headings are as follows:

I	Application and interpretation
II	Supervision and safe conduct of work
III	Safety of working places and means of access
IV	Excavations, shafts and tunnels
V	Cofferdams and caissons
VI	Explosives
VII	Dangerous and unhealthy atmospheres
VIII	Work on or adjacent to water
IX	Transport
X	Demolition
XI	Miscellaneous

The Construction (Working Places) Regulations 1966

As the title implies, the working places regulations are primarily concerned with the safety of working places and the access to and egress from them.

The requirements for scaffolds are dealt with in great detail, and the use of ladders and suspended scaffolds of various types. Widths of working platforms, together with the requirements for guard rails and toe boards are specified. Special requirements are laid down for working on sloping roofs and on or near fragile materials. The use of safety harnesses or nets and the circumstances of their use are also included. A form of report is laid down for the recording of inspections as required by regulation 22.

The importance of these regulations in relation to temporary works will be obvious.

The Construction (Lifting Operations) Regulations 1961

Lifting equipment of one sort or another is involved in many aspects of temporary works. The lifting operations regulations cover the following: lifting appliances and the requirements for their safe operation; the provision, testing and safe use of chains, ropes and lifting gear; special provisions as to hoists; limitations on the carriage of persons by means of lifting appliances; the importance of secureness of loads; and the records that have to be kept.

The Construction (Health and Welfare) Regulations 1966

The specific relevance of the health and welfare regulations to temporary works relates to the requirements for shelters for the taking of meals, and the requirements for the storage and drying of clothing, toilet facilities, the provision of washing facilities and the laying on of a water supply.

Fire Certificates (Special Premises) Regulations 1976

The fire certificates regulations give the Health and Safety Executive powers to require that fire certificates be obtained in respect of any premises of a description specified in part I of schedule 1 of the regulations. The regulations also make provision for exemption from the requirement to obtain a fire certificate, provided that specified conditions are satisfied.

Part I of schedule 1 referred to above includes, in § 15, 'Any building, or part of a building, which either—

(a) is constructed for temporary occupation for the purpose of building operations or works of engineering construction; or

(b) is in existence at the first commencement there of any further such operations or works

and which is used for any process or work ancillary to such operations or works.' Any temporary building on a construction site, therefore, requires a fire certificate unless the conditions for exemption can be satisfied. These conditions are listed in part II of schedule 1.

Clearly, the temporary works in relation to site accommodation needs to take account of the conditions set out above.

General

The above Acts and statutory regulations are the key ones in respect of safety requirements. It must be recognised, however, that there are many other Acts and regulations in existence that may impinge on temporary works. It is the responsibility of the temporary works engineer to become acquainted with all legislation which may affect his actions.

RELATED LEGISLATION

The following list of enactments, while not comprehensive, will provide a general guide as to what type of legislation needs to be explored to see if it is relevant to temporary works activities:

(a) GLC General Powers Act 1966; applies to inner London excavations within 30 ft (9 m) of the highway
(b) Highways Acts; take over control of excavations near the highway in places other than inner London
(c) London Building Acts (Amendment) Act 1939; requirement for party wall award when building against an existing building; safety of buildings regulated by this Act; elsewhere in the UK, sections 76–83 of the Building Act 1984 apply
(d) London Government Act 1963; regulates noise, dust and hours of work; outside London, equivalent bylaws apply.

When working in a particular area of the country, it is most advisable to check if the local authorities have any bylaws which may affect or influence the way in which construction work can be carried out. For example, it is always necessary to obtain a licence from the local authority before erecting any kind of hoarding. If it impinges on the pavement, specific requirements are likely concerning provision of pedestrian access in the roadway guarded by suitable barriers. Warning lights for traffic will be required, and possibly illumination of the temporary footway as well.

If a scaffold has to be erected over a pavement, a licence will be needed, and rules are laid down about the protective measures to be incorporated to protect the public.

In the city of Portsmouth, a licence is needed before a tower crane can overswing the public highway. For this an old local bylaw has been invoked which originally was passed to regulate the brackets fixed to warehouses for lifting bales by rope and pulley to the store-rooms above. Apparently, many used to collapse, causing injury to the public below. By requiring a licence, the structural sufficiency could be established.

City of London (St Paul's Cathedral Preservation) Act, 1935

The St Paul's Cathedral Preservation Act specifies an area around the cathedral designed to protect the cathedral from the effects of deep excavation and the extraction of water from the subsoil. The effect of this Act in relation to temporary works is that no excavation or its support is allowed unless approval has been obtained from the Dean and Chapter; and that no pumping or other abstraction of water shall take place without the approval of the Dean and Chapter. The purpose of the legislation is to protect the cathedral from settlement resulting from alteration of the flow of water in the gravel under the cathedral, or from slippage of soil due to excavation. In practice it often means that the support system for an excavation must be such that it does not interfere with water flow in the ground. Sheet piling in the prohibited area, for example, will not usually be allowed.

Roads (Scotland) Act 1970

Clause 26 of the Roads (Scotland) Act is invoked in Scotland if a contractor wishes to swing a tower crane over the public highway. Amongst other things, all the public utility companies have to be notified and asked if they have any objections. The contractor must submit copies of the replies to the local authority, together with a certification that the crane meets the appropriate codes in its design and stability. Until such documentation is provided, approval to overswing will not be given.

Ancient Monuments and Archaeological Areas Act 1979

Under the Ancient Monuments and Archaeological Areas Act, areas of archaeological importance can be designated by the Secretary of State or a local authority. If construction is to take place within such an area, a period of notice has to be given to the local authority concerned, usually by the developer. The local archaeological investigating authority can then apply to enter the site to carry out investigations or excavations.

Of importance to the temporary works engineer is the ability of the investigating authority to monitor progress of the works as they proceed, and, if something of interest comes to light, to stop the works for proper investigation. As the period allowed for excavation is four months and two weeks, any temporary works supporting the excavation may be in place much longer than the temporary works specialist imagined. All experience to date shows that close co-operation with the archaeologist, including the provision of support to his excavations, will minimise delay to the contract.

SAFETY ON SITE

It will be appreciated that the major part of the legislation relating to construction is there to provide for the health, safety and welfare of the workforce on site. It follows just as positively that those who deal with temporary works—as designers, supervisors, suppliers of equipment, or the operatives erecting or dismantling any item of temporary works— have a duty to comply with all the relevant legal requirements that may be involved. In particular, any temporary works department should be in a position to guarantee that any design, drawings or specifications that it may issue comply with the relevant safety requirements of the law.

Safety always needs to be part of the planning and management of a construction site. It is totally inadequate to see safety as the wallpaper covering the cracks after the planning and management decisions have been made. To assist in ensuring that safety is included in all stages of the construction process, the Health and Safety Executive has recently produced Guidance Note GS 28.[1] As mentioned in chapter 1, the designer is now being asked to look more carefully at what he is designing in relation to the safety of its execution.

It is also necessary for the Health and Safety Executive to be informed in any case where demolition is to take place, as such a site becomes a 'place of work'.

Notwithstanding any licence given by the local authority, the Health and Safety Executive may require alterations to be made to any hoarding or site entrance that may provide a hazard to those working on the site. For example, a particular site was divided into two parts by a main road, and operatives had to cross from one side to the other; the Health and Safety Inspector made the contractor alter the hoardings at the entrance to a splayed-inwards configuration, so that anyone crossing had a better view of oncoming traffic.

CODES AND STANDARDS

There are numerous codes and standards which have either direct or indirect relevance to temporary works. They are referred to and referenced in the chapters where they have specific relevance.

3

Cost and the construction team

All temporary works costs are an addition to the basic labour, plant and material costs of the permanent works. In today's world, where competition for work is fierce, contracts can be lost or won by the solutions adopted in relation to the temporary works necessary. It follows that all those involved with temporary works—temporary works engineer, estimator and site management—need to be cost-conscious at all stages in the design, pricing and execution of the work. For this ideal to be realised, the temporary works designer and all others who may be involved need to possess a number of qualities outside those specifically related to design and detailing of the methods to be used. These further qualities can be summarised as follows:

(a) an appreciation of the benefits of standardisation of methods and equipment in temporary works
(b) a good knowledge of construction plant and methods
(c) the ability to assess where cost really lies, and to understand that on occasions spending money may save greater amounts elsewhere; i.e. an outward-looking approach, taking into account the activities of others
(d) minds which can apply a wide-ranging knowledge of construction technology to achieve the most cost-effective solution to a particular problem
(e) the ability to see how the permanent construction might be adapted to minimise temporary works cost.

Construction management is all about making a profit while giving the client the result he desires, in terms of both quality and cost. Temporary works is an important part of the construction process, in terms of both time and cost, and as such must be recognised as an important part of construction management as a whole.

BENEFITS OF STANDARDISATION
Any company, large or small, general or specialised, that is regularly involved in the provision of temporary works will find great benefits in standardising the equipment that it uses—not only in relation to a specific type of work, but also in use over a number of aspects of temporary construction.

Scaffolding

The type of temporary works which is used the most is probably scaffolding. While subletting of all trades tends to be the order of the day, a recent survey has indicated that, as far as building work is concerned, the main contractor still provides the scaffolding in the overwhelming majority of cases. The way in which this is done will vary: the scaffolding may be provided from the main contractor's own resources, or by subletting to a specialist subcontractor. Whatever the approach used, the objective should still be the same: to minimise cost by careful planning of the scaffolding needs, to improve competitiveness, at the tender stage; it being understood that the maintenance of the required standards to comply with the law at all times must be met.

To achieve this desirable situation, it is essential that careful thought is given to the sequence of scaffolding requirements, and the type of scaffolding most suitable for the use in question. Contractors in specialised types of work may well find that a system scaffold, while more expensive initially, is much cheaper in erection and dismantling costs, so that in the long term the cost advantages will be considerable. Others dealing in one-off work may well see better advantage in conventional tube-and-fitting methods. Where system scaffolds are seen to be to the individual's best advantage, the individual contractor must make up his own mind about which one to choose. One example is shown in Fig. 3.1.

In today's highly competitive market, the hire rate from a specialist subcontractor may well be more competitive than a contractor using his own material.

Further points arise in the chapters on scaffolding and falsework (chapters 6 and 9).

Steel sections

The use of steel sections is a frequent requirement in many aspects of temporary works. For economy, consideration of the best way in which to reduce the sections held becomes important. The question of which sections are the most versatile becomes crucial: a particular section that can be used and reused in a variety of applications will significantly contribute to reducing the cost of any individual temporary works requirement.

For example, this approach can be applied by examining the element of temporary works which a firm does most. Let us assume that it is the support of major excavations, and that the method used is the H-piling (soldier piling) method described in chapter 7. For most situations, three sizes of pile will be adequate as a holding (e.g. universal columns $203 \times 203 \times 60$; $254 \times 254 \times 73$ and $305 \times 305 \times 173$). From these three options, it is possible to design a wide range of temporary works, with full recovery on completion for use in another mode later. How this can work in practice is illustrated by the methods described in chapters 5, 7 and 9, in particular. A specific example is given in Fig. 3.2.

Any company which follows this approach needs to have a charging system which encourages both recovery of the material and care in use.

Fig. 3.1. System scaffolding supporting system form panels: the scaffolding is suitable for access or falsework (Scaffolding (Great Britain) Ltd)

Fig. 3.2 (below). Falsework utilising universal column sections (H-piling) from stock for the support of excavations (George Wimpey plc)

A method that has worked very well in practice is to develop a hire rate for the universal columns on the following conditions. First, the site is charged full cost on delivery.

Secondly, at the end of use the site is reimbursed with three-quarters of new cost, provided that lengths are returned undamaged and more than 4 m long; and damaged ends due to driving etc. are cut off by the site before return to the depot. What length is considered to be economic for return must be decided by an individual company. The 4 m quoted above has been found to be reasonable in practice. Whatever is decided upon, the principle stated above gives a real incentive to recover and return to depot.

Formwork and falsework

Any company that specialises in falsework and formwork will learn very quickly that in this case standardisation of equipment has clear economic advantages. Not only is repetitive use made easier and safer (with better knowledge of the material by the workforce) but performance is also much improved, to the benefit of the operatives and company performance as a whole. More details in this respect are given in the chapters on falsework and formwork (chapters 9 and 10).

Economy is also possible in the formwork field by the use of collapsible lift-shaft forms, where the shape is difficult and accuracy with piecemeal formwork would present considerable problems. In Fig. 3.3 are shown lift-shaft formers that collapse and lift out by the crane. To reset, all that is needed is to reinsert into the shaft, jack out at the base and re-plumb.

Fig. 3.3. Collapsible lift-shaft forms for handling in one piece—both in erecting and striking

ASSESSMENT OF WHERE COST REALLY LIES

It is relatively easy to sit down and arrive at a solution to a temporary works problem. Whether it is the best and most cost-effective solution in overall terms is another matter. It is all too easy to become isolated in one's own speciality. Those designing and making decisions in relation to temporary works need to examine the overall cost equation. Questions to be asked are:

(a) Is the solution the cheapest possible?
(b) If it is, will it work with the methods of construction envisaged?
(c) If it will not, how much will it cost extra to make it work?
(d) As an alternative, would it be cheaper overall to change the construction method?
(e) Is there a case for spending money on the temporary works to save a greater sum of money elsewhere?

In summary, the consequences of the decision concerning the temporary works method must be looked at in relation to operations as a whole. The following case studies illustrate the point.

Case study: trench support

Support is needed for a trench while pipes are laid. The pipes in question are 5 m long.

The temporary works designer cannot consider the support on its own in this case. He must realise that the pipes to be laid are long and will need to be capable of slipping through the struts. If more than one setting of struts is required, the ability to pass pipes down into position becomes even more difficult. Therefore the temporary support must first cater for the pipes. If they cannot be positioned, expensive alteration to the strutting will be necessary. In seeking a solution with standard steel sections, it may well be that the number of sections is theoretically uneconomic. This in practice is much better than buying special sizes for one contract.

While this may sound obvious it is a happening that is not uncommon! A similar situation can arise in raking supports to excavations, in relation to the plant that can be used to excavate between shores.

Case study: railway contract

A major railway loop junction was being remodelled. A new cutting had to be created and an existing one filled up with the material from the new one. Clearly, the newly excavated material would have to be stockpiled until the new cutting and its track were completed.

In the tender planning, it was hoped that the railway company would allow track crossings, to minimise the haulage distance. This the railway company refused to agree to, because the loop configuration in the cuttings gave very bad visibility for flagmen, and inadequate visual warning with vehicles crossing the tracks. The earthmoving was therefore priced on the basis of excavator and lorries using available public roads from one side of the loop to the other, a route of some 8 km.

Fig. 3.4. Bailey bridge crossing of railway line for scrapers (the loop configuration gives the impression that the train is on the wrong track)

With the contract obtained, the whole situation was re-examined. The possibility of putting a Bailey bridge over the tracks at a suitable point on the cutting was investigated. The cost of such a bridge was high, as two concrete abutments were needed, together with an approach road and ramps. It was then realised that a Bailey bridge was wide enough to accept a scraper, and that, with such a bridge, the haulage distance was only of the order of 400 m—well within the economic haul of a scraper. The railway company was approached with this alternative proposal, and, subject to some additional safety measures of minor cost, agreed to the bridge method. The actual situation is shown in Fig. 3.4. The concrete abutments are clearly seen, with the triple–single Bailey arrangement. Plywood sheeting on the sides of the bridge stops earth falling off the scraper on to the line below.

The advantages will be all too clear. The haulage distance for the earthmoving was reduced from 8 km to 400 m, and the plant cost was significantly reduced from excavator and lorries to two scrapers. As a result, the approach roads were not needed, only the approach ramps. As 250 000 m^3 of earth had to be moved twice, the saving was considerable—indeed, to about one-third of the originally estimated cost. This was all a result of spending a good deal of money on the temporary works to make money elsewhere.

ORIGINALITY OF THOUGHT

In the course of his duties, anyone required to deal with temporary works will be faced with many one-off situations. The scope and diversity likely to be met in this field is amply demonstrated in chapter 1. Anyone involved in the solution of such problems needs to have an original mind, capable of applying a wide-ranging knowledge of construction in the solution of unique problems.

ABILITY TO EXPLOIT PERMANENT CONSTRUCTION

A continuing awareness of cost factors (to save temporary works and to give a contractor a competitive edge) is enhanced by a capability to see how the permanent works may be exploited to minimise temporary works. The ability to do this has been greatly increased by the development of such techniques as diaphragm walling, contiguous bored piling and secant piling. The importance of this approach is dealt with in some detail in chapter 8.

Even without the above methods, the permanent works can often be used to reduce temporary works cost. A simple example is shown in Fig. 3.5. On a very restricted site, a means of access for ready-mixed concrete trucks was needed to feed a 1 m³ capacity high speed hoist. The illustration gives a clear picture of how this was achieved.

All the walls seen in the picture are part of the permanent construction. The slabs, too, are permanent. The only temporary works are the central beam in the middle of the sleeper road and the sleepers themselves. To further facilitate the construction and dismantling of the access road, the central beam is a precast unit—easily installed, and easily removed at completion of use.

In situations like these, the Engineer must be a party to the method. Some redesign was necessary to the permanent works to allow the

Fig. 3.5. Adaptation of permanent works to provide temporary access to hoist (George Wimpey plc)

method to work. In particular, the slab edges where the sleeper road starts were made into beams with rebates. These accepted the sleepers in the temporary condition and, on completion of use, provided the bearings for a permanent, simply supported concrete slab. The original design was a continuous slab over the walls, with no beams at all.

MINIMISING COST

It should be clear from the foregoing that cost-consciousness and the ways that cost can be minimised are a key feature in temporary works by the really competitive contractor. Further aspects of this element are examined in most of the following chapters.

KNOWLEDGE OF CONSTRUCTION PLANT AND METHODS

Whatever the degree of involvement in temporary works, a sound knowledge of construction plant and methods is an essential requirement. It is little use designing a temporary ramp to enable plant to get into a basement, and going to great lengths to check the weight involved, if no one remembers to check the width needed!

In another field, provision of falsework and formwork to a major concrete slab cannot be satisfactory if the designer fails to recognise that the concrete is to be pumped and will impose additional stresses on the temporary works: pipeline surge, weight of pipes, and further loadings if a decision is made to use a radial-arm distributor.

Fragmented construction always involves extra cost; and the temporary works content of a contract frequently is a cause of fragmentation by the very nature of what has to be done. For example, in certain approaches to the support of excavations (see chapter 7), a good knowledge of plant and methods will enable those involved with temporary works the better to seek solutions which either minimise or avoid altogether the fragmentation factor.

4

The effect of the site and its boundaries

The need for temporary works can often arise from the features of the site itself and the boundary conditions prevailing. Some items may be quite minor; others may involve considerable expense and, at the same time, affect the way in which the work can be planned. It is important, therefore, when tendering for work, that these aspects are given careful consideration and the anticipated costs allowed for in the price submitted.

SITE INVESTIGATIONS

The importance of a careful site inspection, to establish all the factors that will need to be taken into account in the pricing, cannot be over-emphasised. The inspection should always be based on a checklist format so that nothing is inadvertently missed. A standard printed form is undoubtedly the most effective way of achieving this aim. A typical example of such a form is shown in Fig. 4.1.

As far as temporary works are concerned, in relation to the site and its boundaries, items 1–5 on the site inspection questionnaire are the ones that should be examined and careful notes should be made. From the answers obtained, the extent of any temporary works necessary will become apparent.

ACCESS (OFF SITE)

From the answers obtained to the three questions (Fig. 4.1) under this heading, the temporary works needed could involve the following.

If the local authority imposes weight restrictions on approach roads or bridges, reductions in the capacity of the plant envisaged may be the only way in which to get plant on to the site. This in turn may mean an increased time due to lower output. Where this is not possible—for example, on an opencast coal site, where a walking dragline of a certain size is needed to work the geological conditions existing—the construction of an entirely new road to the site may be the only solution. Such a solution has been needed on a number of occasions in the past. In one case, at least, the construction of a new bridge was needed as well.

In situations where wayleaves over someone's land are inescapable (cross-country pipelines and similar), the need for temporary access roads will arise, if work is to proceed in all weathers. As such temporary

SITE INVESTIGATION FORM (QUESTIONAIRE)
PRE TENDER PLANNING

REGION _____	SITE NAME _____
	JOB CODE NO. _____
SITE LOCATION _____	NEAREST MAIN LINE STATION/AIRPORT
	_____
INSPECTION BY _____	DATE _____

1. ACCESS (Off Site)

   (a) Restrictions on existing roads and bridges to site for heavy plant.

   (b) Restrictions on use of local roads (Reinstatement costs for example if damaged).

   (c) Are Wayleaves required.

2. ACCESS (On Site)

   (a) Overhead obstructions.

   (b) Ground level obstructions.

   (c) Underground obstructions.

   (d) Buildings and trees.

   (e) Old founds. and Basements.

   (f) Watercourses.

3. BOUNDARY CONDITIONS

   (a) Adjacent buildings and trees (Heights and obstruction value).

   (b) Proximity of Railway lines and public roads (Effect on Tower Cranes).

   (c) Safety of the public (Need for covered ways, etc. Cranes over-swing with loads).

   (d) School playgrounds, Parks etc.

Fig. 4.1 (above and facing page). Site investigation form

(e) Adjacent watercourses.

(f) Adjacent or nearby Airfields.

(g) Rights of Access for others and ditto maintenance of services.

(h) Adjacent Mains and Sewers.

4. NOISE

(a) Nearby Hospitals, Schools, Offices, etc.

(b) Restrictions on nightwork.

5. PUBLIC UTILITY SUPPLIES FOR CONSTRUCTION

(a) Water — Availability and Location.

(b) Electricity (Lt. and Ht.) — Availability and location (Check if cable costs involved).

(c) Telephone — Availability and Location.

(d) Foul Sewers — Availability and Location.

6. VISUAL SURFACE GROUND CONDITIONS AND LOCAL GEOLOGICAL FEATURES

7. LOCAL WORKING WEEK
(Degree of operation of 5 day week).

8. LOCAL HOLIDAYS

9. LOCAL WEATHER CONDITIONS

10. REMARKS

roads are generally across country, a system needs to be adopted that can readily be removed at the end of the contract, to minimise reinstatement costs. The use of geotextiles for supporting a hardcore running formation have much to offer, as the textile membrane allows a good recovery factor on the hardcore. The Construction Industry Research and Information Association is currently considering the publication of a useful 'do-it-yourself' design guide for such temporary road construction methods.

ACCESS (ON SITE)
Overhead obstructions

The most common overhead obstructions are high tension electricity cables. Early contact with the Central Electricity Generating Board is the first step in determining the safety requirements in relation to clearances; to ensure that flash-over from cables to plant, vehicles and personnel does not occur, especially in wet conditions, when the flash-over distance is less than when it is dry. There is a legal requirement, in regulation 44(2) of The Construction (General Provisions) Regulations,[1] to take precautions to prevent danger from overhead wires. HSE Guidance Note GS 6 gives considerable detail on this topic.[2]

Once the minimum working clearances have been established, the normal temporary works provision will be as shown in Fig. 4.2. Travelling under the cables should be restricted to defined points, where 'goal posts' are erected on each side of the cable line to define the maximum height that can pass under the cables. Elsewhere, barriers are erected at a

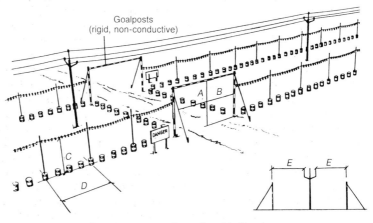

A   Height to be specified by Electricity Board
B   Width to be determined by site conditions (max. 10m)
C   Height 3-6m
D   6m (maximum)
E   6m (minimum)

Fig. 4.2. 'Goal post' protection for overhead cables (Building Employers Confederation[9])

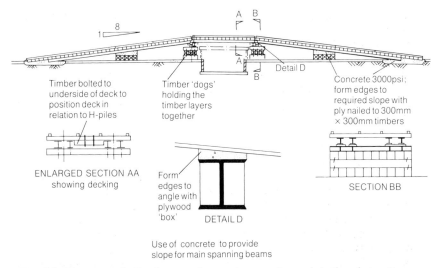

Fig. 4.3. Temporary bridge for spanning service trenches and similar obstructions

safe distance away from the cables to prevent plant or vehicles travelling inadvertently under the cables at that point.

Ground-level obstructions

Considerable variety is possible with ground-level obstructions and each situation has to be considered on its merits. Other than open excavations (dealt with in chapter 7) the most likely obstructions are surface drainage pipes on stools, industrial mains, and similar installations.

The usual need in these circumstances is to provide a form of bridging if access is needed from one side to the other. Barriers may also be needed to prevent damage from new construction operations adjacent to any service pipes, or other installations. Such bridges can readily be provided from standard steel sections that may normally be used for the support of excavations (H-pile sections). Further standardisation can be realised by using timber sections for the deck etc., in line with company sections used for main bearers in falsework. Figure 4.3 illustrates the approach. With a structure as illustrated, all material is recoverable at the end of the contract and available for use in the same or other ways in the future. While not necessarily structurally efficient for the bridging role, the recovery factor for a wide range of other uses makes the solution much cheaper than using material specially bought for the one purpose. While Fig. 4.3 illustrates a typical design, each case, of course, needs to be designed for the conditions in question.

Underground obstructions

A degree of similarity exists between ground-level and underground obstructions. Underground obstructions normally arise from services, cables and so on. The need for any form of temporary protection will only be required if they are sited close to the surface and need protection from traffic passing over, or other forms of vibration. As with ground-level obstructions, bridging across will usually provide the best solution. Whether or not true bridges are needed will depend on the circumstances. Often the use of sleepers spanning across the line will be adequate.

Buildings and trees

Buildings and trees located within the site may affect the choice and operation of plant. In analysing the results of the site inspection, however, questions need to be asked in relation to any protection that may be needed: in the case of trees, to prevent damage from construction operations; with buildings, to avoid damage from falling objects, or to avoid dirt-staining from the new operations. Cleaning up at a later stage can be very expensive.

In the case of trees, all that may be needed is some chestnut fencing, placed at a suitable distance round the tree and suitably supported.

With buildings, much will depend on the particular circumstances. Fans and screen netting fixed to any scaffolding may be enough. Where

Fig. 4.4. Bailey bridge ramp access to basement for piling plant (George Wimpey plc)

dirt-generating activities are involved, plastic sheeting fixed to the scaffold, or to purpose-provided supports if no scaffolding is used, will normally suffice. If sheeting is fixed to the scaffold, due allowance needs to be made for the extra wind-resistance in the design of the scaffold.

Old basements

Where old basements are disclosed, they should be accurately surveyed if it is planned to use them for the support of falsework, storage of materials or support of plant. Judgement will have to be made by a competent structural engineer in such cases. More often, any old basements will have to be removed to make way for the new construction. In many cases, however, the boundary retaining wall is left in place. If this is so, adequate consideration of its stability is necessary until the new boundary wall is in place. Temporary support may have to be provided. This particular topic is dealt with in more detail in chapters 7 and 8.

Access is frequently needed into old basement areas for piling and excavation plant. Such situations are particularly true of city redevelopment sites. As excavation to additional basement depths is usually needed, it is tempting to use some of the available material to form a ramp up to the street level to provide the required access. In many cases, as such sites are usually restricted, such a concept is ill considered. At some time the ramp will be in the way of piling operations, and it will have to be dug out and re-installed in an area already piled. Equally, it will need to be removed altogether at some point in the permanent programme. A far more convenient and economical solution is the provision of a Bailey bridge. It is easily erected and, when the time comes for a move, easily moved by a mobile crane in a few hours over a week-end. Figure 4.4 illustrates such a solution. With this method there is no need to bring back an excavator to remove a ramp at a later stage at extra cost.

Where a Bailey bridge is not readily available, a temporary bridge can be developed using H-pile stock—again an example of the wide use poss-

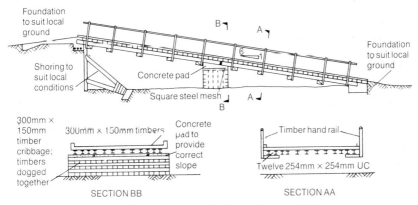

Fig. 4.5. Ramp bridge to basement using H-pile sections and timber

Fig. 4.6. Contiguous pile support to Bailey bridge, plus support to tower crane base (Cementation Piling and Foundations Ltd)

ible of standardised equipment. The general principles of such a bridge are shown in Fig. 4.5. The design of a bridging ramp of this nature must necessarily be carried out by a competent person, and related to the loads anticipated.

Where an excavation is very deep, a ramp may be the only solution. On many civil engineering sites, where there is plenty of room outside the construction area, it may well be possible to have a ramp starting outside the construction zone to minimise its impact on the construction. There will, however, be the cost of reinstatement of the non-construction area, at a later stage, to be taken into account.

Re-creation of space

City redevelopment work usually involves working in very cramped conditions. The new building, at least up to ground level, will occupy the whole of the site area, or a very high percentage of it. The site planning needs to give very careful consideration both to the sequence of construction and to the means of creating space for hutting, storage of materials and unloading facilities.

It is a golden rule, in relation to such sites, that the planning should aim to re-create space at or near ground level as soon as possible. To achieve this objective, the temporary works designer will usually be involved. One solution is to provide some form of temporary steel staging to form an area for unloading, storage and offices. In Fig. 4.6, the contractor has taken advantage of a contiguous pile support system to provide support for a tower crane base, and to add additional piles as

Fig. 4.7. Structural steel structure providing support to space re-creation at road level: Hannover metro interchange station

Fig. 4.8. Re-creation of space by early construction of an area of permanent work (George Wimpey plc)

the foundations for supporting a Bailey bridge which, in turn, is re-creating space at road level. Indeed, this illustration is an excellent example of the use of bored piles as temporary/permanent support as well as pure temporary works. An even more elaborate re-creation of space is shown in Fig. 4.7. All the structural steelwork visible is temporary: to provide room for offices, storage of materials and unloading facilities at a major interchange station on a new metro system in Germany.

An approach of a more limited scale, utilising the permanent structure, is illustrated in Fig. 4.8. Here, site offices have been installed on permanent construction which is not critical to the completion of the project as a whole; and which has deliberately been built well ahead of time.

Watercourses

Maintenance of a well drained site is always of prime importance. The initial site inspection should always examine carefully the state of the ground and, in particular, any existing watercourses. The following questions need answering:

(a) If watercourses exist, is there any local knowledge in relation to liability to flood at certain times of the year? If so, what has been the worst extent?

(b) If no permanent diversions are shown on the drawings, will any temporary diversions be needed? If so, what will be the likely size and extent?

(c) If no diversions are specified, can access be maintained to all parts of the works? Or will temporary bridging of any kind be necessary?

(d) Will water cut-off ditches be needed to protect excavations from

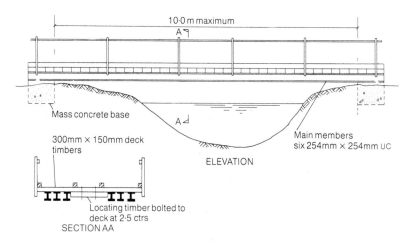

Fig. 4.9. Temporary bridge for stream crossing in standard steel sections

flooding, or to avoid wash-out danger to falsework or other temporary works foundations?

Depending upon the extent of such works as listed above, a proper temporary works assessment and cost can be established. To minimise cost, it is again possible to utilise standard temporary works equipment in the shape of H-piles and standardised timber sections. Figure 4.9 shows such an approach. Design for the circumstances prevailing is, of course, essential.

BOUNDARY CONDITIONS

As listed in Fig. 4.1, the boundary conditions that may affect a site can be quite numerous. While some do not affect temporary works at all, others can demand a good deal of expenditure to satisfy adjoining owners.

Adjacent buildings

Adjacent buildings have to be safeguarded at all times (see chapter 2). As the most common protection needed is from adjacent excavations, this particular aspect is dealt with in detail in chapters 7 and 8.

If demolition has taken place before new construction can begin, any adjacent party walls have to be maintained in a safe and watertight condition until supported by the new works. The requirements in this respect will normally have been agreed by representatives of the adjoining owners and of the owners of the new works. In inner London, the agreement will be established by a party wall award; elsewhere it will be

Fig. 4.10. Shoring to party walls, required by agreement, prior to underpinning (George Wimpey plc)

established under the Building Act 1984 (see 'Related legislation' in chapter 2 for details). The contractor for the new works, therefore, needs to make himself familiar with what has been agreed by others in respect of any temporary works. No two agreements will be the same. Figure 4.10 illustrates a simple case of precautionary shoring to adjacent buildings prior to underpinning the affected party walls.

The need to retain historic facades and to build new structures within the existing facade is now commonplace within most cities. The skills necessary for such work are specialised. The whole subject is dealt with in some detail in chapter 9. Other aspects of adjacent party wall retention arise in chapter 12, under 'Strengthening weak brickwork before shoring'.

The heights of adjacent buildings become important if additional height, and hence cost, is required for a crane to clear the buildings with a safe margin. It should be noted here that a crane overswinging an adjoining property is trespassing, unless the adjoining owner's consent has been obtained in advance.[3] In any agreement reached, there may be conditions concerning provision of protective fans or nets, or other such safety precautions as the adjoining owner may require.

Trees

Trees adjacent to the site boundary mainly impinge on the construction planning as obstructions which may inhibit the use of plant in the best way possible. Because of the height of adjacent trees, crane overswing may be limited in certain areas of the site, and plant siting may not be the most convenient.

If access is needed past trees at the boundaries or just outside, protection against damage is a likely requirement. In such cases, fencing around the base is usually all that will be required.

Work adjacent to railway lines

Special requirements govern the use of cranes adjacent to railway property in the UK, as well as protecting the railway from falling objects etc. Each undertaking has a legal duty to protect the travelling public, and thus has powers to make rules about what goes on on land adjacent to their operational property.

British Rail, for example, publish a handbook for guidance.[4] It contains notes for the guidance of developers and others responsible for construction work adjacent to the British Railways Board's operational railway. The publication lists all those activities which can only be carried out with the agreement and under the conditions of the BR Board. It also lists matters which could endanger the stability of the Board's property or safe running of the Board's railway.

London Regional Transport have no formal booklet, but issue, on request, notes and special conditions[5] which form the basis of their requirements. It is clearly stated that these guidelines are general, and each job or location is treated on its merits. It is, therefore, important that contact is made with the London Regional Transport at an early stage—in the contractor's case, at the pre-tender stage—in order that any specific requirements are established which may require expensive temporary works.

Other railway undertakings should similarly be contacted for their particular requirements at the pre-tender stage.

Both British Rail and London Regional Transport impose conditions on the use of cranes. In BR handbook 36,[4] section 1 states:

> 'The following shall be permitted only if the Board approves, and then only under such conditions as the Board may require'.

This is followed by 1(d):

> 'The swinging of cranes or other plant, equipment or materials over the Board's land'.

Section 4 adds:

> 'In addition, therefore, to Section 1(d), tower cranes should not be erected or used in a position such that in the event of failure they or their loads could fall across railway passenger lines with dense traffic or where passenger train speeds exceed 30 mph. In similar circumstances, mobile cranes, piling rigs and similar equipment should only be erected, and the cranes operated and the sheet piling handled at such times as suitable arrangements can be made for the protection of rail traffic.'

The London Regional Transport special conditions,[5] in relation to cranes, state:

> 'Cranes and any other tall plant are not normally permitted to work in close proximity to the Railway during railway operating hours, where, in the event of a collapse, the crane might fall on to the Railway.'

Close proximity is defined as:

> 'Any mobile or derrick cranes operating within a horizontal distance equal to the length of the crane jib plus 3 metres from the nearest railway boundary'

or:

> 'Any tower cranes or derrick cranes operating within a horizontal distance equal to the diagonal dimension from the foot of the tower to the end of the jib plus 3 metres from the nearest railway boundary'

or:

> 'Any other site or position which, in the opinion of the Engineer constitutes a risk, hazard or danger to the railway'.

The patterns of requirements are very similar, and in practice and pre-cedent, early discussions at the pre-tender stage with the railway in question are essential to determine the specific requirements in the particular circumstances. Additional stability will have to be provided for tower cranes used within the specified distances.

The normal requirement will be that the jib of a tower crane will need to be shortened to avoid any overswing of the railway property; and in addition, the tower stability will have to be increased over that used in the code of practice for the design of the crane.

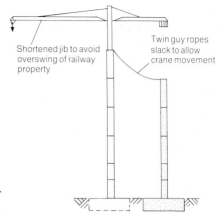

*Fig. 4.11. Secondary base and tower
to improve crane stability*

Figures 4.11 and 4.12 illustrate two solutions to this particular problem. Both solutions have been used in practice, to the satisfaction of all parties.

In Fig. 4.11, the additional stability was needed for a static-base crane. This was achieved by providing an additional crane base some distance away from that supporting the crane itself. On this was erected a section of tower as shown. Between the two towers a linking pair of wire cables was installed, slack enough to allow for the normal sway of the crane in operation. In the event of any failure of the crane tower, the cables would tension and provide additional support against failure of the whole, the effect being to make the crane assembly swing away from the railway back on to the site.

In Fig. 4.12, a rail-mounted tower crane was involved. In this case, improving the overturning stability yet maintaining a free travelling capability was not at first sight easy. The solution accepted by the railway was a fine example of the temporary works engineer's skill. Two suitably sized RSJs were welded beneath the crane's undercarriage, in such a way as to project some distance on one side. To the extremity of these RSJs was welded another RSJ at right angles as shown, creating an outrigger effect. Along the length of the track, and immediately under the outrigger, was constructed a concrete beam, with a 2.5 cm clearance between it and the outrigger. If the crane ever started to topple for any reason, the outrigger would come to rest on the concrete beam. The

*Fig. 4.12. Increasing
crane stability by
outrigger system*

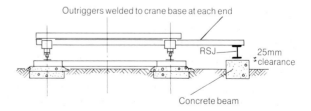

resisting moment to the overturning would immediately increase dramatically and stop any further movement.

Further temporary works will be needed to stop materials etc. from falling on to railway property. The BR rules, in section 3, list items that could endanger the railway or the Board's property, and state that those involved must consult with the Board before the work is planned, and should comply with the reasonable requirements of the Board in respect of, *inter alia*, 'The execution of work and the storage of materials and plant above railway level which could result in plant or materials falling and obstructing the railway whether by accident or the action of vandals'. In other words, the contractor must provide such scaffolding, fans, netting or other means to prevent anything falling onto the railway property.

London Regional Transport's guidance notes say substantially the same thing. Section 4.4 states: 'A protective screen shall be erected by the contractor along the railway boundary, if required by the Engineer. . . . The screen shall be maintained at a level at least 2 metres above that at which the Works are being conducted.'

Safety of the public

The Health and Safety at Work etc. Act, section 3,[6] places a duty on every employer '. . . to conduct his undertaking in such a way as to ensure, so far as is reasonably practicable, that persons not in his employment who may be affected thereby are not exposed to risks to their health or safety'. The effect of this section is to cover members of the public from any risks to their health and safety while going about their business adjacent to the site (i.e. outside the site boundary). It is necessary, therefore, for contractors carefully to consider what forms of temporary protection may be needed to stop anything falling outside the site boundary onto passers-by. Protective fans, netting or covered ways of suitable strength over pavements are the sort of temporary works that need to be examined.

In this connection, it is particularly important that special consideration is given to the protective needs when the adjacent property is a school or school playground. The same need would arise when working adjacent to parks or any place where the public was likely to congregate in numbers, at regular intervals.

This type of protection can become onerous when a right of access across a site has to be maintained throughout the duration of the contract.

CONSTRUCTION NOISE

The Control of Pollution Act,[7] sections 60 and 61, provides for control of and protection from noise generated by construction activities. This act covers those working on the site as well as the public outside the site area.

To meet any noise level restrictions imposed under the Act by the local authority, temporary works may be needed in the shape of baffles,

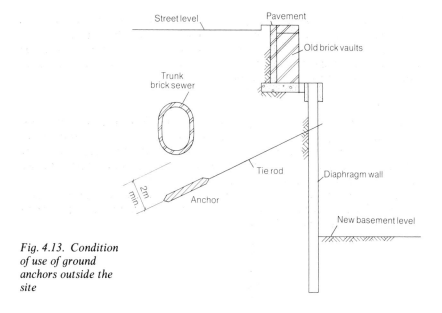

Fig. 4.13. Condition of use of ground anchors outside the site

shelters or other noise-reducing measures. BS 5228[8] provides useful guidance in this respect.

TRESPASS

The courts have established (Woolerton and Wilson v. Richard Costain (Midlands) Ltd[3]) that the overswing of adjacent property by a tower crane jib constitutes a trespass in law, unless prior agreement has been reached with the adjoining owner. This judgement also made it clear that a similar trespass arises if someone encroaches under another person's land.

This point becomes very relevant if, in the upholding of an excavation adjacent to another person's property, it is desired to use ground anchors. The approval of any adjoining owner who may be affected must be sought. If refused, another form of support will have to be adopted, even if less convenient and more expensive to the contractor.

Even if agreement is reached, conditions may be imposed which have to be complied with. An example of such a situation is shown in Fig. 4.13. In this case, the adjoining owner was the City Engineer, who has responsibility for the highway, and at the time in question had responsibility for the sewers which ran under the streets. (Today they would be the responsibility of the appropriate water authority.) While no objection was raised to the use of ground anchors under the highway, two conditions were imposed. First, all ground anchors installed under the road were to be de-stressed on completion of the permanent support. Secondly, no anchor was to pass nearer than 2 m to the major brick sewers running under the street. The effect of these conditions was to increase the cost of the anchors, due to the need to de-stress and in some cases because the anchor length was longer than the theoretical requirement because of the need to be 2 m away from the sewers. In some situations this meant that the angle of the anchor was not the most effective in relation to length required.

SUMMARY

It will be clear from the foregoing that, apart from the more conventional temporary works related to construction, a large number of matters in relation to the site and its boundaries can arise. That they should be identified in the initial site inspection, so that their cost can adequately be established, is clearly of importance.

No attempt has been made to include items related to the site establishment. This is an area worthy of separate consideration, and is dealt with in detail in chapter 13.

5

Plant-associated temporary works

Many items of plant used in construction require the provision of special temporary works for their safe and efficient operation. Such works represent a cost additional to that of the plant itself and the directly associated charges—hire, transport to and from the site, erection and dismantling, and weekly running costs.

Those who design such temporary works need to have a thorough knowledge of the item of plant in question, together with the requirements specified for operating safety (e.g. in relation to foundations for tower cranes, a knowledge of soil mechanics will be essential). Each type of plant will have its own special requirements, which will always have to be assessed against the particular characteristics of any given site.

TOWER CRANES

Tower cranes are normally used in one of three distinct ways: travelling on tracks (rail-mounted); working off a static base; or climbing on the structure being built. Whichever of these modes is used, temporary works will be involved.

Before any design is attempted, in relation to the necessary temporary works for any of the three operating modes above, the best possible information on the ground conditions to be met is required. Even when good borehole and trial pit data is available, additional questions need to be asked; for example:

(a) Has any part of the site been excavated to remove old foundations during demolition or site preparation prior to the crane installation? And backfilled without any serious attempt at compaction?

(b) Were any old cellars or basements backfilled by the demolition contractor? Alternatively, is the area suspect in relation to swallow holes, underground caves or the like?

(c) Is there any possibility of old river beds crossing the site? In central redevelopment sites in major cities such situations are far from unknown.

(d) Is the new construction on piles or a raft?

The final detailing of the track or base will depend on the answers to these questions. With the above in mind, it is now possible to consider the foundation requirements for each type of tower crane operating arrangement.

Rail-mounted tower cranes

All tower cranes require that the base should be truly level. As such, subsidence and any other movements in the supports of the crane need to be kept within very narrow limits to minimise their effect on the operational safety of the crane. It follows that the design of the track for rail-mounted cranes needs to be the responsibility of a competent person, who has adequate knowledge of the local soil conditions, and any special factors that need to be taken into account, as listed above. Once these are established, the following matters must be borne in mind when deciding an appropriate solution:

(a)   The design should aim to minimise the need for maintenance.

(b)   In pursuit of (a), it is desirable to build a degree of insurance into the track design. Thus, if settlement does occur, it will be restricted to a minor order.

(c)   It is a prime requisite of temporary works design that associated costs need to be reduced to the greatest possible degree, consistent with the appropriate factors of safety desired. In the case of track settlement, for example, the design should provide for re-levelling to be as simple as possible.

Track systems

Although the crane maker will give illustrations of the way in which the track can be established, they are clearly stated to be only a pictorial guide, with the contractor being responsible for an actual design suitable for the conditions prevailing. While the contractor has to obtain the information in respect of the soil conditions, the crane maker will provide a tabulation of the loads that have to be resisted from the crane, both in operation and in the out-of-service state. A typical list of loads is shown in Fig. 5.1.

In order to achieve the most suitable and economic answers to the track arrangement, it is desirable to have a variety of approaches that go well beyond the track types usually shown in the erection manual. The different methods that can be adopted will give an answer to most situations, and do this in an economic manner.

Type A. The simplest formation is the use of full length sleepers properly packed with ballast. The disadvantage is that re-packing is required weekly. The compensating advantage is the ability to correct settlement as and when it may occur. Figure 5.2 illustrates this form of track, but with the sleepers bedded on weak concrete. No ballast is needed as the ground conditions are such that settlement is not expected.

Type B. It is frequently necessary to erect a crane on a site which has been partially excavated to remove old foundations, and then backfilled without any real attempt at consolidation. In these circumstances, the track formation shown in Fig. 5.3 is desirable. The key points are

Bogie, loadings (in kN) in and out of operation
Radius: 25m
Basic tower section: 6.85m

Cranes 120HC, 132HC

Number of tower sections: 10			Hook height: 39·4m		
Central ballast required: 62570kg					
Bogie	Crane in operation			Crane out of operation		
	Position of jib					
	I	II	III	I	II	III
A	290	486	111	286	467	105
B	582	486	503	561	467	467
C	324	128	503	286	105	467
D	32	128	111	10	105	105
Horizontal wind force: 44			Horizontal wind force: 83		

Number of tower sections: 11			Hook height: 41·9m		
Central ballast required: 68400kg					
Bogie	Crane in operation			Crane out of operation		
	Position of jib					
	I	II	III	I	II	III
A	305	510	120	294	508	98
B	611	510	528	624	508	508
C	342	138	528	294	98	508
D	37	138	120	0	98	98
Horizontal wind force: 46			Horizontal wind force: 86		

Number of tower sections: 12			Hook height: 44·4m		
Central ballast required: 74200kg					
Bogie	Crane in operation			Crane out of operation		
	Position of jib					
	I	II	III	I	II	III
A	321	534	128	290	550	90
B	640	534	554	699	550	550
C	361	148	554	290	90	550
D	42	148	128	0	90	90
Horizontal wind force: 47			Horizontal wind force: 90		

With 13 tower sections = 46·9 m hook height, the climbing gear has to be lowered. Corner pressure and central ballast remain the same as with 12 tower sections.

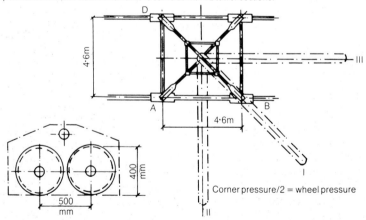

Fig. 5.1. Bogie loadings in and out of operation (Liebherr–Great Britain Ltd)

Fig. 5.2. Tower crane track with full length sleepers (George Wimpey plc)

Fig. 5.3 (below). Sleeper-and-ballasted track over concrete waybeam (George Wimpey plc)

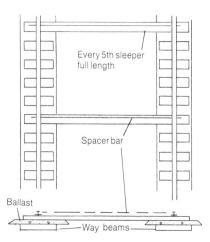

Fig. 5.4. Ballasted track on waybeams

detailed in Fig. 5.4. Reinforced concrete waybeams are constructed as shown; the stub sleeper track is laid on top, with the minimum thickness of ballast between sleepers and waybeam. If, in fact, the waybeam does deflect, the track is capable of repacking to the required level.

The advantages are that ready re-levelling is possible (but the need for this is minimised by the waybeam); that the quantity of timber needed in the sleepers is greatly reduced; and that much less ballast is needed. The disadvantage is the cost of concrete waybeams. Experience has shown that this method works very well in disturbed or made-up ground. The cost of the waybeams is more than justified by the few occasions when any adjustment has to be made to the track.

Type C. As cranes have got bigger, and their capacity has increased, their makers have required that the specified rail must be supported along its entire length. Originally this meant that a timber waybeam had to be inserted between the rail and the sleepers. A better approach is shown in Fig. 5.5. Here the rail is set on top of a universal bearing pile section, and connected to it by means of Lindaptors or similar. With the inherent stiffness of the UBP section, spacers are only needed at about 2.25 m centres. Actual spacing is dependent on the forces involved using a particular type of crane, and the UBP section. To provide an adequate stiffness, the spacers used should be at least 152 × 76 (mm) channel sections.

The resulting assembly is very stiff and it leads logically to the concept of keeping lengths of track permanently assembled to minimise time and cost in erecting and dismantling. A section 6 m long has been found to be easily manageable.

Once the method is established as standard, the track units are capable of employment in a number of ways. Variations are detailed in types D to F below; but in a standard role, the track units are laid on ground beams or ground slabs, depending on the ground conditions (Fig. 5.6). No anchorage to the beams or slabs is needed.

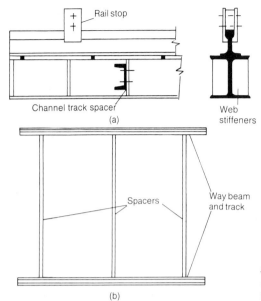

Fig. 5.5. (a) *Integrated rail and steel waybeam;* (b) *use of made-up sections*

Fig. 5.6. Integrated rail and waybeam supported by concrete slab

Fig. 5.7. Integrated rail and waybeam supported by precast concrete pads

Fig. 5.8. As Fig. 5.7 but showing concrete packing to provide level track

Type D. Occasions often arise where it is necessary to erect a tower crane on an existing surface (a concrete-paved area or road or similar). If the area can accept a spread load and is reasonably level, the solution shown in Fig. 5.7 is very economical. The pre-assembled track units of type C are used supported on precast slabs, which are levelled into position on concrete pads (Fig. 5.8). The anchor slots are cast into the precast slabs, so that the rail assembly can be bolted to the slabs and hold them from any movement in relation to the track.

The advantages are that standard pre-assembled track is used, in association with standard precast bearing pads; all is fully recoverable at the end of the contract; the number of bearing pads is minimised by the great stiffness of the rail–UBP assembly. The disadvantages are negligible, as the only costs incurred are those of levelling up and removing the concrete.

Type E. Another situation is similar to that for type D; the only difference is a more sloping or irregular ground surface, which requires a substantial beam to be provided so that a level track can be maintained. Again, the pre-assembled track on top is the most cost-effective answer (Fig. 5.9).

To minimise dismantling cost, the concrete beam is cast in sections with a Flexcell type divider between sections. At the same time, lifting loops have been cast into the top of each beam section. To dismantle, all that is needed is a mobile crane of sufficient capacity to lift up each section of the beam in turn and load into a vehicle for disposal.

Type F. Another variation can be used where a well compacted natural sand base is available (Fig. 5.10). Precast slabs are butted end to end to provide the foundation for the pre-assembled track. For levelling, to avoid excessive accuracy in bedding the slabs, steel shims can be used,

Fig. 5.9. Integrated rail and waybeam supported on levelling beam

Fig. 5.10. Integrated rail and waybeam on precast slabs on sand formation

followed by a cement–sand grout packed underneath the universal bearing pile units.

For the dismantling phase, as in the previous example, the precast slabs are provided with lifting loops. In this way they can be recovered for reuse at another time. The method, therefore, gives almost total recovery and reuse potential.

Static-base tower cranes

The stability of the static-base tower crane is entirely dependent upon the stability of the concrete block that provides its foundation. It follows that the design of such a base needs to be carried out by a properly qualified person, knowledgeable and experienced in structural and foundation engineering.

The prevailing ground conditions are clearly critical, and the base designer must be provided with adequate data in this respect. Just as importantly, the crane maker must supply tabulations of the forces which are developed by the crane and which have to be resisted by the static base. This type of information will be contained in the crane's erection manual and will cover tabulations of dead weight, torque forces in the tower, and the maximum overturning moments generated while operating and in the out-of-service condition. The direction of these forces creating the worst loading will also be shown (Fig. 5.11). It should be borne in mind that when a tower crane is out of service, the jib is left to swing freely with the wind.

Where the ground conditions are bad enough to require the permanent work to be built on piles, it is a good rule of thumb to allow for the crane to be supported on piles at the time of tender. The pricing can cover the cost from the information supplied by the piling contractor. If

Foundation loading   Cranes 120 HC, 132 HC

Jib length 40·45m or 50m

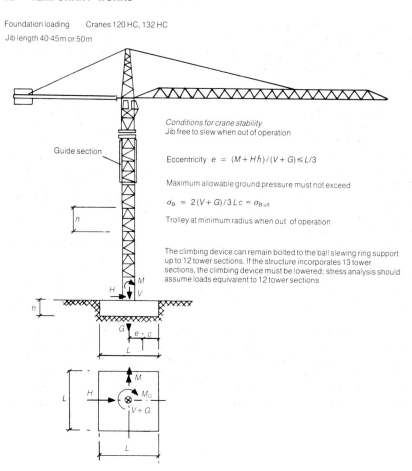

Conditions for crane stability
Jib free to slew when out of operation

Eccentricity $e = (M + Hh)/(V + G) \leqslant L/3$

Maximum allowable ground pressure must not exceed

$\sigma_B = 2(V + G)/3Lc = \sigma_{B\,ult}$

Trolley at minimum radius when out of operation

The climbing device can remain bolted to the ball slewing ring support up to 12 tower sections. If the structure incorporates 13 tower sections, the climbing device must be lowered; stress analysis should assume loads equivalent to 12 tower sections

The loading specifications are getting no own load factor and no hoist load factor

Number of tower sections, n	Hook height, m	Crane in operation				Crane out of operation			
		M, kNm	H, kN	V, kN		M, kNm	H, kN	V, kN	
1	12·6	1013·1	17·4	454·5		936·7	26·5	370·1	
2	15·1	1057·4	18·1	464·8		1056·1	30·6	380·4	
3	17·6	1103·4	18·8	475·1		1167·2	33·6	390·8	
4	20·1	1151·3	19·5	485·5		1302·8	37·5	401·1	
5	22·6	1200·9	20·2	495·9		1454·8	41·6	411·5	
6	25·1	1252·4	21	506·3		1604·2	45·2	421·9	
7	27·6	1305·6	21·7	516·6		1785·5	50	432·2	
8	30·1	1360·6	22·4	527		1931·5	52·5	442·6	
9	32·6	1417·4	23·1	537·3		2083·7	55	452·9	
10	35·1	1476·0	23·8	547·7		2242·3	57·5	463·3	
11	37·6	1536·3	24·5	558·1		2407·1	60	473·7	
12	40·1	1598·5	25·2	568·4		2578·2	62·5	484	

(Torque moment $M_D = 230$ kNm in operation; Torque moment $M_D = 0$ out of operation)

If the crane is erected without climbing device the value for V decreases by about 40kN

Fig. 5.11. Foundation loading (see Fig. 5.17 for definitions) (Liebherr–Great Britain Ltd)

the job is won, the crane piles can be installed at the same time as the structure piles (Fig. 4.6). Alternatively, if the ground conditions are found to be better than the soil report suggested, economies may be possible by using a different type of base.

Cost factors

With the type of tower cranes in use today, a static base is unlikely to be less than 7 m square and 2 m deep. The volume of concrete in the base is therefore not far short of 100 m³. Allowing for an average amount of excavation, formwork to the sides, the reinforcement and the concrete, at least £80/m³ is involved. This gives a minimum base cost of £8000, which is at least 50% of the total erection and dismantling charges for the crane. On completion of the use of the crane, further expense is involved if the base has to be removed. This is almost as much as for putting it there in the first place.

In planning for static bases, therefore, every effort needs to be made to minimise the base cost. One consideration is to avoid the need for removal of the base by siting it below any permanent works that can cover it. However, in these days of small profit margins, the temporary works engineer should always be looking for additional ways of reducing the base cost.

By working in close association with the permanent works designer, it is often possible partially to integrate the base with the permanent works foundations. How this can be achieved is illustrated in Fig. 5.12. In this example, the top level of the base was made to coincide with the top level of the sub-basement floor. As the floor was 1 m thick and provided a continuous thin raft slab over piles below, the top 1 m of the crane base

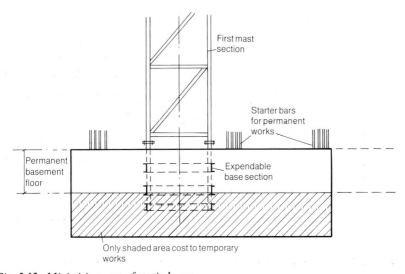

Fig. 5.12. Minimising cost of static bases

Fig. 5.13. Base shown in Fig. 5.12 ready for concrete; expendable crane mast unit visible adjacent (George Wimpey plc)

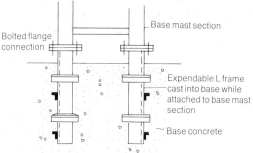

Fig. 5.14. Expendable mast unit

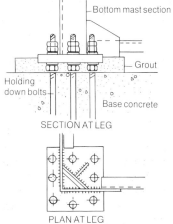

Fig. 5.15. Holding-down bolt method (recuperable base)

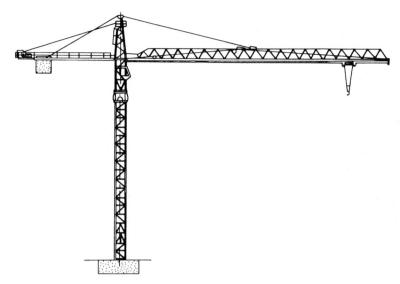

Fig. 5.16. Initial erection of climbing crane on static base (Liebherr–Great Britain Ltd)

became a measured item of the permanent works. As the base size extended beyond the location of six permanent columns, it was arranged to incorporate the starter bars for these columns in the base as well. In this way, the temporary works cost was reduced by nearly half! The actual situation is shown in Fig. 5.13. The expendable base and the first mast section can be seen just above the base waiting for concrete.

Operational matters

Proper precautions need to be taken to ensure that the mast is truly plumb when erected on the base. To provide the best means of seeing that this will be so, the base section of the mast should have an expendable base attached (Fig. 5.14), or the more recent method employing cast-in anchor bolts should be used, with the base section of the mast attached as shown in Fig. 5.15. In either case a good length of mast is available to assist accurate plumbing. The mast should be checked at intervals during concreting and on completion. Useful diagrams are given in CP 3010.[1]

Climbing tower cranes

The main features of the climbing tower crane and its mode of use are shown in Fig. 5.16. The crane is initially erected within the building structure, as a static-base tower crane. Once a specified height has been reached by the structure, the crane is detached from its base and its loads are transferred to the permanent work. As the structure proceeds, the crane is able to 'climb' up the building by means of 'climbing collars' and a special self-lifting mechanism.

The temporary works designer comes into the picture in a number of ways. First, he will be responsible for the static base design. Secondly, although the climbing collars are supplied by the crane maker, the temporary works designer will be responsible for ensuring that the permanent works are able to accept the crane loads brought on to them.

In order to achieve these objectives, the temporary works designer will require from the crane maker the loading factors for the design of the base, as for any static-base crane (as Fig. 5.11, for example); and the loading criteria for the climbing collars, both in respect of out-of-service

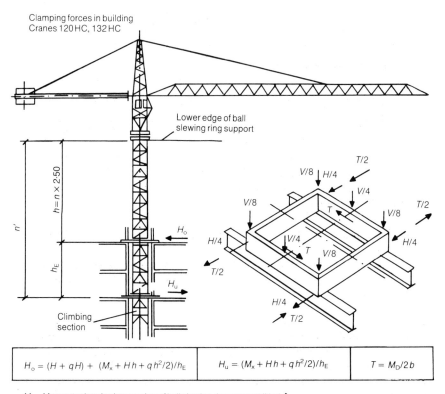

$$H_o = (H + qH) + (M_x + Hh + qh^2/2)/h_E \qquad H_u = (M_x + Hh + qh^2/2)/h_E \qquad T = M_D/2b$$

M_x Moment related to lower edge of ball slewing ring support (Nm)
M_D Torque (kNm)
V' Vertical force of slewing section + ball slewing ring support (kN) } see Fig. 5
H Horizontal force at lower edge of ball slewing ring support (kN)
q Knife-edge load at crane tower from wind or storm:
    0.29 kN/m in operation
    1.26 kN/m out of use, when working below 100m
    1.49 kN/m out of use, when working above 100m
n Number of tower sections above uppermost clamping point
n' Total number of tower sections excluding climbing section
h Height from upper clamping point to lower edge of ball slewing ring support = $n \times 2.5$ (m)
h_E Clamping height; for minimum clamping height see Fig. 5.18
V Total vertical force from complete crane and climbing mechanism = $V + 30.0 + n' \times 10.2$ (kN)

Fig. 5.17. Climbing crane lifted on to structure: forces in building (Liebherr–Great Britain Ltd)

Anchoring forces in building structure

Cranes 120 HC, 132 HC

Load data: H and V in kN; M_x and M_D in kN m

Jib length m	Crane in operation				Crane shut down						
					Hook height 100 m				Hook height 100 m		
	M_x	H	V'	M_D	M_x	H	V'	M_D	M_x	H	V'
25	822	11·4	317	102	755	21·7	238	0	772	25·6	238
30	838	11·4	327	106	644	21·7	248	0	661	25·6	248
35	807	11·4	344	131	549	21·7	266	0	606	25·6	266
40	780	11·4	377	161	757	21·7	298	0	774	25·5	298
45	752	11·4	400	196	739	21·7	321	0	756	25·6	321
50	749	11·4	422	230	696	21·7	344	0	713	25·6	344

The load values stated here do not include any dead load or hoist load factor.

Minimum anchoring height h_E (m)

Tower section above top anchor point	Radius					
	25m	30m	35m	40m	45m	50m
4	6·93	7·33	7·68	7·93	8·05	8·25
5	7·18	7·59	7·95	8·21	8·35	8·45
6	7·44	7·85	8·23	8·51	8·66	8·85
7	7·72	8·14	8·52	8·82	8·99	9·25

Fig. 5.18. Loadings from climbing crane on structure (see Fig. 5.17 for definitions)
(Liebherr–Great Britain Ltd)

conditions and when the crane is climbing (as Figs 5.17 and 5.18, for example).

A tower crane of this type is imposing significant loads on the permanent structure, including torque. Agreement for its use must be obtained from the structural designer at the tender stage.

Cost factors in dismantling

Rail-mounted and static-base cranes rarely involve temporary works in their dismantling. Climing cranes usually will, and the cost will vary in relation to the dismantling procedure adopted. Indeed, the ability to achieve dismantling and any attendant temporary works are key items to be investigated before any decision is made to use such a method. It will be too late when the crane has reached its maximum height, and it is found to be impossible to dismantle it!

In practice, three methods are open to the contractor for dismantling: using a mobile tower crane with a rotary tower and luffing jib; using a dismantling derrick on the roof; and designing and making a special temporary rig for the particular situation. All of these methods have their value in particular circumstances. The criteria for each are as follows.

Mobile rotary tower crane (Fig. 5.19). This is by far the most straightforward method if the circumstances allow. Its use depends on the following considerations.

Fig. 5.19. Rotary tower crane with luffing jib (Sparrows Cranes Ltd)

Fig. 5.20 (below). Dismantling derrick for the removal of a climbing crane from the roof of a structure, in this case 120 m high (George Wimpey plc)

First, a rotary tower crane of sufficient load–radius rating and height must be obtained. Secondly, suitable access must be available; that is, it must be possible to locate the crane close enough on a strong enough foundation.

Thirdly, the roof of the building must be strong enough to accept the weight of the main and counter jibs and the kentledge if the rotary tower crane cannot couple up to the jibs and lower to the ground directly from the operating position. However, there will be occasions when it will be possible to lift the main and counter jibs directly off the crane, thus avoiding the need for any temporary works on the roof of the structure, the only exception being support for the kentledge blocks, which will have to be lowered to the roof before removal to the ground.

Dismantling derricks. Small derricks have been developed of adequate capacity to handle the individual parts of a tower crane from the roof to the ground. In themselves, they break down into parts which are small enough to manhandle and take down to the ground in a standard passenger/goods hoist (Fig. 5.20). Their use depends on the roof structure being capable of providing adequate anchorage in lieu of kentledge, to resist the uplift when in operation. In addition, the roof must be capable of supporting the jibs and kentledge, as these will have to be lowered to the roof before being handled by the derrick (Fig. 5.21). Moreover, a passenger goods hoist of adequate capacity must be available.

Special dismantling rigs. If the two previous methods prove to be impracticable, the use a climbing crane may depend on being able to invent, design and erect a special rig for dismantling purposes. An example of such a rig is illustrated in Fig. 5.22. It was achieved by close co-operation between the temporary works engineer and the contractor's plant superintendent. It utilises the crane's own motors and winch

Fig. 5.21. Temporary works on roof to support jibs and kentledge prior to breaking down into manageable units for the roof derrick (George Wimpey plc)

Fig. 5.22 (above).
Specially designed
dismantling rig for
climbing crane; utilises
the crane's own winches
for lowering (George
Wimpey plc)

Fig. 5.23. Rig shown in
Fig. 5.22 lowering mast
section from roof
(George Wimpey plc)

system, in association with a purpose-made frame holding a cantilever beam for offering the load over the side of the structure (Fig. 5.23). This method is a good example of how to minimise the cost of temporary works. But note that the roof structure must be capable of accepting the loads imposed upon it, or modified to do so.

Anchorages to structures

Whilst the developing design of large capacity tower cranes has enabled greater and greater free-standing heights, there is still a require-

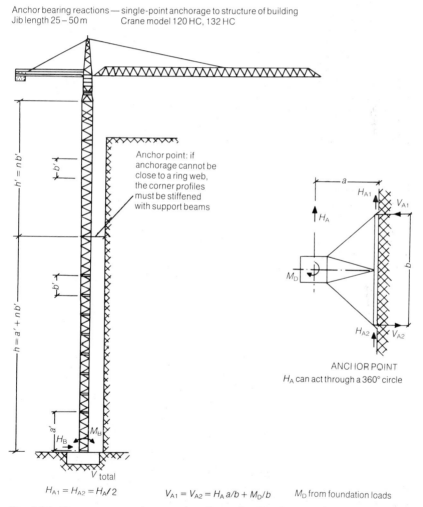

Anchor bearing reactions — single-point anchorage to structure of building
Jib length 25 – 50 m   Crane model 120 HC, 132 HC

Anchor point: if anchorage cannot be close to a ring web, the corner profiles must be stiffened with support beams

ANCHOR POINT
H_A can act through a 360° circle

$H_{A1} = H_{A2} = H_A/2$ $V_{A1} = V_{A2} = H_A a/b + M_D/b$ M_D from foundation loads

Fig. 5.24. Tower crane anchorage: data for anchor bearing reactions (Liebherr–Great Britain Ltd)

ment for cranes to be anchored to the structure when the limits of free-standing operation have been reached.

The particular crane-maker's handbook for any given model will provide the necessary information on how to calculate the loads involved in an anchorage and the forces that will have to be resisted by the permanent works. Figures 5.24 and 5.25 show examples of anchoring to the building and how the various forces can be calculated.

The makers usually have available purpose-made anchor units, designed to resist tension, compression and torque. They are usually made in standard lengths; thus if the distance from the crane to the structure cannot be made to suit, special anchorages will be required. These can be either ordered from the crane maker, or made by the con-

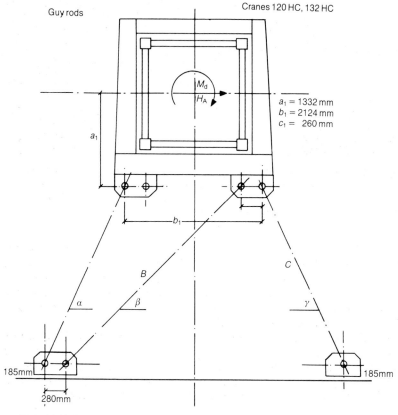

$A = M_d + a H_A / b \sin \alpha$

$B = \{H_A \sin \gamma - [(M_d + H_A a) / b \sin \alpha] \sin (\alpha + \gamma)\} / \sin (\beta + \gamma)$ $a = a_1 - c_1 / (\cot \beta + \cot \gamma)$

$C = \{- H_A \sin \beta - [(M_d + H_A a) / b \sin \alpha] \sin (\alpha - \beta)\} / \sin (\beta + \gamma)$

B_{max} results in case of opposite direction of M_D $b = b_1 - c_1 (\cot \alpha + \cot \gamma) / (\cot \beta + \cot \gamma)$

Fig. 5.25. Anchorage unit: formulae for loadings in members (Liebherr–Great Britain Ltd)

Fig. 5.26. Contractor-designed tie-in for non-standard distance from structure: tri-shores provide strut action while mild steel tension ties at 45° to mast are tightened by bottle screws; spreader beams transfer tie loads from building to the node points of the crane tower (George Wimpey plc)

tractor from designs prepared by the temporary works engineer. As the first option is likely to be expensive and delivery times may be long, the second approach is usually to be preferred. An experienced engineer can make economies by using existing available equipment, while the delivery time is under the control of the contractor. An example of a solution of this type is shown in Fig. 5.26.

Another key role of the temporary works engineer will be in establishing, with the permanent works designer, how the anchorage is to be tied to the permanent works. Such action, of course, must take place at the planning stage. If the structure is not adequate to support the loads involved, another solution in relation to cranage will be necessary.

CONCRETE-PLACING BOOMS

In recent years, a new method has arrived in the world of concrete pumping; that is, the concrete-placing boom, which is capable of climbing up a building in much the same way as a climbing crane (Fig. 5.27). Starting off in much the same way as a climbing crane—from a fixed base—it eventually detaches itself and climbs up the structure, supported by whatever is being built. As with climbing cranes, choice of such a method will depend on the capability of the permanent work to support the loads involved. In this respect, it has to be remembered that the pipeline will be full of concrete in the worst loading condition.

The makers of such placing booms supply loading information in the same way as crane makers. An example is given in Fig. 5.28.

Other versions of the placing boom are mounted on what amounts to a tower crane tower travelling on rails. Design of the track will follow a procedure similar to that used in the case of a travelling tower crane.

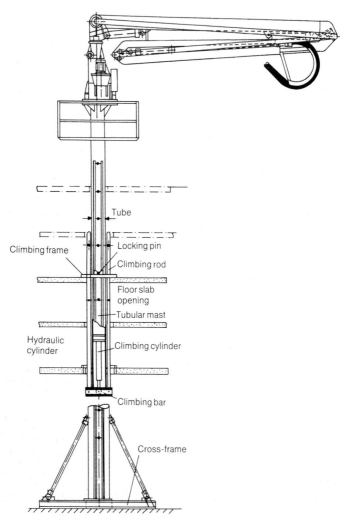

Fig. 5.27. Concrete-placing boom, illustrating climbing action on structure (F. W. Schwing GmbH through their UK distributors Burlington Engineers Ltd)

Load on mast column

Working condition		Wind pressure, W_1, kp	Maximum moment, M_1, kp m	Maximum torque, M_d, kp m	Vertical load, V_1, kp
In operation		—	34000	5500	16000
Dynamic pressure, $q = 30$ kp/m²	Wind along the boom	225	750	—	—
	Wind across the boom	1100	(5300)	5700	—
Out of operation		—	2600	—	15100
Dynamic pressure, $q = 110$ kp/m²	Wind along the boom	825	2750	—	—
	Wind across the boom	4030	19400	4000	—

Load on foundation

Working condition		Wind pressure, W_2, kp	Maximum moment, M_2, kp m	Maximum torque, M_d, kp m	Vertical load, V_2, kp
In operation		34000	34000	5500	20500
Dynamic pressure, $q = 30$ kp/m²	Wind along the boom	700	5190	—	—
	Wind across the boom	1575	(9850)	5700	—
Out of operation		—	2600	—	19400
Dynamic pressure, $q = 110$ kp/m²	Wind along the boom	2570	19030	—	—
	Wind across the boom	5780	36150	4000	—

Fig. 5.28. Loads on mast column and foundation (F. W. Schwing GmbH through their UK distributors Burlington Engineers Ltd)

Fig. 5.29. Slipform on Cormorant gravity platform in construction basin; four tower cranes and four concrete-placing booms are carried on the slipform equipment (Sir Robert McAlpine & Sons Ltd)

Concrete-placing booms have been extensively used in the construction of concrete oil jackets for the North Sea. Associated with slip-forming, the boom assembly has had to be carried on the slipform equipment, in addition to the normal loads and that of tower cranes as well! This aspect is considered in more detail in chapter 10, which deals with formwork generally. Suffice it to say, at this stage, that the loads involved are considerable, and the slipform equipment has to be a good deal stronger than is normally the case. Figure 5.29 makes the point.

MOBILE CRANES

While it is the maker's responsibility to design any mobile crane to be safe and sufficient for the capacities stated, it must be remembered that certain temporary works are the responsibility of the contractor. First, he is responsible for the provision of stable, level areas when lifting. Secondly, when outriggers have to be used, he is responsible for ensuring

Fig. 5.30. Multiple outrigger system for heavy mobile tower crane (Coles Cranes Ltd)

Fig. 5.31. Central batching plant, showing temporary works items (Benford Ltd)

that the bearing available for the outriggers to rest on is adequate for the loads involved. In poor ground, special foundations may be needed.

Thirdly, where a crane is required to work near to an open excavation, the temporary works designer will need to ensure that an adequate surcharge is built into the excavation support system to account for the crane's weight. In general, the temporary works engineer and the planners need to work closely together to make sure that every aspect of the crane's operation has been provided for, as far as any temporary works requirement is concerned.

The adequate consideration of outrigger loads is especially important when heavy cranes are in use. Failure in this respect is a frequent cause of accidents. The driver should normally be aware of the worst-case loading on the outriggers, but it is an added insurance for the temporary works engineer to check for himself the worst-case loading, particularly when very heavy lifts are involved. The multiple outrigger system shown in Fig. 5.30 gives an indication of how big the support capability needs to be, for a mobile rotary mast tower crane of high capacity.

SITE BATCHING PLANTS

While the supply of concrete required for a construction site usually comes in the form of ready-mixed concrete, the larger civil engineering contracts and, on occasion, building sites too, often find it economic to set up their own central batching plants.

In setting up a central batching plant, a considerable amount of temporary construction is needed: foundations for the plant itself; concrete in bin floors, aprons etc.; bin division walls; and drainage, water supply and electric power. All this is additional to the cost of bringing the plant to the site, erecting it and dismantling on completion.

While costs will vary in time and place, studies carried out suggest that the provision of the temporary works items is likely to be in the order of 63% of the total cost of setting up the plant (i.e. the provision of plant and labour and the necessary materials). There is real scope, therefore, for the temporary works designer to try to reduce these costs as far as practicable without sacrificing safety standards.

One area where this can be done is in relation to the bin walls. If a system of soldier piling with infilling timber is used, full recovery is possible for use on another occasion. A further extension to this philosophy is to make such material the same as that used for major earthworks support (Fig. 5.31 and chapter 7).

Unless the site happens to be a sandy one, not much can be done about reducing the cost of the paving to bin areas and hardstandings

Fig. 5.32. Simple mobile hoist needing little in the way of foundation (ACE Machinery Ltd)

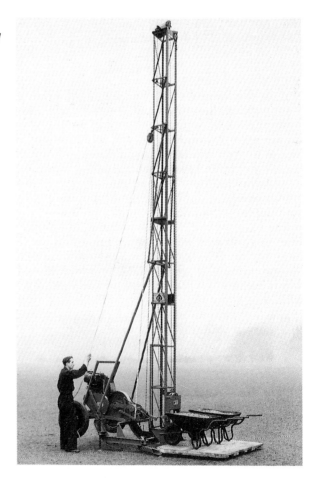

around the mixer. Concrete is necessary to allow washing out at the end of the day's operations. If sandy or gravel conditions exist, the possibility of using precast paving, in large sections (3 m × 3 m, say), can be examined. Certainly in the case of access roads, this is a method used to advantage in Holland, with recovery of the slabs for use elsewhere at the end of the contract.

HOISTS

Temporary works requirements for hoists are in many ways similar to those needed for tower cranes operating in a static mode; that is, the provision of an appropriate foundation and anchorages to the structure. Each type of hoist will have its own special characteristics, and it is important, therefore, that those responsible for the provision of the foundations and anchorages are fully familiar with the characteristics of the hoist to be used.

Fig. 5.33. Twin concrete hoist tower, 120 m high; note anchorages (George Wimpey plc)

The use of hoists is covered by a number of the construction regulations: The Construction (Lifting Operations) Regulations, 1961; The Construction (Working Places) Regulations, 1966; and The Construction (General Provisions) Regulations, 1961. For the temporary works engineer, the lifting operations regulations are particularly important, as they cover the requirements for hoists in relation to enclosure of winches etc., and the safe provision of landings and gates.

In the provision of landings and in the case of passenger hoists, the Health and Safety at Work etc. Act comes into play, as places of work are involved and all safety requirements of the Act need to be complied with. Any passenger hoist is subject to stricter safety requirements than goods hoists, and the temporary works engineer must make himself familiar with the law's requirements in this respect.

Foundations

The hoist maker will provide details of the loadings that will require support, but it is the user's responsibility to provide suitable foundations. With the loads to be supported known, the temporary works designer will have to assess the type of foundation necessary in the light of the prevailing soil conditions. Also, account will have to be taken of the type of hoist in use, and the height to which it has to be erected.

Fig. 5.34. Landing platform at top of tower shown in Fig. 5.33 (George Wimpey plc)

In the case of the small builder's platform hoist (Fig. 5.32), a few sleepers may well be adequate. At the other end of the scale, the twin concrete hoist illustrated in Fig. 5.33 is 120 m high, and the tower surrounding it, to provide a landing for crane skips (Fig. 5.34), is of considerable weight. Design of the foundations and its anchorage to the building is clearly a job for a competent and experienced engineer or structural designer. In between these two examples are centre-slung goods hoists needing a tower, and passenger/goods hoists that do not require a surrounding tower.

Hoists operated by rack and pinion generally have small mast towers and do not need an enclosing scaffold. In such cases the vertical loads are therefore concentrated in a small area of the base. Not only must the design spread the load adequately for the ground conditions, but also it must be adequate to resist the punching shear forces. Foundations for this type of hoist usually take the form of raft slabs containing anchor bolts to hold the mast section in place. The maker will specify his anchorage requirements, and the contractor will have to incorporate these into his base design. A typical base is shown in Fig. 5.35.

Anchorages

All hoists have an operating height above which tying in to the structure will be required, to provide both stability and resistance to wind loadings. Although a necessary feature, such ties are an embarrassment to closing-in the external cladding in the location of the hoist.

The loads to be taken by the ties into the structure are normally stated by the manufacturer for the equipment in question. As with tower cranes, such loads will normally best be resisted by horizontal structural elements such as floors. As the permanent works designer will not have allowed for these forces in his design, he should be consulted about their effect at the planning stage. Any strengthening required to the permanent structure can then be made in good time, and the details prepared of the anchorage elements that need to be cast into the structure as construction proceeds. At the hoist end of the tie, it is usually necessary for the forces involved to be brought back to the nodal points of the tower. As it is unlikely that these will correspond very frequently with floor levels, special collars may need to be designed to transmit loads back to the nodal points.

Figure 5.36 illustrates a tie-in system where the anchorage has to be extended because an external scaffold is required. Designed by the contractor, it needs to comply with the loadings specified by the hoist maker. The most important feature of this tie-in is that it is directly back to the structure.

When considering the number of anchorages that have to be supplied, care is necessary in interpreting the maker's claims about the free-standing height of his tower. For example, a concrete hoist is stated to have a free-standing height of 12 m. From this it may be inferred that ties are only required every 12 m up the tower (or as near to this figure as the floor levels permit). In fact, this may not be the case at all. The

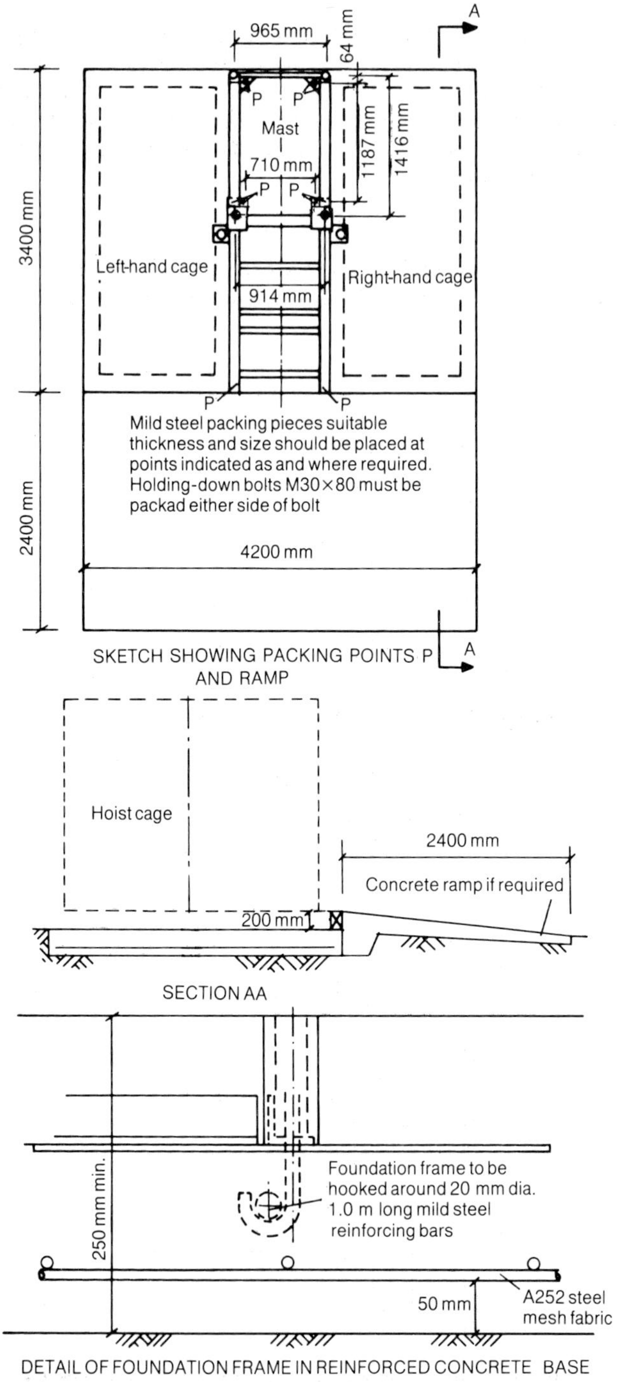

Fig. 5.35. Typical base unit for twin cage hoist (Wickham Engineering Ltd)

headgear and the automatic discharge skip (Fig. 5.37) occupy a given height, h. A further dimension, x, has to be allowed for the discharge chute extension and the floor hopper below it. Then the nearest floor level capable of accepting a tie will be that below the working level. If the manufacturer's free-standing limit is not to be exceeded, the following formula has to be fulfilled:

$$(n + 1) \times \text{storey height} + h + x \not> \text{free-standing height}$$

where n is the number of storeys between ties. What this can mean in practice is demonstrated in the following example, based on Fig. 5.37.

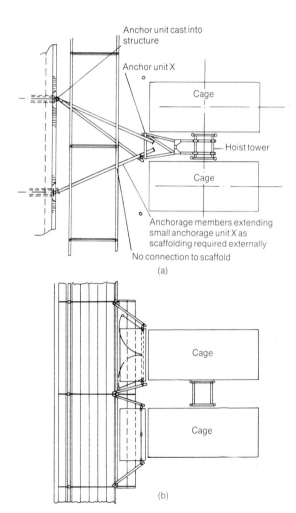

(a)

(b)

Fig. 5.36. (a) Anchorage arrangements for twin cage rack and pinion hoist; (b) as (a) but showing access decking

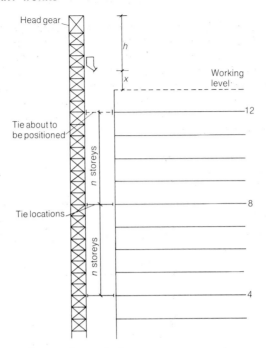

Fig. 5.37. Free-standing conditions for hoists

Let free-standing height = 12 m, h = 3.7 m, x = 2.4 m, storey height = 3.0 m. Substituting these figures in the formula above gives $(4 + 1) \times 3 + 3.7 + 2.4 \not> 12$, or $21.1 \not> 12$, which is absurd. To obey the rules, therefore, it is not possible to put the ties at every fourth floor. The best that can be achieved is to fit ties initially at every floor, and later to remove those in between the standard spacing (every fourth floor). The additional cost in ties and their anchorages will be only too apparent.

When simple cantilever hoists or centre-slung types are in use with a scaffold tower, there is a strong temptation to tie the scaffolding of the tower to the general access scaffolding of the structure. Under no circumstances must this be done. The access scaffolding will be tied in only as is necessary for its own safety. Any hoist tower must be tied directly to the structure.

Access from hoist to building

All hoists must be provided with a safe means of access from the cage to the building, or to the surrounding scaffolding as the case may be. The form that this will take will depend on the hoist type and whether or not it has an enveloping tower. A goods hoist will usually have a surrounding scaffold tower, incorporating a decking arrangement to provide a safe walkway on to the scaffold (Fig. 6.6). With a passenger or passenger/goods hoist, where the driver is required in the cage, a drawbridge mounted in front of the cage gate can be very effective, especially where the structure has no external scaffolding (Fig. 5.38). Constructed in aluminium to avoid too great a reduction in carrying capacity, the bridge unit is pivoted inside the cage behind the line of the gates. When the cage is in motion, the drawbridge is folded back into the cage, but in this position does not greatly interfere with the passengers. A reduction in carrying capacity of one person may be necessary, to account for the slight loss of space and the weight of the bridge unit. On reaching a

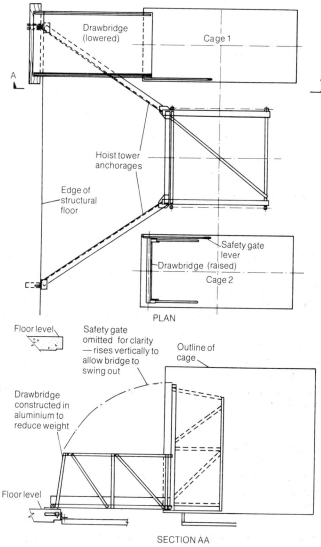

Fig. 5.38. *Drawbridge access from hoist to building*

landing, the safety gate is raised vertically, and the bridge linkage allows the unit to pivot forward on to the structural floor. This method has been used very effectively on very high structures, where no external scaffolding was used. It also has the effect of minimising the amount of any curtain walling that has to be left out.

GENERAL MATTERS

The items of plant considered in this chapter are by no means a complete summary of those that may involve the need for temporary works in their erection and use. While these are the most likely, site planning needs to identify any other items that may need temporary works provision.

Where access is a related subject, reference should also be made to chapter 4. Plant-related temporary works are also considered in chapter 9 (falsework) and chapter 10 (formwork).

In the case of North Sea oil jacket construction in concrete, some rather more exotic plant-related temporary works have arisen. Floating batching plants have been used, with aggregates and cement delivered by water. In other cases, long floating bridges have carried pump pipelines from onshore mixing stations (Fig. 13.14).

6

Scaffolding

Scaffolding can truly be seen as the maid-of-all-work to the construction industry. The great majority of all structures built require the services of scaffolding of one sort or another. So much so, in fact, that it is often taken for granted and not enough care is taken to see that it is erected, used and dismantled safely in proper conformity with the legal requirements. It must always be remembered that scaffolding is provided not only to create a place of work, but also a safe one, which has a safe means of access. Not only must it be safe for those who work on it, but also for those who may be required to work nearby; and, where the scaffold is adjacent to areas open to members of the public, they must be protected from falling objects or materials.

Any scaffold is a place of work, and therefore comes under the requirements of the Health and Safety at Work etc. Act 1974. Specific requirements for scaffolds are given in the Construction (Working Places) Regulations 1966 and the Construction (General Provisions) Regulations 1961 made under the Factories Act 1961 (chapter 2).

Scaffolding can also be affected by many other Acts, regulations, bye-laws and other statutory requirements. It must be recognised, however, that it is the responsibility of anyone dealing with scaffolding to make sure that any relevent legislation has been complied with.

The code of practice which covers scaffolding in its access and working role, and in special structures, is BS 5973.[1] This code superseded CP 97 parts 1 and 3. It is very wide-ranging and detailed in all aspects of scaffolding design and construction. It is clearly a must for all those involved in scaffolding, whether designer, detailer, contractor or erection supervisor.

BS 5974[2] is also relevant when suspended access equipment is needed.

BS 5975, the code of practice that deals with falsework, also contains a great deal of information relating to the use of scaffolding as falsework. Its use in this role is dealt with in chapter 9.

An introduction to scaffolding and the requirements of the code is given in an Institution of Civil Engineers Works Construction Guide.[3] For those involved in design, a book *Falsework and access scaffolds in structrual steel*[4] provides valuable additional guidance and information. Many of the design tables in this book result from experimental work carried out by its author.

As so much documentation is already available in relation to statutory requirements, design methods and specifications covering the material to be used, this chapter is primarily devoted to practical and commercial considerations, which never seem to be dealt with elsewhere. The contractor who requires a scaffold, or is responsible for providing one for the use of others, is well advised to make sure that a number of important matters are properly dealt with, starting from the initial planning to the final realisation on site, and the scaffold's subsequent use. Failure to do so may well involve unnecessary cost and jeopardise site safety. The matters referred to can be divided into a number of quite clear divisions, as set out below.

ESTABLISHING REQUIREMENTS

The initial contract planning needs, amongst other things, to evaluate the requirements for scaffolding and associated matters: hoist towers, ladder towers, loading-out platforms, and so on. In this study the contract document needs to be examined carefully to establish the extent to which provision of access and working platforms is specified for subcontractors.

An experienced estimator or planner will be conscious, at the pre-pricing stage, of the need to relate progressive erection of a scaffold to the envisaged rate of construction. If neglected, sections of the scaffolding may be erected far too early, with unnecessary hire cost being incurred. On buildings of considerable length (e.g. factory sheds) an external scaffold may be needed for the cladding (brickwork, sheeting or whatever may be specified), together with the external plumber.

To provide a full length scaffold in these circumstances usually means that large sections will be unused for much of the time. By providing a mobile scaffolding considerable cost can be saved. A typical example is illustrated in Fig. 6.15 for the brick cladding of a warehouse. Achievement of full height brickwork, two bays at a time, is possible because the columns project beyond the line of the brickwork. Minor errors in horizontal coursing will not be apparent. When using such an approach, full advantage of the possibilities should be taken. Note that a small hoist is included in the mobile unit.

For lateral movement, the scaffold's castor wheels sit in face-up channels reasonably levelled. As the scaffold is not of great weight, movement can be achieved without elaborate levelling of the channels.

In order that a systematic approach is adopted to provide a clear brief when requests for quotations are called for, it is desirable to formulate a standard method of presentation which can be filled in in relation to the specific needs of a particular contract, to provide a briefing 'method statement'.

METHOD STATEMENTS

The procedure for drawing up a method statement should have the following aims and benefits. First, effort should be saved in compilation by the use of standard preprinted forms covering most situations. Those relevant to the particular situation then merely need filling in with the details of what is required.

Secondly, no doubt should be left in the mind of the subcontractor as to what he is pricing.

Thirdly, a breakdown of elements should be allowed (i.e. hoist towers, ladder towers etc. should be priced separately from the main scaffold run). By avoiding an overall lump sum, savings/increases can be evaluated where necessary by reductions/increases in the items provided.

Fourthly, the attention of those pricing the work should be drawn to any unusual features that have to be dealt with and allowed for. Thus consideration should be given to any sections of scaffolding needed to provide access around awkward odd sections of the perimeter of the structure, where fans or safety nets are needed and protective sheeting may be required; also to any requirements related to the protection of the public (protective netting, pavement gantries, brick guards etc.—see later section).

From the foregoing, it will be apparent that the objective of an effective method statement is to achieve an accurate and detailed price. In so doing, the risk of arguments over claims for work not covered in the invitation to quote can be greatly reduced or avoided altogether. The discipline required in preparing such a method statement also makes for more effective management (i.e. more careful consideration of what is wanted—often with considerable saving).

Of further importance in relation to improved management is the setting of the timescale for the scaffolding to be on site. It is not unknown for specialist scaffolding firms to make a good deal of their profit from contractors overrunning the stated contract period and attracting the additional hire rate per week—which is always greater than the weekly rate in the contract period.

Site managements need to keep just as accurate a check on the scaffold programme as they would on construction items. Indeed, it has always been this author's view that scaffold periods should be as much part of a construction programme as any item in the bill of quantities.

SAFETY CONDITIONS

When a method statement has been prepared, and specialist scaffolding firms are asked to quote, it is desirable that a standard form of quotation should be used; this should include a section on safety conditions. The object here is to make sure that everyone is aware of the basis of design and who is responsible for what. (This is particularly important in respect of establishing who is going to provide the foundations and anchorages to the building.)

Some years ago the National Federation of Building Trades Employers (now the Building Employers Confederation) produced a model form of quotation for the hire, erection and dismantling of scaffolding. Use of the current edition[5] is fully supported by the National Association of Scaffolding Contractors. Within this document are a number of matters which are of importance in relation to temporary

Fig. 6.1. Safety conditions: model form of quotation for scaffolding (Building Employers Confederation and National Association of Scaffolding Contractors)

MODEL FORM OF QUOTATION FOR THE HIRE, ERECTION AND DISMANTLING OF SCAFFOLDING

(Owners)   From: Name _____

Address: _____ Our Ref: _____

_____ Your Ref: _____

(Hirers)   To: Name _____ CONTRACT QUOTATION _____

Address: _____

_____ Date _____

Dear Sirs,

(Job Identification)

We thank you for your enquiry dated_____ and have pleasure in submitting the following Quotation for the hire, delivery, erection, dismantling and return of scaffolding. This Quotation is subject to the Model Conditions of Contract for Hire, Erection and Dismantling of Scaffolding, which are deemed to be incorporated in our Quotation, and to the other conditions overleaf.

Yours faithfully,

1. LOCATION

_____

The Hirers shall ensure that the ground is cleared and ready for the erection of equipment by the date on which erection is to begin.

2. DESCRIPTION AND SPECIFICATION OF THE WORK

Including full details of type of materials and uses of scaffolding. For loading specifications see Clause A of the Safety Conditions.

_____

_____

_____

_____

_____

_____

_____

_____

3. LADDER ACCESS

_____

4. MINIMUM PERIOD OF HIRE

_____ weeks, commencing _____

and terminating _____

SAFETY CONDITIONS

A. LOADING SCAFFOLDING(f)

In order to comply with Clause 2 of the Quotation the Scaffold Structure will be constructed on a

_____ (m) (_____ ft) x _____ m(_____ ft) nominal grid and is designed to support safely

_____ No. working platforms with a distributed load of _____ kN/m^2

(_____ lb per ft^2) per working platform. This loading MUST NOT be exceeded.

B. LOADING – SUPPORT SCAFFOLD/FALSEWORK(f)

In order to comply with Clause 2 of the Quotation the Scaffold Structure will be constructed on:

  *a _____ m(ft) x _____ m(ft) grid

  * as shown on drawing No. _____

It is designed to support superimposed vertical loads(g)

  On each standard of _____ tonnes

  As figured on Drawing No. _____

The loadings stated above MUST NOT be exceeded

Without limiting in any way the Owners obligations and liabilities for properly designing the support scaffold/falsework structure, horizontal loading due to wind, side surge and inclined forces have been allowed for:

(a) Wind _____

(b) Side Surge _____

(c) Inclined forces _____

(f) Safety Conditions A and B are alternatives, delete one as appropriate.
(g) Delete one of the following two lines and complete the other.

C. ELECTRICITY CABLES

The Hirer is responsible for ensuring that any electricity cables in the vicinity of the Scaffold Structure have been isolated or insulated to the satisfaction of the local Electricity Board before commencement of erection.

D. WORKING PLATFORMS

If components of working platforms (e.g. scaffold boards, hand rails or ladders) are moved as the Work proceeds, after the Owners shall first have placed them in position, it is the responsibility of the Hirers or of the employers of labour using the Scaffold Structure to ensure that it complies with the Regulations at all times. Scaffold boards must not be used for any other purpose than as part of the Scaffold Structure

continued overleaf

Fig. 6.1—continued

E. FOUNDATIONS

Unless otherwise agreed to the contrary it is the responsibility of the Hirers to ensure that the ground and/or foundations provided for the Scaffold Structure is/are adequate to support the loads to be applied. The Owners shall supply to the Hirers adequate information in respect of any loads imposed on the foundations to enable this to be done. Prior to erection, the Owner will inspect the site and surfaces available before carrying out their work and will inform the Hirer of the loading to be applied and any apparent problem. Subject to this, the Hirer is responsible for any failure of the Owner's work due to a settlement of the subsoil or other defects in the foundations or base which would not be reasonably apparent to the Owner. The Hirer relies on the skill, care and expertise of the Owner in the undertaking of such inspection and advice given as a result of making the same.

F. ANCHORAGES

It is the responsibility of the Hirers to ensure that sufficient anchorage points suitable for a positive tie into the structure are made available either in accordance with B.S.I. Code of Practice No. 5973, as from time to time amended, or to a method agreed between the Hirers and the Owners. The Owners shall be responsible for ensuring an adequate number of such anchorages and their effectiveness.

The Hirers shall be responsible for ensuring that sufficient anchorage points are available during the period of the scaffold erection, use and dismantling.

G. TIES AND BRACINGS

Adequate ties and bracings will be supplied by the Owners. Ties and bracings shall not be removed or interfered with by the Hirers. If it is necessary to alter ties or bracings, this must be carried out by the Owners or by a qualified scaffolder with the agreement of the Owners.

H. CLADDING

No tarpaulins or other types of sheeting are to be fixed to the Scaffold Structure without the prior written consent of the Owners.

I. HANDING OVER CERTIFICATE

(a)   Upon completion of the erection of the Scaffold Structure the Owners shall upon request issue to the Hirers a Handing Over Certificate stating that the Scaffold Structure has been supplied and erected in accordance with the Contract and complies with all Regulations including any design requirements governing the design erection adequacy stability and safety of Scaffold Structures.

(b)   Where the Contract provides for the handing over of sections of a Scaffold Structure such certificate as is referred to in Clause I(a) above shall be issued with reference to such sections upon their dates of completion.

Provided that where a Scaffold Structure has been erected in accordance with the design of the Hirers the issue of a Handing Over Certificate pursuant to these Conditions shall not relieve the Hirers of any responsibility with regard to design. Nevertheless in such a case the Owners shall be responsible for ensuring that the Scaffold Structure is erected in accordance with the Hirers' design.

J. STATUTORY INSPECTION

Whereas the Owners will ensure that the Scaffold Structure is soundly and adequately constructed for the purpose requested by the Hirers and that when constructed it will comply with any applicable Regulation, the Owners cannot undertake to carry out the statutory inspection of the Scaffold Structure or to sign the Register of Scaffold Inspection (Form F91) (Part 1) Section A. Under Regulations these matters are the responsibility of the employers of labour using the Scaffold Structure.

works associated with scaffolding; in particular, the three pages illustrated as Fig. 6.1. The first part shown covers a general statement of what the scaffolding contractor is offering to provide and makes reference to the loading specifications covered in the safety conditions. These are shown in the remainder of the figure.

From these conditions the following will be seen. A clear statement is given of the loading for which the scaffold is designed. Also given are the loads which will be brought down by each standard and for which foundations will be required. (Scaffolding firms do not usually expect to be responsible for foundations, as they will be unaware of the ground conditions and whether or not any excavation has taken place in the area prior to the erection of the scaffold.) With the information suppplied, the contractor who has asked for the quotation can then determine the needs for the foundations.

The scaffolding contractor is also showing if horizontal loads have been allowed for, and their magnitude.

The model form makes the firm statement that all anchorages for tying the structure will be provided by the hirer.

The scaffolding contractor agrees to give a handing-over certificate for an agreed section of completed scaffold, which confirms compliance with all applicable statutes and statutory instruments governing the design and erection of scaffold structures. Statutory inspections, from then on, become the responsibility of the employers of labour using the scaffold.

The value of this document in establishing where responsibility lies in a positive way will be obvious.

For any contract that is let using these model conditions, the companion document, *Model conditions of contract for the hire, erection and dismantling of scaffolding*[6] should be used.

Safety of the public

The Health and Safety at Work etc. Act[7] requires, in section 3, that every employer must conduct his operations so that any persons not in his employ are not exposed to risks to their health or safety, so far as is reasonably practicable. The public at large clearly are included in this section.

When considering the needs of scaffolding for any contract, the contractor supplying the scaffolding must consider what action, if any, he needs to take to protect those not in his employ from any risks. If the site is immediately behind the pavement, the most pressing question will be the risk of materials, tools or other items falling out of the site on to the pavement or road. To avoid such risks, various options are open:

(a) the provision of fans or safety nets carrying fine netting to catch any material etc. that may fall (Fig. 6.2)
(b) the use of brick guards to stop material being accidentally knocked off a scaffold
(c) draping the whole working area of the scaffold with fine netting (Fig. 6.3)

Fig. 6.2 (above). Safety netting carrying fine netting to protect persons below from falling items, as well as providing a catch net for operatives working on the structure

Fig. 6.3. Draping of whole structure in fine netting to stop any tools or materials falling on to the public or vehicles

Fig. 6.4 (above). Pavement gantry, fully boarded, and illuminated, with brick guards; baulk timber at curb to protect scaffold from being struck by vehicles; use of drape netting

Fig. 6.5. Well erected scaffolding, but no brick guards

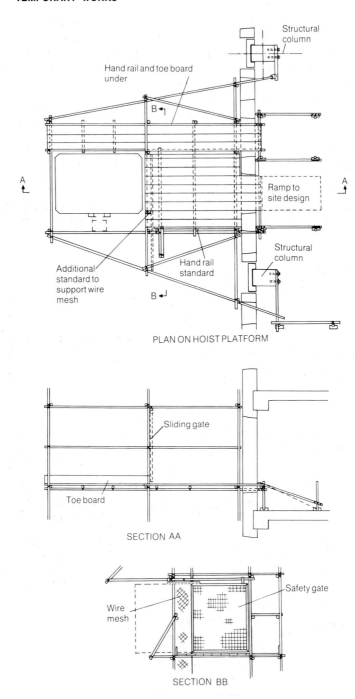

Structural column

Hand rail and toe board under

B

A

A

Ramp to site design

Structural column

Additional standard to support wire mesh

Hand rail standard

B

PLAN ON HOIST PLATFORM

Sliding gate

Toe board

SECTION AA

Wire mesh

Safety gate

SECTION BB

Fig. 6.6. Standard detail for platform hoist requirements

(d) where it is necessary to have a scaffold spanning over a pavement, the provision of a pavement gantry, adequately boarded to prevent dust or objects falling on to the public below (Fig. 6.4)

(e) any special methods in the light of unusual conditions that cannot be safely covered by the methods above.

Each site will have its own risk characteristics, and will need to be considered individually. Figure 6.5 illustrates a well erected scaffold, with hand rail and toe boards. What is missing is any form of brick guard to stop the brick stacks being knocked off the working platform. The working places regulations are often misunderstood in this respect.

ACCURACY AND SPECIFIC REQUIREMENTS

The method statement approach can be speeded up if the main contractor, or whoever else is responsible for seeing that a scaffold is provid-

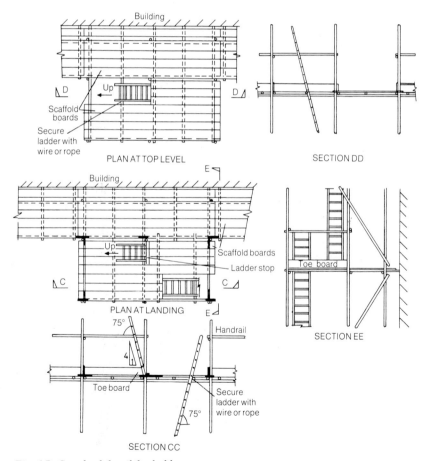

Fig. 6.7. Standard detail for ladder tower

ed, has a set of standard details to which he wishes the supplier of scaffolding to conform. One drawing, for example, should set out good practice requirements in relation to plumb and level of members, bracing, tie spacings and locations, and so on. Other drawings can conveniently detail standard ladder towers, hoist towers suitable for the company's hoists, and any other details which are found to occur over and over again. Two examples of such standard details are given in Figs 6.6 and 6.7.

While a comprehensive code exists, and most scaffold firms are very experienced, the contractor in charge of the site needs to remember that, under the Health and Safety at Work etc. Act, he, as well as the specialist subcontractor, has a responsibility for any scaffold that may be erected. Not only will he have to carry out statutory inspections as required by the Construction (Working Places) Regulations 1966 but also he will have to assure himself that what has been provided is safe and sufficient for the purpose for which it has been erected.

While most access scaffolds are designed to very large factors of safety, the organisation or person in control of the site should establish a rule determining when a specialist scaffolding contractor should be asked to provide calculations and drawings for checking purposes. For complex configurations, the circumstances should also be established when a clear drawing to a large scale, showing all couplers, should be provided. (Some examples of this latter situation are given in BS 5973.[1])

It has been found in practice that an effective guide to the situations where calculations and drawings should be provided is as follows.

(a) Calculations should be provided for an access scaffold above 20 storeys.
(b) Calculations and details should be provided
     (i) for any scaffold that cantilevers out of a structure, or where a truss-out method of support is used for a scaffold above
     (ii) for any scaffold required to carry heavy loading either overall or in highly localised points.

(Item (ii) applies particularly in falsework, and is dealt with in chapter 9.)

SCAFFOLD TIES

The code deals very comprehensively with the tying-in of scaffolds to the structure. There are, however, a number of matters that can usefully be commented upon or emphasised, from a practical point of view.

Ties through windows

The code makes a good deal of the method of using ties through windows, as it is the method traditionally used in building. While the illustrations show that the method is positive in every respect, the disadvantages are not mentioned—even though they have a very serious effect on the safety of the scaffold. These are as follows.

First, the presence of the tubing inside the building means that internal finishes and decoration cannot be completed until the external scaffold has been removed; or at best, small areas will have to be left until much later and completed at considerable extra cost.

Secondly, the internal areas cannot be made fully watertight, as the glazing cannot be completed until all ties have been removed.

Thirdly, and perhaps most importantly, the physical presence of an effective tie being in place cannot be established on weekly inspections, without going into every room involved (in the case of dwellings) or every partitioned area (in the case of commercial or industrial buildings). There is a great temptation to save trouble and not inspect every tie internally. This leads to the fourth point: if following trades get to know that the internal fixing of a tie is rarely inspected, there is a temptation to release the tie so that plastering or finishes can be completed on one visit. This is something that happens all too often.

It follows, therefore, that ties are better kept to fixings which relate to the outside of the structure. Examples are given in the code, but some need examination in relation to their ability to resist lateral loads as well as horizontal ones (i.e. tension and compression forces). Ties should also have an adequate resistance to bending: settlement of scaffold foundations is not unknown!

Fig. 6.8. Use of scaffold cranes; need for independent anchorage, even if fixed on the scaffold (ACE Machinery Ltd)

Ties for handling plant

On a structure of any significant height, there will be a need to tie in hoists or their towers to the structure; also, any items of equipment used for lifting purposes directly attached to the scaffolding itself (e.g. gin wheels and midget scaffold cranes; Fig. 6.8). In the case of hoist towers it is particularly important that such structures are tied directly to the structure being built and not by way of the scaffolding provided for access and working purposes. The rule becomes crucial where a hoist tower is associated with a putlog scaffold. If the tower was attached direct to the scaffold, very little outward movement would be needed to disengage the putlog blades from the wall of the building.

In the case of civil engineering structures, cast-in or drilled anchor fittings will almost always be the appropriate solution. Whilst not yet at anchorage height, the passenger/goods/concrete hoist shown in Fig. 6.9 will have to be dealt with in one of these ways. As the structure is a slipformed group of silos, the drilled anchor method will be most likely—after the slipform has passed.

Mention also needs to be made of the use of loading-out towers associated with the handling of materials by forklift truck. It is a

Fig. 6.9. Passenger goods hoist on slipform construction; in this case anchorage is direct to structure after slip has passed anchor position

*Fig. 6.10.
Loading-out
towers; must not
be anchored to
working scaffold
(Kwikform Ltd)*

common failing to tie such towers to the scaffold. This must not be allowed to happen. The tower should be sited at least 300 mm away from any scaffold. Then, if the tower is inadvertently struck by the materials handler, no damage will be done to the scaffold or the brickwork being built. If the tower was too close, and if, for example, the scaffold was a putlog one, the whole of the brick or blockwork could be pushed over (Fig. 6.10).

SAFETY NETS, EDGE PROTECTION AND PROTECTION FROM FALLING OBJECTS

Considerable sums of money can be saved on many tall structures if they can be constructed without the use of scaffolding. In so doing, however, proper arrangements have to be made for the provision of a safe place of work and access to it. The method of making the workplace safe will depend on what it is that is being built.

Slipform construction

By its very nature, slipform construction is designed to obviate the need for large quantities of scaffolding. Nonetheless, safe working platforms have to be provided at three levels: at the pouring level, at the base of the forms, and at a level low enough to allow final finishing of the concrete surface when it has had time to go off somewhat (Fig. 6.11). All of these stagings, and the means of access to them, must comply with the legal requirements already quoted.

Fig. 6.11. Arrangement of access scaffolding in slipform construction (Sir Robert McAlpine & Sons Ltd)

Fig. 6.12 (below). Edge barrier when no external scaffold in use

Tall buildings

For a tall building, provided that it is designed so that the structure and the cladding can be erected from the inside, no scaffolding is needed to allow the work to proceed. Nevertheless, adequate safety protection must be provided, to avoid both operatives and materials falling out of the structure.

The usual procedure in these cases is to provide a form of barricade at the structural working level, normally bolted down to the previously constructed floor. In the example shown in Fig. 6.12, the wire netting screens are designed to provide a safety barrier for those fixing steel to columns, fixing the formwork, and pouring the concrete. This is achieved by the barrier being one and a half floors high.

On completion of the operations above, the screens are removed and table forms installed for the floor construction. They are provided with edge guard rails and toe boards as required by the regulations.

In this way, the edge safety is mainained at all times. On completion and until the cladding is in place, an edge barrier with suitable hand rails and toe boards is required.

As a secondary precaution on very tall structures, safety nets should also be installed. Two British Standards cover the use of such nets.[8, 9] The first deals with the requirements for the nets themselves, and the second with the way in which they should be rigged. It is usual to install such nets below the structural working level, and raise them progressively as construction proceeds.

Objects falling from a tall structure can reach the ground a long way from its base, particularly when strong winds are blowing. If scaffolding is being used, fans should be provided progressively up the structure.

Fig. 6.13. Safety nets deployed below slipform to gravity platform towers (Sir Robert McAlpine & Sons Ltd)

Table 6.1. Basic checklist for scaffold inspection (tubes and fittings)

Description	Inspection	Action
Foundations	Walk round the perimeter of the scaffold and check for (i) subsidence of the ground (ii) cavities underneath sole plates (iii) dislocation of base plates	(i) Rectify with adjustable base plates (ii) Fill with concrete (iii) Restore in place
Standards	Stand back in front of each standard and check for (i) plumbness (ii) any signs of buckling in first 3–4 lifts	(i) and (ii): stop using scaffold in the affected section until made good
Horizontal bracing	Check in first 3–4 lifts the position of ledgers and transoms First lift is of extreme importance, and the standards must be effectively braced in both directions at ground level Vertical distance between horizontal bracing in the first lift must not be greater than in subsequent lifts	Replace any missing bracing
Diagonal bracing	(i) Transverse bracing to alternate pairs of standards may be fixed either to ledgers or direct to standards (ii) Facade bracing to be fixed to transoms with right-angle couplers and extended from the ground level	As above
Scaffold ties	Check ties in first 3–4 lifts (i) Each tie must be fixed to both ledgers as near to standards as possible (ii) Horizontal spacing must not exceed three bays (iii) Vertical spacing should be at each storey height starting from the first floor, or at every other lift of the scaffolding	Replace any missing tie
Scaffold ties	Check the position and fixing of all scaffold ties	As above

Decking	(i) The working platform should be closely boarded, each board having at least three supports (ii) Boards should be butted and they should oversail their last support by at least 50 mm but not more than 150 mm. Lapping is permissible if bevel pieces are provided to prevent tripping (iii) Precautions should be taken to hold down decking in high winds (iv) Additional scaffold board to be placed between the inner standard and the face of the building when the open space exceeds 300 mm	Do not use scaffold until (i), (ii) and (iv) are rectified (iii) Nail steel straps to hold boards together
Guard rails and toe boards	(i) Both guard rails and toe boards should be fixed to the inside of the outer standards and remain in position before decking is removed (ii) Guard rails should be fitted at not less than 0.9 m and not more than 1.15 m above the decking (iii) Toe boards should be at least 150 mm high above the decking and the clear spacing between the guard rails and toe boards should not exceed 0.75 m *Stacked material needs special consideration*	The decking must not be used until conditions (i)–(iii) are complied with
(a) Standards (b) Ledgers (c) Transoms (d) Diagonal bracing (e) Scaffold ties	Make sure that the members (a)–(d) are not supporting any other loading, vertical or horizontal, coming from external structures like cranes, hoists, loading towers, rubbish chutes etc. These structures should be designed as independent load-carriers with separate ties to the building	

continued overleaf

Table 6.1—continued

Description	Inspection	Action
(a) Safety nets and fans (b) Weather-protection	When (a) and (b) are incorporated in the scaffold, the detailed relevant drawings should be available from the subcontractor for checking purposes	
Ladders	Every ladder must stand on a firm and even base and be supported only by the stiles. The ladder must be securely held in position at top and bottom by fixings to the stiles. The ladder should project at least 1 m above the landing platform. Inspect all rungs for soundness	
Extended scaffold skeleton	(i) Make sure that vertical and horizontal joints in tubes are staggered (ii) Not more than one lift can be erected above the scaffold ties	
Mixed construction of steel and alloy scaffold	No mixing is permitted of steel and alloy scaffold components of the same designation All standards must be made either in steel or alloy Similar requirement applies to ledgers, transoms, bracing and ties Hand rails must be made of the same material as ledgers	The final arrangement to be checked by a competent engineer

Their design is fully dealt with in BS 5973.[1] A wise secondary precaution, especially where structures are being erected without scaffolding, is to drape the upper working levels—where cladding has not yet been erected—with a fine netting, to prevent material being inadvertently thrown out during clearing up or by pure accident. Where safety nets are in use, they can be covered by a fine mesh to achieve the same object.

The principles above can readily be adjusted to suit civil engineering structures; for example, Fig. 6.13 shows safety netting carried on slip-form to high towers of a gravity oil platform.

CHECKING OF SCAFFOLDING

The model form of quotation already discussed makes it quite clear that the weekly checking of scaffolding required by the regulations is the responsibility of the employers of labour using the scaffold. In practice, this means the main contractor.

Many site managers—and, indeed, their subordinates—are ill prepared for this role. On a large site, the problem of how to deal with the statutory requirement—short of having someone spending all his time examining every tube and fitting—often seems insuperable. The answer to this problem is really quite simple. It is based on identifying the key factors in any scaffold which make the scaffold safe or not. These can then be tabulated, and set alongside the form of inspection needed, and the action to be taken if the scaffold is found wanting. A basic checklist for tube-and-fitting scaffolds is shown in Table 6.1.

Scaffolds of a proprietary type (usually called 'system' or 'framed' scaffolds) present fewer problems than tube and fittings. Most have methods of connection which do not require the tightening up of bolts of one kind or another. The connections used cannot be achieved unless the components are properly spaced and plumb, in most instances, and rely on wedge action or a simple drop link operating through a hole in the frame scaffold unit. The main points for checking are therefore the following: foundation sufficiency; anchorages in place, and to the number specified; specified diagonal members in place, and the regulations complied with in respect of toe boards, hand rails and ladder fixing.

SHORT-TERM SCAFFOLDS

In the past, tubular and system scaffolds in particular have found extensive application for short-term use, mobile units being used for internal services installation, cladding (both internal and external), column formwork installation, pouring the concrete in the forms, and much other work.

More recently, however, a minor revolution has been taking place. The growing varieties of the 'aerial work platform', together with 'mechanical access systems', have necessitated a rethink where mobility and short-term use are involved.

When the timescale of use is small, the ability to bring in a mobile work platform or scissor-lift unit, for work within their physical range, on hire, often means that the cost involved is significantly less than that for erecting and dismantling a suitable scaffold. Moreover, the scissor-lift types are usually designed to be capable of elevating materials as well as men, so that hoist and erect are carried out by one item of equipment (Fig. 6.14). As it is dangerous to generalise, it is useful to have a tabulated form of cost comparison that will ensure a fair and reliable comparison with static forms of scaffold access (Table 6.2).

Table 6.2. Cost comparison format for scaffolding versus mechanical access*

£

Mechanical access means
Hire of equipment: £   p.w. ×   weeks =
Fuel and lubrication: £   p.w. ×   weeks =
Transportation: £   per hour ×   hours =
Operator: £   per hour ×   hour week ×   weeks =
Hire of back-up equipment (e.g. generator): £   p.w.
        ×   weeks =
Fuel and lubrication of back-up equipment: £   p.w.
        ×   weeks =
Provision of mains electricity source, plus any cabling =
Mains electricity charges =
Low pressure gas charges =
Labour—dismantle, move and re-erect (if not in subcontract):
          man hours × £   =
          Total cost of mechanical means =   £ _____

Scaffolding or other static means of access
Hire of scaffolding etc.: £   p.w. ×   weeks =
Labour—erect and strike: man hours × £   =
Labour—dismantle, move and re-erect: man
          hours × £   =
Transportation (including driver): £   per hour
        ×   hours =
Estimated losses =
Lump sum subcontract price—materials plus labour =
Allowance for remedial work to floors etc. =
          Total cost of scaffolding etc. =   £ _____

Effective cost of mechanical means
Total cost of mechanical means =
Contract time savings†—deduct   weeks' prelims
        × £   p.w. =
Effective cost of mechanical means =   £ _____

Potential savings
Cost of scaffolding etc. =
Cost of mechanical means =
Savings by use of mechanical access means =   £ _____

* Hourly labour rates are to be those representing the *overall cost to the company of employing the operative.* Where plant hire rates are quoted 'per hour', the figures to be inserted for weekly hire must obviously relate to the proposed hours worked. Fuel and lubrication calculations must likewise follow the same pattern.
† *Not* operational time savings.

The method in Table 6.2 holds good equally well when comparing traditional scaffolding with the portable or fixed work platforms, which provide a substantial length of working platform capable of climbing up and down a vertical mast.

SPECIAL SITUATIONS

Situations can arise where the scaffolding solution is very different from the usual standardised approach. In such circumstances, it may be possible to save a great deal of money; or, by applying expert design, to speed up the overall construction process on the contract in question. Two examples illustrate the point.

The first case study concerns a warehouse in precast concrete construction which had to be clad in brickwork. The main columns projected beyond the line of the brickwork. Instead of a full scaffold being erected to one elevation, a mobile scaffold was devised to cover two bays of the elevation (Fig. 6.15). As it was of light construction, standard castors were used, and upturned channel section was adopted as the

Fig. 6.14. Scissor-lift equipment as short-term-use replacement for traditional scaffold

Fig. 6.15 (above).
Mobile scaffolding for
building cladding

Fig. 6.16. Cantilever
support to scaffold 26
floors high; fan
protection for those
working below

Fig. 6.17. Scaffold collapse due to lack of ties and bracing

track: as such it only needed to be roughly levelled. Incorporated in the mobile unit was a small hoist for handling mortar and bricks.

The saving by the use of this method was considerable.

The second case study, in a central redevelopment project, concerns a 28-storey tower block surrounded by low rise construction. The tower design was such that an external scaffold was essential. If it had been erected from the basement level, no work would have been possible on the low rise area until the scaffold was dismantled from the tower, and the whole project would have been delayed.

To overcome this difficulty, it was decided to cantilever out the scaffolding from the second-floor cantilever as shown in Fig. 6.16.

In a situation of this nature, special care is needed in the design of the cantilever anchorages and in the detailing of the supports for the scaffold standards. As the cantilever members are carrying 26 floors of scaffolding, the anchorage is crucial. In the situation illustrated, suitable anchor bolts were cast in when the cantilever structure was concreted. In this way a positive anchorage was achieved. The ends of the cantilevers were then linked together, with a channel at the extremities to provide rigidity. The scaffold standards were carried in upturned channels welded to the cantilevers, so that there was no possibility of slipping off.

The result was very successful, with the low rise construction able to proceed at the appropriate time.

It will be clear that those responsible for scaffolding need to be imaginative in their approach, as considerable savings can be achieved, or awkward programme situations resolved, by not just accepting the standard method.

FINAL NOTE

Scaffolding is an item of everyday use in temporary works. Lack of care can result in death or injury to human beings. Or at least a very expensive replacement problem (Fig. 6.17).

7

Support of excavations

Excavation is involved in most types of new construction; as well as in works involving alteration and modernisation. An excavation normally requires to be supported, in order to provide safe working conditions for those employees who may work in or adjacent to the excavation; to protect adjacent property; and to facilitate the execution of the new works.

LEGAL REQUIREMENTS

As far as personal safety of employed persons is concerned, the Health and Safety at Work etc. Act[1] requires that all employed persons are to be protected against risks to their health and safety. More specifically, The Construction (General Provisions) Regulations, Part IV,[2] which deals with work in excavations, shafts and tunnels, requires in section 8 (1) that:

'An adequate supply of timber of suitable quality or other suitable support shall where necessary be provided and used to prevent so far as is reasonably practicable and as early as is practicable in the course of the work, danger to any person employed from a fall or dislodgement of earth, rock or other material forming the side or the roof or adjacent to any excavation, shaft, earthwork or tunnel.'

Section 8 (1) (a) adds that the regulation shall not apply

'to any excavation, shaft or earthwork where, having regard to the nature and slope of the sides of the excavation, shaft or earthwork and other circumstances, no fall or dislodgement of earth or other material so as to bury or trap a person employed or so as to strike a person employed from a height of more than 4 feet [1.2 m] is liable to occur.'

The effect of the above regulations is that all excavations which are more than 1.2 m deep have to be supported, unless the sides are excavated to a safe batter or are in unfissured rock with level bedding planes.

In addition, section 10 (1) lays down that:

'No timbering or other support for any part of an excavation, shaft, earthwork or tunnel shall be erected or be substantially added to, altered or dismantled except under the direction of a competent person and so far as possible by competent workmen possessing adequate experience of such work.'

The above regulations cover when support is necessary, and the need for competent persons to carry out such activities. It is just as important to recognise that the design of such supports must be carried out by persons competent to do so, as well.

Rights of support

Manson, in an article on rights of support,[3] states that 'The natural right of support is defined in Halsbury's *Laws of England* as giving every owner of land as an incident of his ownership the right to prevent such use of the neighbouring land as will withdraw the support which the neighbouring land naturally affords to his land'.

It follows that any adjacent excavations must not cause withdrawal of support to the adjoining land or cause damage to buildings which may rest upon it.

Agreements with adjoining owners

Where new construction is to take place adjacent to or near to existing structures, the requirements vary greatly from place to place. Those for inner London are probably as demanding as any, and well illustrate the need for anyone involved in temporary works to make sure that they are fully informed about any legislation, bylaws etc. that may affect their activities.

Inner London

Taking the case of inner London, the following Acts have to be complied with.

The GLC General Powers Act 1966 deals (among other things) with excavations within 30 ft (9 m) of a highway. Elsewhere in the UK, the same control is taken over by the Highways Acts.

Under part VI of the London Building Acts (Amendment) Act 1939, a party wall award has to be agreed between adjoining owners when new construction is to take place against an existing building. The award will contain details of the measures required to protect the existing building while the adjoining property is being developed, both in respect of stability and against the effects of the weather. The temporary works engineer must ensure that he is fully acquainted with the contents of such an award, as the temporary works required will be specified. The architect is usually the person who agrees the party wall award with the adjoining owner's representative.

Safety of buildings is regulated in London by the London Building Acts (Amendment) Act 1939; elsewhere in the UK by sections 76–83 of the Building Act 1984.

If a building owner wishes to place his foundations at a lower level than the adjoining owner's and within 10 ft (3 m), or below an angle of 45° and within 20 ft (6 m), or in any case where a party wall is cut into, underpinned, raised etc., notices must be given under part VI of the London Building Acts (Amendment) Act 1939 (Fig. 7.1). Elsewhere common law applies, but quite often building owners and adjoining

Fig. 7.1. Underpinning to adjacent building; temporary shoring in background required by party wall award

owners (or rather their representatives) agree to operate the procedures under part VI.

Demolition may involve temporary works of one kind or another. It is covered by bylaws in inner London in respect of noise, dust, hours of work etc., made under the London Government Act 1963. Equivalent bylaws occur in the 26 different areas of England and Wales. Notice of demolition must be given to the local authority under section 80 of the Building Act 1984 (but not in inner London). Notice must also be given to the Health and Safety Executive when the demolition site becomes a place of work under the Health and Safety at Work Act 1974.

Elsewhere in the UK

Requirements in relation to agreements with adjoining owners vary considerably across the UK, and may not be as onerous as in the inner London situation. Temporary works engineers should always check with the local authority in question if in doubt.

Damage to existing services

There will be many occasions when public utility services are adjacent to or cross an excavation. The contractor carrying out an excavation has a duty in law not to damage such services. Such a duty is found in the tort of negligence.[4] For negligence to be proved, three essential elements are involved: duty of care; breach of that duty of care; and damage resulting from that breach of care. Unless all three elements are present, negligence cannot be proved, and no negligence arises.

In order to be sure that all precautions have been taken, it is prudent for a contractor engaged in any form of excavation to use his best endeavours to establish the true location of any services which may be in the vicinity of his work. Taking the information off a public utility company's map is not enough. Such maps are rarely accurate to within a metre as to position, and just as inaccurate in relation to depth. Where any form of excavation is to cross a service, the service should be exposed by careful hand excavation, or alternatively, by calculation from visually available points on either side of the proposed line of the excavation.

Failure to comply with a few simple rules can cost the contractor a great deal of money if a key service is disrupted (e.g. telecommunications cables).

Because a contract is out in the country is no excuse for failing to do an adequate survey before excavation is commenced. Gas and petroleum pipelines now abound underground, as do communications cables.

Noise regulations

When consideration begins of the methods of support to be used, and the way in which they are to be installed, the effect of the Control of Pollution Act 1974[5] must be taken into account. In this Act, noise is a pollutant, and sections 60 and 61 deal with the control of noise on construction sites.

Under this Act, local authorities have the power to set noise limits for any particular contract; for example, to specify plant that may or may not be used; to specify the hours during which the works may be carried out; and to specify the level of noise from the premises or any specified point on the premises. This can be of considerable importance when contemplating the use of sheet piling or any other potentially noisy activity in relation to excavation and its support. Those involved in the method planning need to be properly informed of such noise restrictions, at the tender stage. (See also later sections of this chapter.)

Section 61 covers the ways in which prior consent can be negotiated. As one of the ways is through the Architect or Engineer, at the time of obtaining planning consent, a careful study of the contract documents needs to be made at the tender stage to see if specific levels have already been fixed and may limit the choice of method. If not, the contractor will need to contact the local authority and come to an agreement on noise levels—at the tender stage!

Related legislation and bylaws

A check should also be made to see if there are any other Acts or local bylaws which may affect decisions related to the method of support to be used. The City of London (St Paul's Cathedral Preservation) Act 1935[6] is a good example in relation to the support of excavations. It is discussed in some detail in chapter 2.

A further matter of some importance, in connection with the actual installation of support works, is an offshoot of the Construction (Lifting)

Regulations 1961. A certificate of exemption can be issued to make the installation of trench supports and whatever is to go in the trench more efficient. It is known as the Certificate of Exemption CON(LO)/1981/2 (General), Excavators, Loaders and Combined Excavators/Loaders.

The certificate of exemption allows the use of the above equipment temporarily as cranes, solely by the secure attachment of lifting gear to the bucket, or to part of the machine specifically designed for the purpose, for work immediately connected with the excavation. Specific conditions are laid down and have to be met if the certificate is to be issued. Any equipment used in this way must have a certificate uniquely identified with the particular item of plant to which it applies. It, or a copy, must be on site at all times that the machine in question is being used in the crane role.

The limitations to the above use are that the excavator can off-load support material and handle it into the excavation; and it can off-load pipes from a delivery vehicle adjacent to the excavation and lower pipes into the excavation. It must not be used for general unloading or the handling of other materials unconnected with the excavation.

Numerous other pieces of legislation and regulation can be related to the support of excavations, and those associated with the provision of temporary works on a site need to make sure that they are complying with any that may be relevant.

BASIC TYPES OF SUPPORT

The ways by which the support of excavations can be carried out, can be reduced to three basic types: double-sided; single-sided, with raking support; and simple or modified cantilever. Each type has a role to play, and the characteristics of each are as follows.

Double-sided support

The basic features of double-sided support are illustrated in Fig. 7.2. In this method, the sheeting against the ground, the walings and the struts perform the function of maintaining a *status quo* situation when a trench has been excavated. The forces due to earth pressure, from one

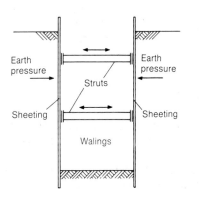

Fig. 7.2. Double-sided support · all forces horizontal

Earth pressure

Struts

Sheeting

Walings

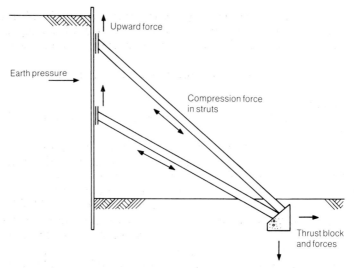

Fig. 7.3. Raking support inside excavation: vertical forces as well as horizontal; total forces in rakers > horizontal earth pressure

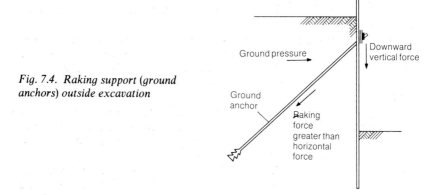

Fig. 7.4. Raking support (ground anchors) outside excavation

Fig. 7.5. (a) Cantilever support; (b) propped cantilever support

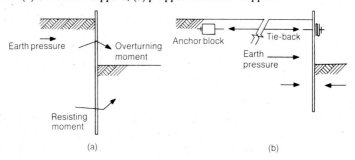

side of the trench, are collected by the sheeting and transferred through the walings to the struts. Here they are opposed by an equal and opposite force from the other side of the excavation, so that equilibrium exists.

With this type of support, all forces involved are horizontal.

Single-sided, with raking support

Two types of raking support are possible and are illustrated in Figs 7.3 and 7.4.

With this method, the sheeting system collects the forces due to earth pressure and again transfers these through walings to the struts, or ground anchors. In this case, however, the struts or anchors are inclined, as no opposite face is available. Where struts are used, the loads coming down them have to be resisted by a suitable foundation. This in turn must be of an adequate design to transfer the loads to the earth in a safe manner. In the case of ground anchors, the anchor design must be adequate to resist the loads coming upon it.

In either case, the loads in the struts or anchors will be greater than the horizontal forces resisted. In addition, the raking nature of the support will induce a vertical force into the support system as a whole. Any design must evaluate the size of such a force and make sure that an equal or greater resisting force is provided.

Failure to provide for these vertical force restraints can have catastrophic results.

Two known cases, in the author's experience, of sheet pile walls inadequately toed into the ground resulted in the whole assembly rearing upwards, causing total collapse of the support system. In one case, it was only gardens that fell into the excavation. The other, in the centre of London, resulted in half a side street falling into the excavation, together with lamp posts and cables, and, worst of all, fracture of a water main, which flooded the basement excavation to a depth of some 3 m. The cost of reinstatement in such cases is not cheap for the contractor, and the various authorities involved are not amused!

With ground anchors, the vertical force acts downwards and one may be forgiven for thinking that the system is fail-safe. While to a degree this is so, it must be remembered that any downward movement associated with a notionally fixed-length anchor will inevitably cause the top of the support system to move inwards. Such movement may well be enough to cause settlement to the adjoining ground of a magnitude sufficient to cause damage to service facilities adjacent. One case of downward movement known to the writer occurred in Canada. Here a soldier-pile support system actually moved downwards 1 m. The resulting horizontal movement inwards of the support was 200 mm.

Simple or modified cantilever support

Provided that a sheeting material has sufficient section modulus, there is, in theory, no reason why a cantilever method cannot be used, avoiding the need for any form of propping. In practice, however, all such cantilever methods will deflect to an unacceptable degree if used near adjoining structures. The only direct way such deflection can be avoided would involve a section modulus so big that its use would be uneconomic.

The disadvantage of cantilever methods can be overcome if the propped cantilever system is adopted. Figure 7.5 illustrates both methods. The propped cantilever approach has many useful applications; while the pure cantilever can only be used in locations where some movement and settlement can be tolerated (e.g. in open-field site conditions).

STANDARD AND DESIGNED SOLUTIONS

In the past, much of the support of excavations was carried out by 'timbermen'. Such persons were men of long experience in the world of excavation and its support. They could be relied upon to timber trenches, in particular, in a safe and efficient manner. Their capability was based on long experience, often passed down from one generation to another, of what any particular type of ground condition demanded by way of support for a safe condition. No design as such was done: the methods used were rule of thumb learnt the hard way, or what might be termed standard solutions. In today's world, the concept of standard solutions can be enlarged by the availability of proprietary equipment for which the makers provide tables for use in various types of ground.

Table 7.1. Recommended limitations on the use of standard solutions

Criteria

Standard solutions should only be used for the support of excavations:

  (a)   where open cut not exceeding 6 m in depth is feasible
  (b)   with double-sided support, in non-water-bearing ground, excavation not exceeding 6 m in depth
  (c)   in shallow pits not exceeding 6 m in depth
  (d)   in water-bearing ground, where water problems have been eliminated by other means (e.g. well-pointing), within the limitations of (b) and (c).

Procedures

In the above situations the procedures below should be followed.

When deciding the batter of an open cut excavation, proper account must be taken of the material and its characteristics and the safe slopes recommended in *Trenching practice*[7] or *Timber in excavations*[8] or chapter 8 of the BEC safety manual.[9]

Do not assume that excavation in rock is necessarily stable. Look for sloping strata, fissures and loose material after blasting. Support unless absolutely sure that the material is stable.

Supervision should make sure that persons erecting or removing supports have been adequately instructed on the method to be used.

Where proprietary methods are being used, the procedures must be strictly in accordance with the manufacturer's instructions.

All relevant legislation must be complied with.

Equally, any suitably qualified person can develop designs of a standard character for use in specified ground conditions.

While some situations can safely be left to the use of appropriate standard solutions, particularly in relation to trench support of limited depth, it is equally clear that other situations arise where detailed design by persons with the necessary skill is essential.

The support of excavations, therefore, can be divided into two distinct categories: situations which can be dealt with by standard solutions; and conditions which require the support to be individually designed by persons competent to do so. For safety in use it is essential that clear parameters are established to indicate when standard solutions can safely be used and when special design is necessary.

On re-examination of the basic types of support, and the comments made for each, it becomes clear that only double-sided support can be safely considered for use in the context of standard solutions. Even then, some limitation on depth needs to be applied. All the recent publications in this field are in agreement that the use of standard solutions should be limited to trenches and shallow pits not exceeding 6 m in depth. To delineate the division more clearly, Table 7.1 sets out the criteria in detail, together with the procedures that should be followed when using standard solutions.

STANDARD SOLUTIONS

With Table 7.1 in mind, some further consideration of standard solutions is necessary; in particular, to establish where suitable guidance can be obtained.

Until the late 1970s, the industry was ill served by authoritative guidance in relation to temporary works in general and the support of excavations in particular. Happily this situation, in relation to excavations, has now been remedied by a number of publications from the Construction Industry Research and Information Association, the Timber Research and Development Association and the Building Employers Confederation.[7-11] Of these, *Timber in excavations, Proprietary trench support systems* and *Trenching practice* are particularly relevant to the standard solution approach. They should be read in conjunction with the Building Employers Confederation safety manual,[9] chapter 8, which deals exclusively with safety in excavations.

Timber in excavations and *Trenching practice* primarily cover what could be called traditional methods of trench support: timber and trench sheeting for the side sheeting, timber for the walings, and timber or adjustable steel struts for the strutting. Both publications describe in detail the method of installation and use, and give checklists for checking the work at all stages. Both have broken new ground in advice on the support of excavations and are to be recommended unreservedly.

Proprietary systems

The Health and Safety at Work etc. Act lays great stress on the provision of a safe place of work. Too often the installation of trench support involved risk to those installing it. Accidents to workers in this field was depressingly high, usually because operatives worked in the trench to erect the support without the protection of previously installed support.

Pressure to improve this situation led to the development of 'proprietary systems'. In recent years, the growth of such systems has been considerable. Those now available have been well documented in an authoritative report from the Construction Industry Research and Information Association,[10] to which reference should be made. The document contains comparisons of the various systems and their modes of use, and lists the names of suppliers.

The available systems fall into a number of well defined groups: hydraulic struts associated with waling systems (usually in aluminium to save weight); shields or boxes which are dragged along the trench as work proceeds; box or plate supports; and special methods.

Hydraulic struts with walings

A typical system of hydraulic struts with walings is shown in Fig. 7.6. The objective is to provide a strut–waling assembly which can be

Fig. 7.6. Aluminium walings with hydraulic struts; lowered into trench as a unit, and struts operated by hydraulic pump seen on right (Mechplant Ltd)

*Fig. 7.7. Manhole
support system
(Mechplant Ltd)*

lowered into the trench and hydraulically stressed against the sheeting without the need for an operative to enter the trench at any time.

While the initial cost is high, such systems have found favour with contractors where the supported length of a trench can be kept short and a rapid turnover of the equipment can be achieved; in this way the hire rate of the equipment becomes economic. The ability to do this has been greatly helped where, for example, specifications allow testing of pipes in short lengths; and not having to test between manholes only.

These systems normally only cover the support of trenches up to 6 m deep. Installation must be strictly in accordance with the manufacturer's instructions and limitations of use. The manufacturers of this equipment also market manhole supports operating in a similar way (Fig. 7.7).

The waling members are made in aluminium, both for lightness and to allow them to take up the line of the trench when strutted against the sheeting. The aluminium, being resilient, straightens out on removal. Figure 7.6 shows a three-strut section, but wider-spaced two-strut units are also available to provide greater access room for long pipes.

Shields or drag boxes

As the name suggests, shields or drag boxes are designed primarily as a protection to persons working in an excavation rather than an excavation support. The side sheeting and the strutting which keeps the sheeting apart provides a rigid box. As the work proceeds, the box is pulled forward by the excavating machine to the new working area.

Such boxes are simple to make and, as they are rigid structures, require little maintenance. Inevitably, though, they are heavy, and the excavator has to be of enough power to pull them forward in the trench. A typical example is shown in Fig. 7.8.

Box and plate lining systems

Not to be confused with shields or drag boxes, box and plate lining systems are designed for support and not just protection. Boxes here mean strutted support walls of a modular nature, which can be positioned by machine, and built up vertically and laterally (Fig. 7.9). They are not designed to be dragged along the trench.

Plate lining methods work on the principle of installing a pair of vertical members and linking struts at set intervals, between which heavy plates slide into position (Fig. 7.10). As the excavation proceeds, so the plate elements can be pushed downwards and further units added from above.

With either of these methods, cross services present a problem, as the run of the system has to be interrupted. Other methods for support have to be used in this area.

Box and plate lining systems are expensive and their economy is dependent on speedy progress to minimise the hire rate per unit run of trench.

A further need for a good rate of progress is the fact that, if left in position for too long, some difficulty may be experienced in extracting the equipment.

Fig. 7.8. Drag-box protection in action (GKN Kwikform Ltd and Jayville Engineering Ltd)

Fig. 7.9 (above). Box support system (Scaffolding (Great Britain) Ltd, distributors of Krings linings)

Fig. 7.10. Plate lining method (Scaffolding (Great Britain) Ltd, distributors of Krings linings)

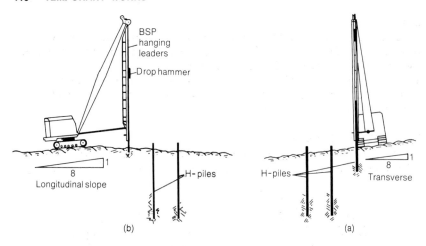

Fig. 7.11 (above).
Principle of driving
H-piles

Fig. 7.12. View of
driving in progress

Special systems
Many contractors have their own designed methods and in some cases they are available for hire. The main piece of equipment of this type in the UK is the Ramshor. Of some magnitude, it is a hydraulically operated machine for installing vertical sheet piles. The equipment is self-powered and self-propelled. Its disadvantages are the considerable weight and size and the lengthy time to set up.

DESIGNED SOLUTIONS

With the criteria established for standard solutions, it follows that all other situations require that the support should be designed by a person

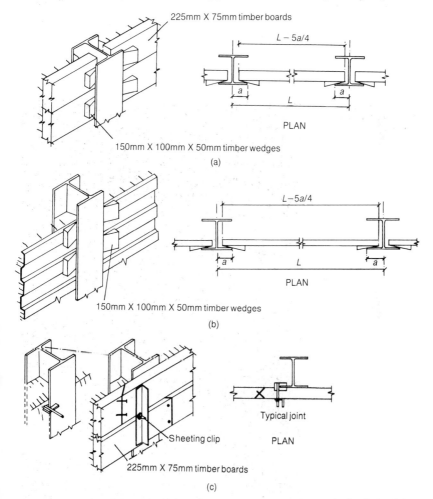

Fig. 7.13. Methods of attaching timbers to H-piles: (a) timber tucked in behind face flange; (b) trench sheeting tucked behind face flange; (c) random-length timber clipped to face flange

or persons competent to do so. While the methods of support for run-of-the-mill situations are dealt with in great detail in the publications already referred to,[7–11] further consideration is necessary in relation to bigger schemes, where the traditional support systems are no longer appropriate, either technically or in terms of cost.

On an international basis, two methods of support stand head and shoulders above all others: steel sheet piling, for conditions of free water in the ground, and H-piling (soldier piling) where no free water exists. The dry condition support is taken first.

H-piling or soldier piling

Sometimes also known as the Berlin wall method, the H-piling or soldier piling technique of supporting excavations, in dry conditions, is the most universal worldwide. This is not really surprising, as the method has important advantages, both structurally and in its flexibility of operation and use.

Basic system

Universal column sections (H-sections) are driven into the ground before any excavation is commenced. The usual method is by drop hammer and hanging leaders (Figs 7.11 and 7.12). While the H-section is to be preferred, it is not uncommon to see substantial I-sections in use as well.

Once the piles are in position, excavation is commenced, and the exposed ground between the piles is timbered or sheeted from the top

Fig. 7.14. Arching effect with H-piles before sheeting inserted

downwards. A number of methods can be used; the most common are illustrated in Fig. 7.13. Of these, the timber tucked in behind the face flange of the pile is far and away the most common around the world. The other methods all have their uses in particular circumstances and will be described in relation to specific applications.

The advantages of the H-pile system are considerable and can be listed as follows.

First, the main support structure is in place before any excavation takes place.

Secondly, the method of timbering is flexible. A decision on whether to use full timbering, hit and miss, or other combinations is not integral with the design. The ground can be dealt with as found. Considerable economy can result. If time shows that closer timbering should have been used (earth swelling between boards), the matter can be rectified without trouble. All that is needed is limited excavation between the offending timbers, and additional timbers inserted.

Thirdly, due to an arching effect between the piles, the loads on the horizontal timbers are not as great as would normally be expected. A saving in timber section results.

Fourthly, having the steel faces of the H-piles visible on the inside of the support system provides a surface to which other members can be welded to create additional flexibility in use.

Fifthly, by the very nature of the predriven piles, the support can be effectively tailored to go between services or other obstructions without risk of damage to them.

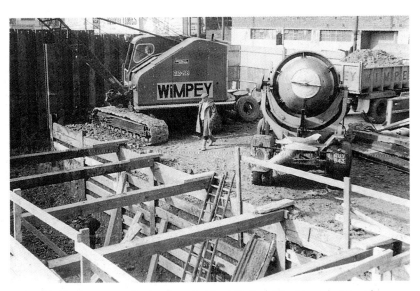

Fig. 7.15. Timbering to suit the ground: hit and miss with wider spacing at lower levels

How these characteristics work in practice, and the advantages that accrue, are dealt with in the following sections.

Main supports in place before excavation

While, in theory, the sheeting can be positioned when the excavation is only deep enough for installation of one horizontal board, in practice most people dig out to a greater depth before attempting to install the sheeting. The value of the main supports being in place already is best seen if some of the side of the excavation should fall in before the sheeting can be positioned (Fig. 7.14). The arching effect that results is clearly seen and the large tipper lorry is in no danger of falling into the excavation, in spite of the fact that the material that has collapsed is old filled ground sitting on top of gravel. This could be said to be the first fail-safe mechanism of the method as a whole.

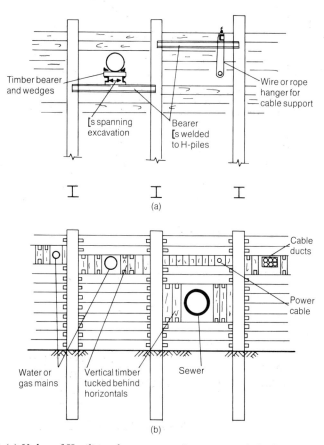

Fig. 7.16. (a) Value of H-piling when support of services needed; (b) flexibility of H-piling when dealing with services passing through the support

Flexible method of timbering

A major advantage of H-piling is that the timbering is not part of the overall design parameters, other than the span that it will achieve for a given anticipated load. If the ground is found to be much stiffer than anticipated, the amount of horizontal timbering can be reduced from, say, full timbering to half timbering (Fig. 7.15). If with time this decision is found to be a mistake (e.g. if clay begins to squeeze between the half timbering), the situation can easily be remedied. All that is needed is to excavate between the in-place timbers and insert additional timbers in the miss spaces.

Cases are not unknown where, when excavation had reached the blue London clay, the material was so hard that timbering could be left out

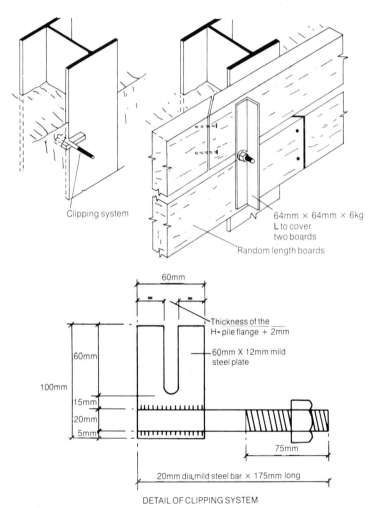

Fig. 7.17. Use of random-length timbering: clipping method

Fig. 7.18 (above).
Random-length
timbers in action
(George Wimpey plc)

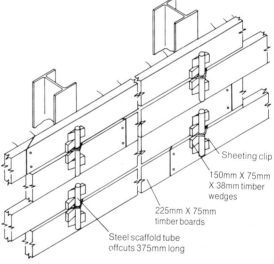

Sheeting clip

150mm X 75mm
X 38mm timber
wedges

225mm X 75mm
timber boards

Steel scaffold tube
offcuts 375mm long

Fig. 7.19. Clipping
system to cope with
pile location errors

PLAN

altogether. It is much easier to make such decisions when a retrieval is possible if the idea turns out to be wrong.

The great flexibility possible with the timbering stage is a great advantage if support is needed to an excavated face across the paths of a number of service ducts, cables or pipelines. Provided that the locations of all services are properly determined beforehand—preferably by hand excavation actually exposing them—the individual piles can be driven with confidence between the services. Timbering the face can then be arranged to suit the local conditions. Figure 7.16 illustrates the way in which this is done.

While the cut-to-length tuck-in board method is far and away the most used worldwide, it is also possible to use random-length boards. In the right situations this approach is the most economical in timber: cutting to length is avoided and only minimal preparation of the excavated face is needed. The key to this way of use is in the clipping system. One method is shown in Fig. 7.17. It is really self-explanatory and is shown in action in Fig. 7.18. Another method, shown in Fig. 7.19, is designed to overcome a frequent problem in H-piling practice—that of error in pile location. As can be seen, the pile can twist in relation to the wall line, but the clipping arrangement will still be effective. Specific details of this clip for various sizes of H-pile are given in Fig. 7.20.

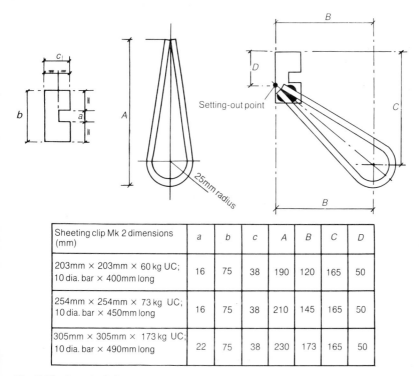

Sheeting clip Mk 2 dimensions (mm)	a	b	c	A	B	C	D
203mm × 203mm × 60 kg UC; 10 dia. bar × 400mm long	16	75	38	190	120	165	50
254mm × 254mm × 73 kg UC; 10 dia. bar × 450mm long	16	75	38	210	145	165	50
305mm × 305mm × 173 kg UC; 10 dia. bar × 490mm long	22	75	38	230	173	165	50

Fig. 7.20. Detail of clip sizes

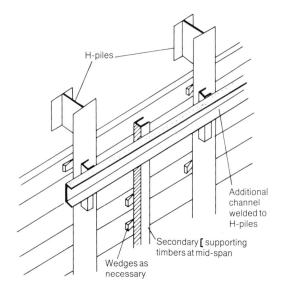

Fig. 7.21. Retrieval capability with H-piles

The value of steel faces

The fact that the inside flange of the H-pile is visible from the inside of the trench (in the standard timbering method) provides further flexibility. Being able to weld on other steel elements has many advantages.

First, where services cross the excavation, support is often needed and frequently specified. Suitable steel bridging members can readily be supported off the soldier piles (Fig. 7.16(a)).

Secondly, if the worst should happen and the span for even full sheeting has been miscalculated, and the timbers are bulging under the pressure of earth, additional support can be introduced by welding members to the faces of the H-piles as shown in Fig. 7.21. That this is possible is due to the fact that the H-piles themselves are not normally ever fully stressed.

Thirdly, the attachment of steel walings and struts presents no problem, other than making sure that the welders employed work to a laid-down standard. In view of the safety aspects involved, Lloyds'-certified welders should be used. The same requirements should apply when dealing with raking struts and bearings for ground anchors.

This 'weldability' property of H-piling creates the ability to widen the application of H-pile support beyond the simple support so far illustrated. The following case studies serve to illustrate the further flexibility of this much-used method of earthworks support.

Case study: retaining wall

In a central development project, a retaining wall had to be constructed immediately behind the pavement, under which were old vaults. The new basement was deeper than the vaults, and the consulting engineer required a heel to be provided to the wall. Figure 7.22(a) illustrates

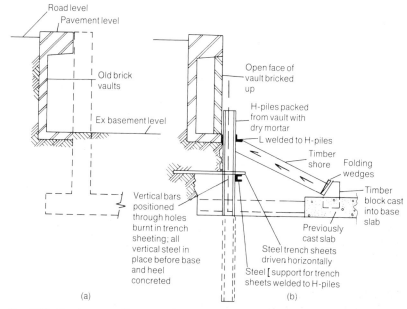

Fig. 7.22. Retaining wall case study: extension of H-pile use—(a) existing and new work; (b) initial stage

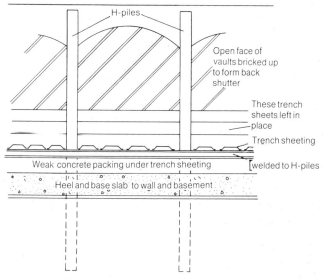

Fig. 7.23. Retaining wall case study: elevation on completion of toe to wall (reinforcement in place not shown)

the existing condition, with the new wall superimposed. Clearly, support was required both to stop undermining the vault foundations and to avoid any possibility of the vault falling into the new basement area.

Stage 1 of the method adopted is shown in Fig. 7.22(b). H-piles were driven opposite each dividing wall of the vaults, with raking shores supported off the basement slab, previously completed to a convenient distance from the boundary wall.

Stage 2, the construction of the toe under the pavement, is shown in Fig. 7.22(b) and Fig. 7.23. To provide a safe working environment for the operatives mining out under the vaults, a channel section was first welded across the H-pile faces at a suitable height. Using this as a support, steel trench sheeting was driven horizontally, as shown, to a distance adequate to provide safe support when the heel area was excavated. Those doing the mining-out, therefore, had a steel-sheeted roof over their heads.

With excavation complete, the toe and upstand to the wall were constructed. When set, the space between the heel and the trench sheeting was filled with weak concrete, the ends of the sheeting were burned off and the channel member was removed.

For the construction of the remainder of the wall, a number of matters had to be taken care of. From the illustrations so far, it is apparent that

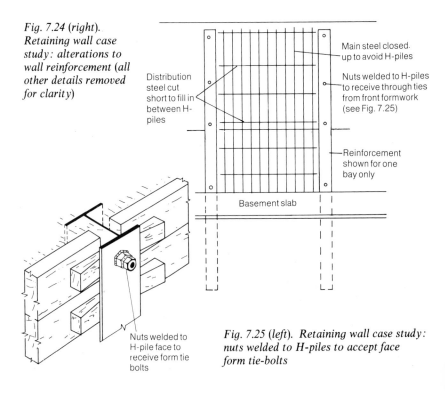

Fig. 7.24 (right). Retaining wall case study: alterations to wall reinforcement (all other details removed for clarity)

Distribution steel cut short to fill in between H-piles

Main steel closed up to avoid H-piles

Nuts welded to H-piles to receive through ties from front formwork (see Fig. 7.25)

Reinforcement shown for one bay only

Basement slab

Nuts welded to H-pile face to receive form tie bolts

Fig. 7.25 (left). Retaining wall case study: nuts welded to H-piles to accept face form tie-bolts

the H-pile system was within the wall thickness. By agreement with the Engineer, this was left in place, and acted as part of the cantilever reinforcement. As the wall main steel was all vertical (cantilever design), no alteration was necessary. All that had to be altered was the horizontal distribution steel at the back of the wall. Instead of random lengths, the bars were cut to fit in between the H-pile spacings (Fig. 7.24). Before the wall was poured, the raking shores were removed. (Once the heel had been constructed and the void backfilled with concrete, the stability of the old vaults was secure.)

To save a lot of concrete being wasted, the vaults were bricked up at an early stage, so that a back shutter was available. As only a front shutter was needed for the wall, a further detail possible with the H-pile system is shown in Fig. 7.25. Nuts were welded to the H-pile face, into which the shutter tie bolts were screwed. By this means, awkward raking shoring to the forms was avoided.

Case study: raft foundation

The construction of a 28-storey office building required a raft foundation, 3 m thick, supported on 195 bored piles 750 mm in diameter. The top of the raft was 2.8 m below the ground level. In plan, the raft dimensions were 34 m × 27.75 m. Overlaying the whole site area was an exist-

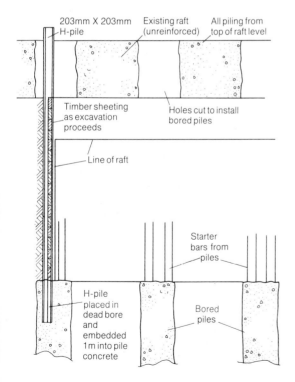

Fig. 7.26. Raft foundation case study: installation of H-piles to raft excavation support

ing raft of unreinforced concrete, on average about 700 mm thick. For the construction of the raft, an excavation 5.8 m deep would be involved, for which support would be necessary.

When the method of support was considered, study of the site boreholes showed that a black silt would be encountered in the lower levels of the excavation. Because of this, considerable concern was felt about the ability to achieve a satisfactory bottom anchorage for the H-pile method preferred. Indeed, it was felt that whatever method was used the problem would be the same. The way in which the problem was resolved was a joint effort between the contractor and the Engineer. To stabilise the bottom of the H-piles, it was suggested that they should be embedded in the top of the outside line of bored piles, when they were installed. To enable this to be done, the Engineer, who had shown these piles just inside the raft edge, agreed to move them outwards to be half on and half off the raft. With this arrangement, there was room for the H-piles to be located (Fig. 7.26). There was, of course, no reason why this should not be done, as in their original position the piles would have been supporting only half the weight of all the others.

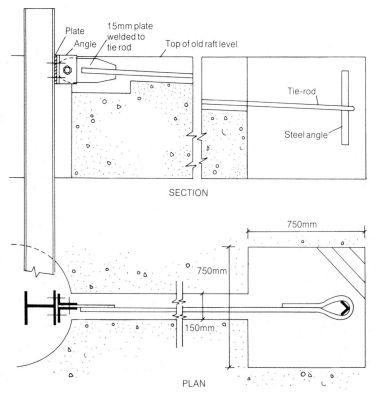

Fig. 7.27. Raft foundation case study: top ties to H-pile supports

With the bottom safely secured, the tops presented no problem at all. It was agreed that all the bored piles should be installed from the top of raft level, and holes cut in the raft to allow this to be done. With the H-piles established in the dead bore of the pile, it was then merely a question of how to support the tops. The solution was a classic example of the temporary works engineer exploiting the characteristics of the site to make savings in temporary works cost.

Figure 7.27 shows the method of tying back the H-piles, utilising the existing concrete raft as a very large external waling. Slots were cut in the raft, ending in holes 0.75 m square and the thickness of the raft in depth. Once the tie-rods were installed, the whole was reconcreted.

In this case study, we have an almost perfect example of temporary support installed for nothing! Only the materials, plus the cost of the tie-back excavation and the subsequent concrete backfill had to be paid for.

It is also a very good demonstration of what has already been mentioned about exploiting what the site may have to offer, in order to minimise temporary works cost. The final icing on the cake occurred when the excavation took place. Very wet silt was encountered, which subsequent enquiries showed was the remains of an old London river, long since filled in. Without the solution of bottom anchorage, problems would undoubtedly have arisen in relation to the stability of the support as a whole. Figure 7.28 shows the site when the excavation was almost finished. It also demonstrates the wisdom of leaving the old raft in place to provide a weatherproof access around the site for as long as possible.

Fig. 7.28. Raft foundation case study: site as completed (George Wimpey plc)

Fig. 7.29. Underground tank case study: support of H-piles by anchor piles and ties

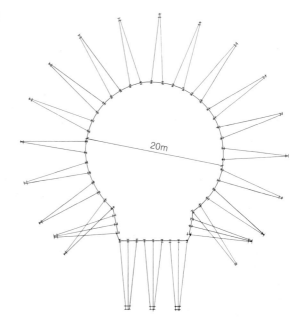

20m

Fig. 7.30 (below). Classic use of sheet piles: caissons for the Barton pier, Humber bridge (John Howard and Co.; Freeman Fox Ltd)

Case study: underground tank

If the H-piling support is in use on a site where the excavation to be supported is well away from the site boundary, an economical tie-back system can be provided without the need for raking shores, or use of ground anchors to give a clear site.

A situation of this nature arose where a deep excavation (10 m) for an underground tank had to be supported. The solution is indicated in Fig. 7.29. Although a large number of tie-backs were needed, they cost a good deal less than any other supporting method considered.

Case study: excavation in clay

An excavation in London Weald clay had taken place and was supported by H-piles. The initial impression of the ground on excavation was that it only needed hit-and-miss horizontal timbers. In wet weather, however, it was found that the clay was bulging between the timbers. This situation was remedied by adding in the miss timber to provide full timbering. Continuing wet conditions, coupled with very heavy traffic loading adjacent to the support system, led to further bulging, even with full timbering, and some action had to be taken, to safeguard the integrity of the support.

The steel face of the H-pile provided the solution. The arrangement of steel channels shown in Fig. 7.21 was established, which halved the distance that the original timber had to span. Each board was removed in turn and the soil re-excavated to leave the board flat when replaced.

Steel sheet piling

Interlocking steel sheet piling has long been a major tool for the support of excavations and, more particularly, for caissons in tidal or

Table 7.2. Advantages and disadvantages of steel sheet piling

Advantages
Interlocking and basically watertight
Good section modulus against bending
Capable of many uses when well looked after
Ideal for 'cut-off' situations where water-bearing ground overlies an impermeable stratum
The only real answer for cofferdams and caissons in tidal and deep-water locations
Can be used when a second barrier is desired against water penetration in deep basement construction in water-bearing ground

Disadvantages
Initial capital cost high
Driving cost high, as whole supported area has to be driven, plus required penetration
Expensive driving plant needed
Special measures needed to meet noise levels set by local authority
Not always watertight; may need expensive caulking

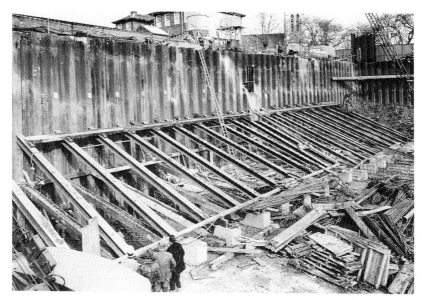

Fig. 7.31. Steel sheer pile support to large basement; to remain part of the permanent construction, with retaining wall cast up to it (ground was unsuitable for ground anchors; the disruptive effect of internal raking shores is only too obvious)

Fig. 7.32. Sheet piling in the cut-off role; in the background, ground anchors used to keep escalator shaft area clear (successors to Acrow Engineers Ltd)

deep-water locations (Fig. 7.30). While it is not always as watertight as may be claimed, judicious caulking is normally all that is necessary to make it so.

In terms of design and use, the advantages and disadvantages are summarised in Table 7.2. From this it will be clear that use of sheet piling is more restricted in economic terms than use of H-piling—which is cheap

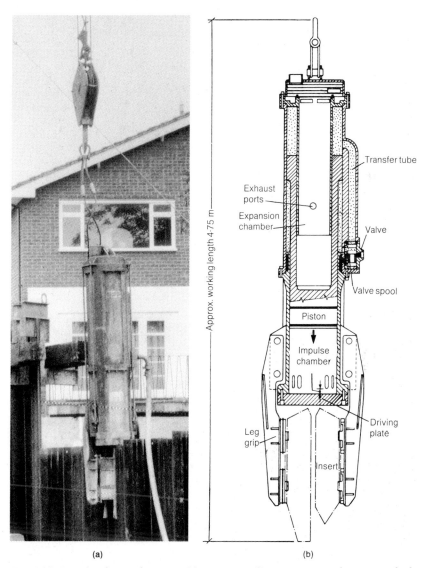

(a)   (b)

Fig. 7.33. Impulse driving hammer: (a) in action; (b) cross-section showing method of operation (BSP International Foundations Ltd)

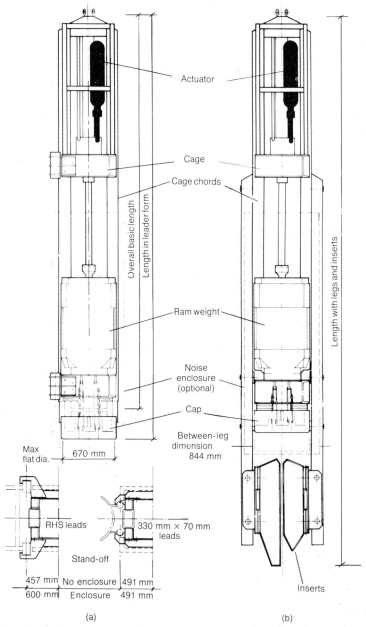

Actuator

Cage

Cage chords

Overall basic length

Length in leader form

Ram weight

Noise enclosure (optional)

Cap

Between-leg dimension 844 mm

Length with legs and inserts

Max flat dia.   670 mm

RHS leads   330 mm × 70 mm leads

Stand-off

457 mm No enclosure 491 mm
600 mm Enclosure 491 mm

Inserts

(a)   (b)

Fig. 7.34. Hydraulic hammer: (a) leader operation; (b) suspension operation (BSP International Foundations Ltd)

to drive, using simple driving equipment, and for which the initial capital cost is far less. Nonetheless, in the right situations no other support material can equal it.

Figure 7.31 illustrates the use of sheet piling initially as part of the temporary works supporting a deep basement. The concrete retaining wall was to be built right up to the sheeting, and the sheet piles were to be left in as additional protection against water penetration. The basement had to be especially dry as it would contain telecommunications equipment when the building was complete. In the event, the combined wall leaked in several places, and considerable trouble had to be taken to stop the leaks. In many ways it provided an object lesson to the contractor. If the specification is clear about non-leakage, money spent on caulking the piling before the concrete wall is cast is money well spent.

Figure 7.32 shows sheet piling in the cut-off role (gravel overlying clay) in the construction of the Victoria line in London.

Driving of sheet piling

Since the introduction of the Control of Pollution Act,[5] local authorities have been empowered to impose noise levels on construction sites (see start of chapter and chapter 2). Before the introduction of the Act, sheet-piling was a noisy operation, both to those doing the installation and to the public at large. One effect of the Act has been to stimulate manufacturers of driving equipment to produce quieter driving hammers, so that sheet piling can still be used in the temporary support role, even in suburban locations.

In order to comply with likely noise limits in urban areas, one firm has developed what is called an impulse hammer (Fig. 7.33). This machine, operated by compressed air, is designed so that steel sheet piling can be installed by normal panel driving methods without objectionable noise and without the need for expensive screening. This desirable objective is achieved by providing an air cushion between the ram and the driving plate which avoids actual impact. Although the air cushion reduces the peak forces, it increases the duration of the applied force. The nature of this driving pulse enables a wide range of piles to be driven in pairs in average conditions without pile damage.

The firm mentioned above also manufactures hydraulic hammers (Fig. 7.34) which can be provided with enclosures which cover the striking area. It is claimed that these noise enclosures can reduce noise output to well below that of diesel hammers. It is also claimed that such noise emission levels are in line with Government legislation and can be used in the urban environment without undue problem. Figure 7.35 shows the hammer in action. The simple but effective pile frame for holding the piles in position while pitching and driving is an example of good temporary works.

Vibratory hammers are also available for the driving of sheet piling. Although the noise level is small, it is necessary to consider the environmental effects of the vibration itself. Excessive vibration can be very unpleasant to the public who may be close to such operations.

Fig. 7.35. Hydraulic hammer in operation (BSP International Foundations Ltd)

OTHER METHODS

The methods of excavation support described in this chapter are those in which physical structural members are involved, these being removed on completion in most cases. In the appropriate circumstances, support to excavations can be achieved without any physical structural additions at all. Four such ways exist:

  (a) if space is available, by excavating to a safe batter, the over excavation and its subsequent replacement being deemed the temporary works
  (b) the use of well-pointing to dry out and stabilise water-bearing non-cohesive soils
  (c) ground freezing, usually by the use of liquid nitrogen—a specialised, expensive process, but where it is the only solution it is the means of doing the job
  (d) chemical stabilisation—again a specialist process suitable in special circumstances, which have to be determined by experts.

Apart from the first method, all are specialised operations and depend on the ground conditions being suitable for their use.

In the following chapter consideration is given to support methods where the permanent works initially act as a temporary works, creating considerable savings in cost.

8

Use of permanent works as temporary support of excavations

Where deep excavations and their supporting walls are involved, construction of retaining walls by conventional methods is usually both time-consuming and expensive. This is largely due to the temporary works needed to build them. Even by the use of H-piling or steel sheet piles, cost is difficult to reduce.

Developments in construction technology have, however, made it possible to re-examine the whole concept of retaining wall construction for deep excavations. A number of methods now exist which allow the deep excavation to have the permanent support wall in place before any excavation is started. With these methods, the only requirement for temporary works is to provide temporary lateral support until the permanent construction is at a stage to fulfil the permanent needs of lateral support. As a result, considerable economies are possible in the overall cost.

Where such approaches are used, it must be recognised that contractual boundaries need examination to make sure where permanent construction design ends and where temporary works begin. Clear traditional fields of responsibility tend to become blurred, and adequate discussion between the parties needs to take place to clarify any grey areas. This point is dealt with in more detail later.

AVAILABLE METHODS

A number of techniques allow the installation of the perimeter walling to a deep excavation, or the structural element of a retaining wall, without the need for any significant temporary works until the excavation is commenced. Indeed, in the case of retaining walls, any support needed is usually included in the permanent works design. The methods amenable to this approach fall into three basic categories: diaphragm walling, contiguous bored piling, and secant piling.

Diaphragm walling

Most people in construction today are familiar with diaphragm or bentonite walling. For those that are not, the fundamental principle involves excavating a trench on the line of the required wall and to the required width, and keeping the sides from falling in by keeping the trench filled at all stages with a mixture of bentonite (fuller's earth) and water. Why this should retain the sides of the trench for considerable depths and in almost any soil is a complex matter and is not discussed here. Those who want to know more about the subject are referred to a number of papers published on the topic (see bibliography for the chapter). Once the excavation is complete, the bentonite liquid is displaced by concrete to provide the retaining structure.

Diaphragm walling cannot start until 'guide walls' have been installed. As the name suggests, they are there to determine the line of the wall and also its width. They are constructed in concrete and are usually 1 m in depth. Their construction is normally the responsibility of the main contractor. They are clearly temporary works. A procedure for their construction is given in chapter 12. It must be remembered that the inner leaf of the guide walls has to be removed early on in the excavation adjacent to the wall. This will involve cost, and ways of minimising such expense are given in chapter 12 as well.

With the guide walls in place, the specialist contractor can start work. The precise methods of installation vary with the firm concerned, and new developments are always taking place. Figure 8.1 is a stylised and generalised presentation of how a diaphragm wall is established in position. Sophisticated hydraulic grabs, rotating-wheel cutters or other means are used to excavate the trench to the width and depth required.

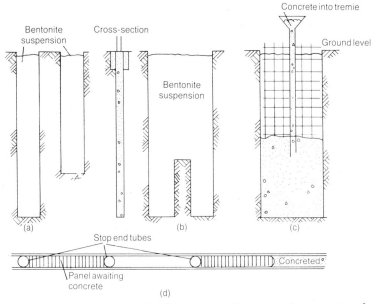

Fig. 8.1. Construction sequence for diaphragm wall: (a) stage 1, excavation of panel—excavation kept filled with bentonite suspension; first one side then the other side of bay; (b) stage 2—centre of panel excavated; panel on completion full of bentonite; (c) stage 3—reinforcement inserted and concrete-pouring in hand; as concrete is placed, so bentonite is displaced; (d) panels in plan showing use of steel tube stop ends (singly or double)

As excavation proceeds, the trench is filled with bentonite liquid, so that at all times the trench is kept full. The excavation is carried out in bays, convenient to the contractor carrying out the work. A 'hit and two miss' bay construction is normally used, unless the Engineer requires a wider spacing to maintain the stability of adjoining boundaries.

When the excavation of a bay is complete (and full of bentonite), prefabricated reinforcement is lowered into the excavated area, displacing the bentonite as it does so. The displaced bentonite is run off and pumped back to storage tanks. Depending on the condition of the ground, the bentonite can be used a number of times before it has to be thrown away and new material introduced.

Concrete is now poured into the trench excavation by means of a tremie, the concrete displacing further bentonite as the pour proceeds; eventually all the liquid is displaced. Circular tubes, the same diameter as the trench width, are provided as stop ends to the hit bays to create curved ends to the pour. Later pours will fit into these curves and form watertight joints.

The advantages of this method of construction are as follows. First, installation is free from vibration and excessive noise. Secondly, no separate support of the earth face is needed. Thirdly, walls can be constructed with the minimum disruption to adjacent areas.

Fourthly, such walls serve a dual purpose: they avoid the need for temporary sheeting to the excavation and become the final structural element of the retaining wall. Some form of internal facing is normally provided, for cosmetic purposes.

Fifthly, if the design calls for the diaphragm wall to be permanently supported by ground anchors, the only temporary works cost will be the guide trench walls and the removal of the inner one when excavation commences.

Sixthly, as already mentioned, such walls are substantially watertight.

The installation of diaphragm walls needs the use of a specialist subcontractor, who will also be responsible for the wall design to meet the loads specified by the Engineer.

If the diaphragm wall is to be supported by the structure to be erected inside the basement area, temporary support for the wall will be needed until the permanent structure is ready. This clearly becomes temporary works and has to be priced as such. Figure 8.2 shows a specialist contractor's solution to the temporary works requirement, which is both elegant and economical. It is an excellent example of the diaphragm wall and the unobstructed working space it provides, allowing greater efficiency and the saving of money in the construction of the permanent works.

Contiguous bored piles

In a contiguous bored pile wall, conventional concrete bored piles are merely installed as close together as possible to provide a curtain; this supports the excavation before becoming part of the permanent structure. The method of installation is usually on the 'hit and miss' basis, the gaps being filled in afterwards.

Fig. 8.2. Diaphragm wall to deep basement with temporary steel waling support (Cementation Piling and Foundations Ltd)

Fig. 8.3 (below). Contiguous bored pile support to site perimeter (Cementation Piling and Foundations Ltd)

As no continuous contact is possible, the use of contiguous piles in basements has to be restricted to situations where naturally dry soil conditions exist, both in the permanent and temporary phases. When used as the main structural element the piles look unsightly; any finish has to be obtained by cloaking the face with in situ concrete, brickwork or other cladding. When used in retaining walls outside basements—for roads or other external situations—concrete surfacing can provide weep holes to allow egress for any water seeping through the piles themselves.

Figure 8.3 illustrates a typical contiguous bored pile support to a building basement. In this case, the piles are in cantilever and need no additional temporary support. (In this picture the tower crane base adopts the principle put forward in chapter 5 for minimising the static base cost by making it part of the basement slab.) Any further temporary works needed will depend on the finish required to the piles in the final state. If the face is to have a skin of concrete, formwork will be needed as an item of temporary work.

In order to extend the use of contiguous piling to water-bearing situations, one specialist piling company is currently developing a method where contiguous piling is associated with a jet-grouting seal. The principles of the method are illustrated in Fig. 8.4. The advantages claimed are that the economics of a contiguous piled wall are combined with the ability to seal the clutches in areas where water ingress may be a problem.

As with diaphragm walling, contiguous bored piling is an operation for specialists. Where the main contractor is responsible for any temporary support of such piles, knowledge of the specialist's design calculations, the loadings allowed for, and anticipated points of support is essential.

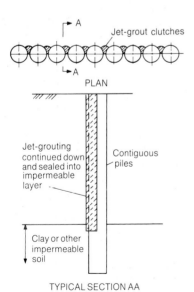

Fig. 8.4. Jet-grouting of contiguous bored piles (Lilley Construction Ltd)

Secant piling

Secant piling is a development of the bored pile technique. The name secant arises from the fact that adjacent piles cut into each other, forming a cut-out in the shape of a secant. By this principle, watertight walls can be achieved.

Until recently only one type of secant walling was available. Now two specialist companies market secant piling, each having its own characteristics for solving problems. The methods used are different and are described separately.

Libore secant piling

The equipment and method of Libore secant piling were developed by W. Lawrence & Son (London). The Libore rig is capable of boring through almost all strata and subsurface conditions, dry and water-bearing, including sands, ballasts, clays, sandstones, marls and shales. A universal type of rock-breaker is also available to deal with boulders. The rig is designed for heavy duty operation and is specially designed for the precision boring necessary with secant piles. The equipment can form retaining walls in restricted areas with minimum disturbance to adjoining property, services and people.

The rig operates by forcing a casing into the ground by rotary oscillation combined with vertical loading. The soil forced within the casing is excavated by a hammer grab. Within this sequence, the soil is supported at all times. When concrete is being placed, the tube is kept in motion. Every so often the extraction of the tube is reversed to ensure that concrete is not adhering to the tube, and to ensure that the annular space of the tube displacement is properly filled.

The first stage of the secant pile technique involves boring alternate piles (female) on centres less than twice the diameter of the selected tube

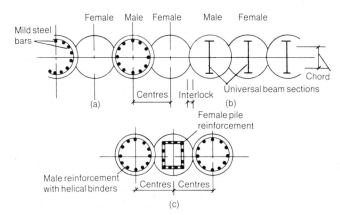

Fig. 8.5. Principle of Libore secant piling (Lilley Construction Ltd); all piles have circular shape as cast inside steel linings: (a) light construction—male piles reinforced with mild steel bars; (b) heavy construction—both piles reinforced with universal beam sections; (c) heavy construction using reinforcement only

Fig. 8.6. Deep shaft construction with secant piles (Lilley Construction Ltd)

size. In the second stage, the gap is closed and the interlock is formed by boring the male piles: with the power of the boring equipment and the hardened teeth of the cutting edge, sectors of the female piles are cut away; and in the subsequent filling of the male piles, the surfaces are bonded together to form a solid wall. Figure 8.5 illustrates the principle.

The equipment used in this form of piling is much heavier than for normal bored piles, and in consequence the result is more expensive. The value of the method is where a heavy wall is needed—in terms of bending resistance—in water-bearing or hard-digging ground: it is used in heavy civil engineering work, in deep basements requiring heavy support resistance, and in ground conditions not suitable for normal boring techniques or the grabbing method of constructing diaphragm walls. A recent excellent example of its use is at the new British Library in the creation of a perimeter wall with secant piles up to 30 m deep.[1] Figure 8.6 illustrates its use for the construction of a deep shaft.

Stent Wall secant piling

While the Libore secant pile method has been around for a considerable time, the Stent Wall secant pile is very new. The method is quite different from the Libore technique. The wall consists of alternate bentonite–cement–PFA piles and reinforced concrete piles, which interlock to form a continuous wall. The advantages claimed are that this wall allows the more economic contiguous pile construction techniques, yet provides the water and granular soil retention properties of traditional secant walls and diaphragm walls. Savings of up to 35% are said to be possible.

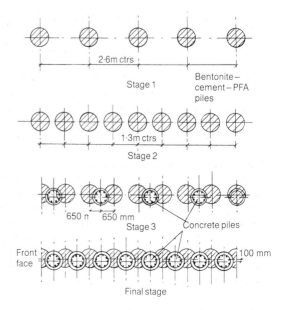

2·6m ctrs

Stage 1

Bentonite–
cement–PFA
piles

1·3m ctrs

Stage 2

650 mm   650 mm

Stage 3   Concrete piles

Front
face   100 mm

*Fig. 8.7. Principle of Stent
Wall secant piling (Stent
Foundations Ltd)*

Final stage

The method of installation is illustrated in Fig. 8.7. The bentonite–cement–PFA piles are constructed before the concrete piles, and are spaced 1300 mm apart along a line which is 100 mm outside the line of the concrete piles. The concrete piles are constructed midway between the bentonite–cement–PFA piles, parts of the latter being bored out during the construction process.

Adjacent bentonite–cement–PFA piles are not constructed the same day, as they are only 1300 mm apart: the minimum distance between piles of this type constructed in any one day is 2600 mm. The intermediate concrete piles are constructed only when the bentonite–cement–PFA piles have gained sufficient strength to allow boring to proceed; this is usually at least three days after the adjacent bentonite–cement–PFA piles have been constructed.

A bentonite mixture of 50 kg bentonite to 1000 litres of water is pre-mixed and stored. The bentonite–cement–PFA pile is constructed by sinking a steel lining and boring out the required depth. The pile bore is then filled with the bentonite slurry. At this stage, a funnel mixer consisting of a 150 mm airlift pipe with a mixing hopper on the top is inserted into the pipe bore. By the injection of air into the mixture from the bottom of the pipe, the bentonite slurry flows up into the mixing hopper; it returns to the top of the pile bore through an outlet at the base of the hopper. The required quantities of cement and PFA are added to the bentonite slurry in the mixing hopper while the slurry is circulating, and mixing continues for ten minutes after the last of the cement and PFA have been added. On completion, the steel casing is withdrawn.

The concrete piles are produced by vibrating a liner to the required level and boring out with an auger rig; reinforcement is lowered into place, the bore is filled with self-compacting high slump concrete, and the pile casing is withdrawn.

The first wall of this type was installed in Kingston upon Thames in 1985.[2] It formed the perimeter wall of an underground car park. As excavation proceeded after the wall was installed, parts of the first basement floor slab were used as temporary struts to the Stent Wall piles. These strips of floor were provided with intermediate support from steel sections cast into column piles at appropriate centres. Subsequently the steel sections were used to form part of the permanent column.

CONTRACTUAL RELATIONSHIPS

Where permanent works are to be used as temporary works, the contractual relationship is usually one of two types. In the first, the consulting engineer specifies one of the methods of support listed above, and requires the contractor to provide temporary support for the locations and loadings shown on the working drawings. In the second, the contractor puts forward a diaphragm wall or piling solution to save expensive temporary works, and to make his tender more attractive compared with the method shown on the tender drawings.

Consultant specifying support

In the first arrangement, a division of responsibility arises. In design terms, the permanent side of the use of one of the three methods is clearly the responsibility of the Engineer. The temporary support, until the permanent construction takes over, is contractually the responsibility of the contractor. It is the interface that potentially creates the problem. The contractor is asked to design temporary works to loadings given by someone else. What happens if these loadings are not correct, and the temporary works fail? Who carries the blame?

The simple answer to the questions raised above is clear. The contractor must ensure that the loads to which he is designing are realistic. In order to do this, he should always ask the Engineer for a copy of the calculations for the permanant works that have to be supported. If this may seem presumptuous, it must be remembered that the Engineer is used to dealing with a final situation: the loads to be carried by the structure on completion. The loads to be supported in the temporary situation can be quite different. How things can go wrong, with the best will in the world, are illustrated in the two real life examples given below.

Case 1

In designing the support for a diaphragm wall, the contractor asked for the span that the diaphragm wall had been designed for. The answer given was the distance between the top of the basement slab and the line of support shown on the contract drawings. What had been completely overlooked was the fact that the diaphragm wall would have to span a much greater distance in the temporary condition, as shown in Fig. 8.8. Calculations by the contractor's temporary works specialist indicated that if this mistake had not been picked up, the diaphragm wall would have bowed inwards by as much as 40 mm while the basement raft was being constructed. Although total failure would not have arisen, the bow in the wall would have been very noticeable and cracks would have been visible. Three parties would have been involved in the resulting post mortem: the diaphragm wall specialist (having designed the wall), the contractor and the Engineer. How much better it was that the problem was analysed in advance, and remedial action taken without rancour.

Remedial action required the installation of a second line of ground anchors, to break the span to a more acceptable figure.

Case 2

A diaphragm wall had to be temporarily supported and was located immediately behind the pavement on a major London thoroughfare. The loading to be supported was specified. As the support was to a major highway, the temporary works designer queried the basis of the loads quoted. Were they derived from MoT HA or HB loadings on the highway? He was told that the less onerous HA had been used, to mini- mise the temporary works support cost. This was challenged for the fol- lowing reasons. The temporary support would be in place for nearly a year. Within that time it was possible that an abnormal load would pass down such a main highway. If, as a matter of engineering judgement, such a possibility was foreseen, it would be irresponsible not to account for such a situation. In the circumstances HB loading should be adopted.

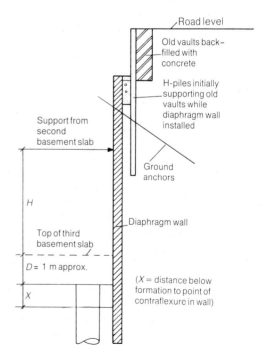

Fig. 8.8. Design of diaphragm walls—need to account for temporary conditions during basement construction: temporary span of diaphragm wall is $(H + D + X)$ m—which makes a big difference in deflections

To this argument the Engineer eventually agreed, and recalculation of the loads to be supported was carried out.

Contractor's proposal

Where a retaining wall design is a conventional one, the contractor's analysis at the tender stage may indicate that the temporary works needed to support the excavation would involve high cost. Further study may show that the use of bored pile walling or diaphragm walling as the permanent wall, supported by ground anchors or other means, achieves a significant saving; even though the wall may have to be faced with an additional skin for cosmetic purposes. Such a totally different approach from the contract design will have to be submitted as an alternative to the contract drawings, with a saving offered. In this way the contractor can improve the attraction of his bid. If the Engineer is satisfied of the validity of the suggestion, he may accept the alternative, and the saving.

The design responsibility now becomes that of the contractor, as do all associated temporary works. The Engineer will still want to approve all calculations, however, as he remains the client's representative, and the projected method will become measured permanent works. The alternative is for the Engineer to take over the design himself. What is crucial is the need to have complete agreement between the parties involved before any work starts, so that future arguments do not arise in relation to where responsibility lies.

CASE STUDIES

The following case studies have been selected to illustrate the way in which the use of permanent works can play a major part in reducing temporary works cost in the support of excavations, and, indeed, in reducing construction time, to the benefit of the client.

Redevelopment with three basements

A large central development site in London had two basements over the whole site and a third basement in a small part of the area. Existing brick vaults supported the first basement perimeter, and diaphragm walls supported the entire area of the site perimeter below this level, including the area occupied by the third basement. Although the diaphragm walls were installed, no other work had taken place when the building was let, and the tenant wanted the earliest possible completion.

When a detailed study was carried out to see how the contract time could be reduced, it became clear that the third basement area was a delaying factor. Further study indicated that if the second basement slab could be completed before the third basement, and the latter mined out underneath while work was going on above, six weeks could be saved on the contract period. The Engineer and the contractor therefore set about devising a method by which this change could be achieved.

It was clear that if the second basement slab was to be completed before any of its supporting columns were in place, in the third basement area, some form of temporary support would have to be devised. After a

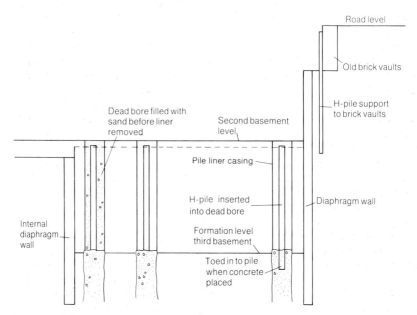

Fig. 8.9. Temporary H-pile support: method of installation

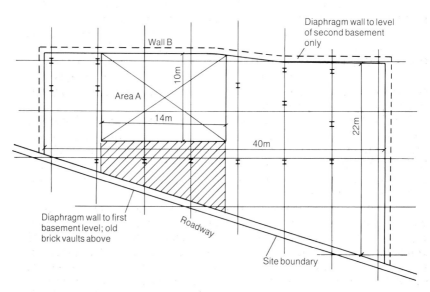

Fig. 8.10. Layout of H-piles in third basement area

number of possibilities had been considered, it was felt that the cheapest answer would be to provide what amounted to temporary columns capable of being put in place before the second basement slab, over the third basement, was constructed.

To achieve this desired result, bearing in mind that the building as a whole was supported on piles, it was decided to insert an H-pile in selected piles at cut-off level when the piles were installed, and their liners still in place. By this method the H-piles could be bedded in the wet concrete at cut-off level (Fig. 8.9). Once the pile concrete had hardened, the dead bore was to be filled with sand and the liner removed. The H-piles could then be used to support the second basement slab. Their location in relation to the third basement area is shown in Fig. 8.10. While the slab was being concreted, starter bars were to be included for the permanent columns, so that they would be in place when needed. To provide for the column below as well as above, the starter bars were to go both ways—up and down. (These can be seen in Figs 8.12 and 8.13.)

Figure 8.10 shows the third basement area: the area is surrounded by diaphragm walls; away from the site boundary these rise to the level of the second basement slab only. As the planning progressed, it was obvious that a hole of some size would need to be left in the second basement slab, both to remove the excavated material from the lower basement, and to let in the Drott excavators to do the mining-out. The area involved is shown as area A in Fig. 8.10. Consequent on this decision, the shaded area of the slab had to be redesigned as a deep horizontal beam, to pick up and transmit the earth pressure from the perimeter wall back to the second basement slab and across to the opposite wall, passing *en route* over the low-level diaphram wall marked B.

At all stages in the development of this revised scheme, the Engineer and the contractor maintained a close liaison, each agreeing the needs of the other party and making sure the whole was practical and as economical as possible. In the event the method worked extremely well. This case involved only a limited area: much greater areas have been mined out adopting the same basic principle.

One further matter had to be dealt with before construction could commence. The site as handed over was open to approximately first basement level, as single basements had been present in the demolished buildings previously on the site. How then would the excavation below the second basement slab be carried out, and the excavated material removed from the site?

The solution is a further example of the need to re-create space at ground level on restricted sites. Figures 8.11 and 8.12 show the temporary bridge built to support a large tipper vehicle, together with a 22RB grabbing crane for lifting out the excavated material. What should be noted in this solution is the way in which H-piling is used to provide support at one end of the bridge (itself an extension of the temporary support for the second basement slab below) and—although not readily apparent from the photograph—the main spanning beams as well. While the span could certainly have been achieved with less steel of a different

Fig. 8.11 (above).
Re-creation of space
for removal of
excavated material
(George Wimpey plc)

Fig. 8.12. Grab in
action (George
Wimpey plc)

Fig. 8.13. Excavation of third basement and installation of second line of ground anchors (George Wimpey plc)

section, the H-piles came from stock holdings in the contractor's depot and would be returned there at the end of the day, with no damage and a full refund of the hire rating percentage realised (see chapter 3 under 'Steel sections').

Excavation to the third basement was carried out by Drott crawler excavators paring out the material under the slab and bringing it to the open area from whence it could be lifted out by the grabbing crane and loaded into lorries on the access bridge.

In this type of construction method, a number of points of detail need emphasising. First, where mining-out is to take place, the slab under which it will all happen should be cast on plywood or hardboard laid level on a bed of sand. The point, of course, is to avoid heavy pieces of blinding falling upon the Drott drivers' heads!

Secondly, the contractor and the Engineer must work closely together in achieving the final solution. Each should agree the details of the other.

Thirdly, the method of providing full continuity for the column concrete needs careful examination for the circumstances in question. The best solution may not be the same in all cases (cf. case study below—redevelopment with five basements).

The method as described worked very well in practice and fully justified the trouble taken. While on a limited scale in this instance, the method in principle can be applied to much larger areas, or used to provide H-pile support to horizontal strutting where the span calls for king piles. Figure 8.13, taken from underneath the slab, perhaps gives a better feel of the working conditions. The boring rig is installing a second row of ground anchors before the full depth of the basement is excavated. This, in fact, is the situation quoted earlier in the chapter in case 1 of the section on contractual relationships.

Fig. 8.14. Diaphragm wall in Barton anchorage, Humber Bridge (Freeman Fox Ltd)

Barton anchorage, Humber Bridge

A much more unusual use of a set of diaphragm walls as temporary works—which were finally left in place—occurred in the construction of the Barton anchorage of the Humber Bridge. Diaphragm walls were used in the large excavation area within the anchorage in order to split it into strips and so control the heave and softening of the fissured clay beneath (Fig. 8.14). The figure also shows the precast struts and their in situ packing to the diaphragm walls; and the steel rod hangers to prevent the struts dropping into the excavation in the event of movement in the walls. The upper level was similarly dealt with, but this is not readily obvious from the illustration.

Redevelopment with five basements

The third study relates to a very restricted site, where the structure occupied the whole area. Five basements were called for, above which was a theatre, with commercial development above that. There were roads on three sides, and an existing building on the fourth. Clearly, the way in which the excavation would be supported was critical.

This particular contract is, in its way, a classic of how designer–contractor co-operation can solve a difficult support problem by utilising the permanent construction in unconventional ways, to the maximum degree possible, and in this case virtually doing away with temporary works altogether.

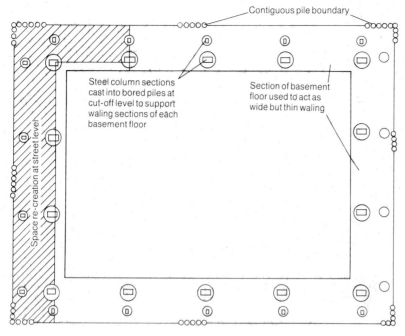

Fig. 8.15. General arrangement of excavation five basements deep

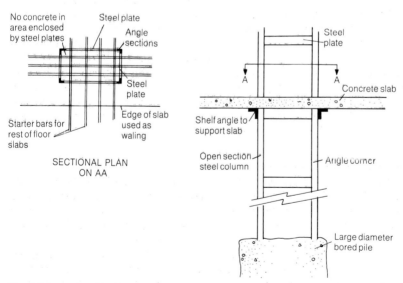

Fig. 8.16. Steel columns to provide temporary support (if shelf angle support for slab is inadequate for permanent situation, floor reinforcement can pass through open area of steel column and link into column when it is poured)

Fig. 8.17 (above). Perimeter waling slabs complete to full depth (photo J. Mustajew)

Fig. 8.18. View of the site showing space re-creation at ground level (middle to upper left) (photo J. Mustajew)

The initial decision involved surrounding the site with contiguous bored piles, to ensure that the main structural elements of the support system were in place before any excavation was commenced. The use of piles in this way was nothing special: what was remarkable was the way in which they were supported and the site was excavated.

The whole structure was founded on piles of various diameters. In particular, those round the perimeter of the theatre were of very large diameter, as they would have to carry the loads of the commercial development above. Figure 8.15 shows the site in plan, with the main perimeter piling and the very large diameter piling some distance inside the site. All other piling has been omitted for clarity. It was decided to utilise these piles as the foundation for the supporting members for internal walings formed from parts for the permanent floors at each level.

At the time that the piles shown were installed, steel column units fabricated from steel angles and plate (Fig. 8.16) were lowered into the pile liners until they were suitably embedded in the wet concrete at the cut-off level of the pile. When the concrete had hardened, the liner was removed and the dead bore was backfilled with sand or other suitable material. The steel units were made to conform to the outside dimensions of the permanent columns. Once all columns had been dealt with in this way, excavation was carried out to the formation of the first basement slab. The perimeter of this slab was then concreted, to a width that encompassed the large diameter piles with their steel column inserts (Fig. 8.15), the top of which had been arranged to coincide with the underside of the first basement slab. To support this slab, the columns were provided with shelf angles, on which the slab sat.

Once this stage was reached, excavation commenced in the area not concreted down to the formation level of the second basement slab. At this point, mining out under the floor-cum-waling could be started. When this was complete, the procedure for the first basement slab was repeated, and so on until the fifth basement level was reached.

The general approach is clear from Fig. 8.17. A Drott excavator is visible bottom centre of the picture. As in the case of the first case study, arrangements are needed to remove the excavated material heaped by the Drotts in the centre of the site. The grab used for this purpose is clearly visible to the left of the excavator. Once again the need arises to re-create space at ground level early on. Figure 8.18 shows the operating platform supported off the steel columns. Its extent is also indicated in Fig. 8.15. On this operating platform can be seen the excavator fitted with grabbing equipment for lifting out the spoil. The platform is also being used for the unloading of materials.

When the excavation is complete to the bottom level, the lowest floor slab is cast. At this point, steel fixing can begin both to the columns until now buried and also to those with the steel columns already in place. In the latter case, remembering that the steel frame was made to the external dimensions of the columns in question, all that is needed in relation to formwork is flat panels anchored to the steel, when the size is automatically established. As no concrete exists inside the steel frame, the column can be poured in the conventional way. When this is complete, the central infill area of the floor in question can be completed. The procedure is then repeated for each of the basement levels.

Figure 8.15 also shows details that can be adopted at the column–floor connection in the final situation.

Commentary

In the final analysis, the whole of the actual support method is dealt with by utilising permanent construction, with the partial exception of the steel columns finally buried in the permanent work; 'partial' because the icing on the cake of this method is the fact that the steel column corner angles in fact provide the corner protection to the columns normally specified in structures where vehicular damage to the columns is possible!

The only true temporary works that had to be provided were the structural requirements for the re-creation of space at ground level.

Piccadilly Line extension

This example of the use of secant piling is from the Piccadilly Line extension from Hounslow West to Hatton Cross, with a tunnel section continuing the line to Heathrow Central.

The particular section in question was designed to be constructed by cut-and-cover construction. The first 2255 m were carried out in secant piling, with the remaining 335 m in conventional box construction between sheet-piled walls, with substantial strutting holding the sheet piles apart.

Secant piling in this case study relates to the method using the Libore equipment.

Although Libore secant piling is expensive because of the heavy equipment used, it has particular advantages over diaphragm walling and contiguous bored piles. In this situation, the cut-and-cover construction was under existing roads, it passed through water-bearing gravel, and the piles had to be driven in areas where many abandoned services had been left behind after diversion. Libore secant piling can provide a virtually watertight wall; because of its heavy boring equipment it can readily go through old sewers, water mains and ducts without any prior removal of such services being necessary; and most importantly in this case, secant pile construction can be used to open up a section, and reinstatement can be carried out very rapidly. This was important in this case as 1828 m were in a residential area.

In this situation, the extra cost was outweighed by the advantages. Away from the residential areas, the cheaper sheet piling and conventional concrete box construction was adopted.

The details of how the secant pile section was dealt with are fully described by Mundy.[3] Briefly, the piles were installed and then capped by a concrete beam and held apart by a reinforced concrete roof slab. Formwork was avoided by use of inverted T-beams, into which reinforced concrete was poured. Once the roof slab was mature, the excava-

Fig. 8.19 (above).
Completed
cut-and-cover tunnel
at Heathrow:
track-laying in
progress (London
Regional Transport;
Lilley Construction
Ltd)

Fig. 8.20. Secant piles
in metro construction
in Germany

tion took place from underneath, with the mucking-out dealt with by conveyors. In this way, disruption to residential streets was only necessary during the installation of the piles, capping beams and roof slab. When this was complete, the road could be reinstated and the tunnel excavation carried out without impinging on the public at all.

By using this heavy piling, no temporary works were needed at all. Figure 8.19 shows the completed tunnel, and track-laying in progress.

As in the three previous case studies, the final method can only be achieved as a joint effort between Engineer and contractor.

Figure 8.20 shows a similar situation in the use of Libore secant piles in the construction of a metro system in Hannover, Germany. In this illustration, the secant piles form the permanent wall to the cut-and-cover tunnel. They are temporarily supported by the structural steel walings and struts in the foreground until the concrete roof slab is in place. The in situ concrete waling outside the steel one is to ensure that strut loads are fully distributed to the curved pile faces. Copybook use is made of H-piling to support the temporary tunnel end and areas both above and behind the secant piling.

Motorway interchange

As part of the M40–M25 motorway interchange, a long and high retaining wall was called for to support the side of a hill. Traditional construction in such circumstances would have involved excavating in a wide trench, suitably supported, to allow the wall to be constructed before any other excavation could be carried out. The method would have been both time-consuming and expensive.

The problems with conventional construction were recognised, and the wall design was based on the use of contiguous bored piles. Support to the wall involved two rows of ground anchors (Fig. 8.21).

Once the piles were installed, excavation could proceed down to the level of the first waling, with the support maintained by the contiguous piles acting in cantilever. The waling construction is shown in Fig. 8.22; in particular, the in situ concrete used to ensure full load contact with the curved pile surfaces. In the same illustration can be seen the anchor end plates, and in one case the stressing jack in position; also the grout tubes for entry of grout once the tendons have been stressed.

With the first waling constructed and the ground anchors stressed, excavation could proceed to the next waling level, where the procedure was repeated.

At this stage no temporary works as such had been needed. It was only at the cosmetic stage—where the piles were to be hidden by a skin of in situ concrete—that formwork to the face was needed; the only real temporary works in the construction of the wall as a whole (Fig. 8.23).

A similar solution is shown for a building site in Fig. 8.24. The value of using ground anchors to achieve an obstruction-free site is only too apparent. The savings achieved in not having any support obstructions in the way of the permanent construction are considerable. The construction can be planned as a whole rhythmic process, without having to

*Fig. 8.21. Contiguous bored pile retaining wall with ground anchor support
(Eastern Region, Department of the Environment and Transport; Sir William
Halcrow & Partners; Tarmac Construction National Contracts)*

*Fig. 8.22. In situ concrete walings and anchor jack (Eastern Region, Department of
the Environment and Transport; Sir William Halcrow & Partners; Tarmac
Construction National Contracts)*

Fig. 8.23. Formwork to wall facing (Eastern Region, Department of the Environment and Transport; Sir William Halcrow & Partners; Tarmac Construction National Contracts)

Fig. 8.24. Contiguous bored piles and ground anchors to provide unobstructed work site (Cementation Piling and Foundations Ltd)

leave out bits and pieces and come back to fill them in at a later stage, at greatly increased cost. All of this is quite apart from the avoidance of any temporary works and their cost; together with a saving of contract time.

Redevelopment on a sloping site

A new building had to be erected on a very restricted site in the centre of Birmingham, as part of post-war redevelopment. The site was triangular, with a drop of some 9 m from one end to the other. One side was bounded by a railway tunnel. The building was circular and founded on a circular raft, which in turn sat upon a bored pile foundation. The site as a whole was occupied by basements and ancillary structures up to first floor level at the deepest part of the site. Figure 8.25 shows the basic situation.

In considering the construction methods to be adopted, it speedily became apparent that the support of the two deep sides of the site was going to present some difficulty. Any support for raking shoring would have to use the circular raft as a foundation. Radiating from the raft to the perimeter excavation, the shoring would greatly restrict the areas of wall that could be constructed—with the resultant delay on the infill wall sections, and complications in building the central parts of the permanent structure which would support the external wall when the temporary supports were taken away.

Discussions with the Engineer ultimately led to a solution that not only saved time and the client's money, but produced a method, probably unique, of building a retaining wall from the top downwards!

The key to the method is shown in Fig. 8.25. All the perimeter piles at the two deep sides of the site were moved outwards to line up with the

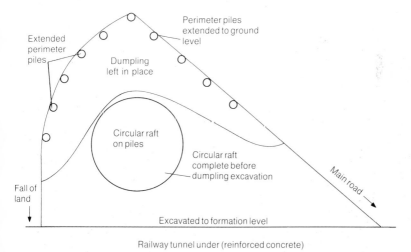

Fig. 8.25. Extended bored piles on deep side of site: extended piles had increased reinforcement to cover their earthworks support role

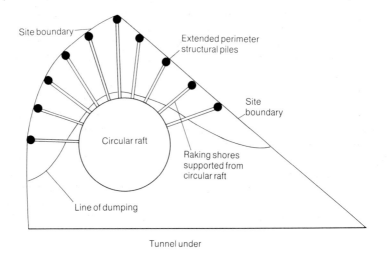

Fig. 8.26. Raking shore support to extended bored piles

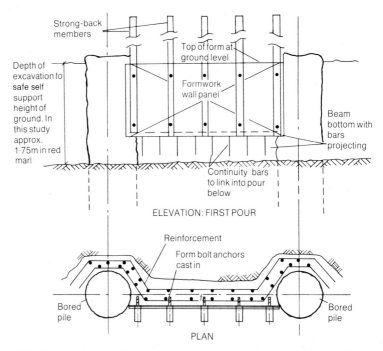

Fig. 8.27. Excavation, reinforcement and formwork to first (top) lift of wall

perimeter wall. The design was altered to increase their reinforcement so that they could support the earth pressure expected from the deep excavation sides. Finally, in installation, the pile bore was concreted up to ground level. The object of all this change was to make the bored piles act as soldier piles in the normal earthwork support sense. These were to be supported by raking shores, rising from the circular raft in the centre of the conical-shaped initial excavation (Fig. 8.26). Once this stage had been completed, the retaining walls were started. A lift of wall—the top lift—was excavated between two soldier piles, formwork was erected in the position shown, and the reinforcement was detailed to span between soldier piles and link round the back of them (Fig. 8.27). For each lift, a bottom was provided to the wall form. Through this were passed starter bars for linking into the pour below at a later time (Fig. 8.27). Once the wall lift had matured, excavation continued below, and the sequence was repeated until the desired formation level was reached (Fig. 8.28). Once the walls were complete, the central permanent support structure was

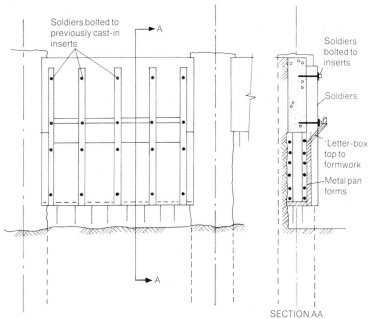

1. Form is in same way up as for first pour
2. Secured as cantilever from first pour by soldiers
3. 'Letter-box' top provides head of concrete to ensure, when vibrated, no gaps with previous pour and full penetration behind piles
4. Projecting concrete cut off when form is struck
5. Projecting face of pile and irregularities in concrete face masked by brick skin in final basement finish
6. Sequence repeated to depth required

Fig. 8.28. Downward sequence of wall casting

commenced and the temporary shores were progressively removed. For cosmetic reasons, the inside of the retaining wall was finished off with a brick skin to cover the face of the piles projecting from the wall face.

Today, ground anchors would undoubtedly have been called into play, with soldier piles of the H-pile variety.

An outdated example perhaps—but the approach to upside-down construction can be applied to soldier pile construction just as well as in this case. It may provide an answer to a problem somewhere!

CONCLUSION

It should be clear from the examples given in this chapter that the technologies of diaphragm walling and the various forms of piling that can, today, provide in situ forms of excavation support, have revolution-ised the means of supporting deep excavations of all kinds. Temporary works costs have been greatly reduced in such circumstances, if not removed altogether in some situations. The temporary works engineer needs to be sure to keep up to date in this area of ground engineering.

9

Falsework

Falsework—in its development, the divisions into which it can be broken down, and future development trends—bears a resemblance to the support of excavations, covered in chapters 7 and 8. Starting as something that was left to carpenters to organise, the need for proper design grew as the structures to be supported became more complex and involved the support of heavy loads (the parallel being the timberman having to give way to soil mechanics and design calculations when depths became much bigger and earth pressures greater). At the same time, it became clear that there was room for standard solutions as well as designed ones. To complete the parallel with excavation support, current trends in bridge design, in particular, are those which minimise or avoid the need for falsework, just as has happened in the use of permanent works as temporary works in the support of excavations.

Falsework is defined in BS 5975[1] as 'Any temporary structure used to support a permanent structure while it is not self-supporting'. This definition is not entirely satisfactory as it can be construed to include the support of permanent construction such as diaphragm walls and the like until they are fully supported by permanent works. It is not generally accepted that such temporary support comes within the classification of falsework.

A more satisfactory definition, in this author's mind, would be: 'Falsework is any temporary structure, in which the main load-carrying members are vertical, used to support a permanent structure and any associated raking elements during its erection and until it is self-supporting.' The significant difference is the emphasis on the main supports being vertical. Figure 9.1 illustrates the point and makes a clear distinction between falsework as generally understood, and such areas as the support of earthworks and the raking shoring of buildings.

The importance of creating such distinctions also relates to the use of the term Falsework Co-ordinator in BS 5975, where it is clearly related to the supervision of work within the revised definition given above. Other temporary works have clearly defined roles of their own, and are usually covered by British Standards codes specifically related to the topic in question (e.g. excavations, scaffolding).

The main legislation relevant to falsework, requiring statutory compliance, is Health and Safety at Work etc. Act 1974, Factories Act 1961,

The Construction (General Provisions) Regulations 1961, The Construction (Lifting Operations) Regulations 1961, The Construction (Working Places) Regulations 1966, and The Construction (Health and Welfare) Regulations 1966.

ADVISORY COMMITTEE ON FALSEWORK

As construction of bridges (the main user of heavy falsework) grew more sophisticated, so the falsework involved became more complex, in terms of the load distribution and the stability requirements necessary. In the period from the late 1950s to the early 1970s a growing number of falsework collapses took place in countries around the world—many spectacular in character and involving loss of life and serious injury. Collapses occurred even in countries where a proof checking system operated.

In the UK, matters came to a head following the collapse of the falsework to the viaduct over the River Lodden in Berkshire in 1972. Three men were killed and ten injured. The Government of the time set up an advisory committee on falsework with the following terms of reference:

'To consider and advise on the technical, safety and other aspects of the design, manufacture, erection and maintenance of temporary load-bearing

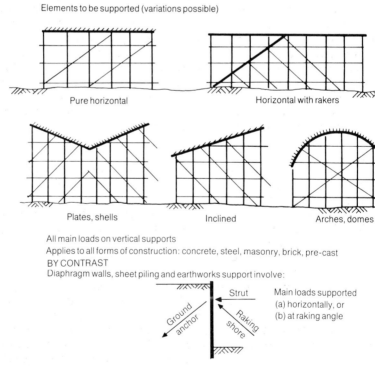

Fig. 9.1. Revised falsework definition

falsework used to support formwork or permanent structures, particularly bridges, during construction, and, in particular, to:

(a) identify any inadequacies in present knowledge, standards and practices, recommend such steps as may be needed, and indicate an order of priority;
(b) draw up an interim technical criteria, for use in advance of the publication of a British Standard Code of Practice, together with such procedural guidance as the Committee may consider appropriate;
(c) recommend what research and development should be carried out in the short and long term; and
(d) advise as to the training, organisational and manpower implications of the Committee's recommendations.'

This advisory committee—the Bragg committee—issued an interim report in 1974;[2] its final report (dated June 1975) was published in 1976.[3]

Currently with the Bragg committee, a British Standards code of practice committee was established in order to prepare a definitive code on falsework as rapidly as possible after the Bragg report was published. In the event, the code took much longer than anticipated and was not published until 1982.

CODE OF PRACTICE FOR FALSEWORK

The *Code of Practice for Falsework*, BS 5975,[1] which resulted from the Bragg report, is undoubtedly the most comprehensive document on this subject anywhere, at the present time. It should be essential reading for anyone who may have any association with falsework, and all falsework schemes should be required to be designed in compliance with it.

The code covers the whole spectrum of activity involved in the design and execution of falsework: materials and components; loads applied to falsework; foundations and ground conditions; design; work on site; and standard solutions; together with many useful appendices and tables.

In one particular it is unlike any other code, in that there is a first section dealing at some length with procedures.

Procedures

It is increasingly common for more than one party to be involved with any falsework. The increase in subcontracting has increased the number of organisations involved, under the general control of the main contractor, or, in a growing number of cases, the managing contractor. In addition, the falsework may be hired from a specialist supplier, who may provide the design for the use of his equipment, or at least a tabulation of design data; in some cases there may be more than one supplier of proprietary equipment. The design and procedure of the whole or part may be carried out by the main contractor, with subcontractors doing all the work of erection and striking; alternatively, subcontractors may handle everything, including the formwork. Whatever the arrangement adopted, many different trades will be involved, including carpenters, scaffolders, steel erectors, labourers and steel-fixers. Even the falsework design may be by the main contractor, the subcontractor, the equipment supplier, or someone who is a separate party altogether.

The possible permutations are considerable and it is for this reason that the code lays great emphasis on the need for having formalised procedures so that responsibility is clearly established for the component parts and the falsework as a whole. In section 7.2 of the code, the main items for which responsibility needs to be established are listed as

'(a) the design brief (see clauses 8 and 41);
(b) the concept of the scheme;
(c) the design, drawing out and specification of the falsework;
(d) the adequacy of the materials used;
(e) the control of erection and dismantling on site, including maintenance;
(f) the checking of design and construction operations;
(g) the issuing of formal permission to load and dismantle the falsework (see clause 13).'

Within this same section, the code points out that appropriate procedures to implement the above can be established to suit the scale of the falsework involved. It goes on to say:

'Of equal importance is the need to ensure that the various responsible individuals do not work in isolation from each other but rather that there is some means adopted to provide effective coordination of all tasks. It is therefore recommended that a falsework coordinator be appointed whose duty it should be to ensure that all the actions required are supervised and performed in accordance with the recommendations of this code (see 10.2).'

The falsework co-ordinator's principal activities are seen as:

'(a) coordinate all falsework activities;
(b) ensure that the various responsibilities have been allocated and accepted;
(c) ensure that a design brief has been established with full consultation, is adequate, and is in accord with the actual situation on site;
(d) ensure that a satisfactory falsework design is carried out;
(e) ensure that the design is independently checked for;
   (1) concept
   (2) structural adequacy
   (3) compliance with the brief
(f) where appropriate, ensure that the design is made available to other interested parties, e.g. the structural designer;
(g) register or record the drawings, calculations and other relevant documents relating to the final design;
(h) ensure that those responsible for on-site supervision receive full details of the design, including any limitations associated with it;
(i) ensure that checks are made at appropriate stages covering the more critical factors (see 40.3 and clause 50);
(j) ensure that any proposed changes in materials or construction are checked against the original design and appropriate action taken;
(k) ensure that any agreed changes, or corrections of faults, are correctly carried out on site;
(l) ensure that during use all appropriate maintenance is carried out;
(m) after a final check, issue a formal permission to load if this check proves satisfactory;
(n) when it has been confirmed that the permanent structure has attained adequate strength, issue formal permission to dismantle the falsework.'

It will be clear from the above that the code places great importance on the formalisation of procedures as a means of creating safety in the design and execution of the falsework as a whole entity.

FALSEWORK DIVISIONS

As with the term support of excavations, the range covered by the term falsework is extremely wide. At one end of the scale come a few telescopic props holding up the soffit of formwork to the lintel over an opening (Fig. 9.2), while at the other end are complex structures of considerable height and weight for the support of bridges (Fig. 9.3), such structures as these clearly requiring great skill and experience for their design.

With such a wide range of operations, it is helpful if some form of division or categorisation can be evolved to make the consideration of falsework more logical and less unwieldy. In terms of area, the greatest amount of falsework carried out by far is that related to the support of floors in commercial and residential property, and it supports loads that are relatively light and evenly spread over the area to be supported. With such conditions, pre-prepared design tables can be used to provide safe answers to the support needed. Such an approach follows the same line as that for the support of excavations (chapter 7) under the heading of standard solutions. The *Code of practice for falsework* recognises the validity of standard solutions and devotes a section to examples of how this principle may be applied. It singularly fails, however, to give any lead as to the point of division between situations where standard solutions are applicable, and those requiring design by persons competent to do such work.

While a division between the two is less easy to define than in the case of the support of excavations, it is this author's view that the following provides a sound basis from which to start:

(a) Standard solutions may be used for the support of floors and beams where the loading is of the type normal in commercial and residential concrete construction, and where the height of support is low (within the range of standard telescopic props).

(b) All other situations require design specific to the circumstances, by persons competent to do such work.

STANDARD SOLUTIONS

The guidance on standard solutions in the code is very limited. As the great mass of falsework falls into this category and, today, the bulk of such work is carried out by many small firms specialising in the erection of formwork and falsework, some further guidance was clearly necessary. The matter was taken up by the Construction Industry Advisory Committee, through a working party. As a result, a guidance booklet dealing specifically with the standard solution approach has been produced by the Health and Safety Executive.[4]

Standard solutions may take the following various forms.

Fig. 9.2. Falsework to beams over openings: not to be recommended!

Fig. 9.3 (below). Structural steel falsework to bridge structure (George Wimpey plc)

(a) Company details for standard tabulated loadings.
(b) Standard details and tables provided by suppliers of proprietary equipment.
(c) Standard designs given in textbooks or relevant codes of practice, together with Health and Safety Executive guidance notes or other authoritative sources.

Whichever form is used, a design brief should first be prepared to establish and record the loads that the falsework will have to support at all stages in its use. The items to be considered are listed in detail in the code, in the Designed Solutions section, under the heading Design Brief.

A word of warning is necessary when using standard details, however. If components from a number of sources are to be combined to provide the complete falsework solution, someone needs to be appointed to make sure that the methods in association are compatible, and that the interface between components from different sources has been properly examined to ensure that they link together correctly, with the same strength characteristics. This is particularly important when using proprietary equipment carrying heavy loads that need to be transferred to the contractor's own equipment. (A number of well known failures have been traced to this sort of mismatch.)

Many firms offer proprietary falsework systems, many of which include the formwork that goes on top. Figure 9.4 illustrates such a combined method; in this case, using metal-framed panels with plywood

Fig. 9.4. Completed falsework and formwork proprietary system (Scaffolding (Great Britain) Ltd)

Fig. 9.5. Proprietary falsework system for traditional timber and plywood decking (Scaffolding (Great Britain) Ltd)

Fig. 9.6 (below). Aluminium propping and bracing in association with aluminium beams and plywood decking formwork

faces on top of a system scaffolding support. In Fig. 9.5, the support system provides only the beams on to which the soffit formwork can be laid, either as plywood sheeting or in the form of waffle pans or trough formers. A further approach becoming popular with the smaller form-work specialists is the use of aluminium beams supported upon props or proprietary scaffolds: the beams contain a timber insert to which second-ary joists and plywood can be nailed; they are light to handle, and with proper care they have a very long life as the primary support member, compared with timber beams (Fig. 9.6).

In spite of the availability of proprietary methods, many formwork firms still prefer to use the conventional timber, ply and telescopic prop approach. The capital investment cost is less and it is recouped quicker: an important matter, in times of small profit margins.

Whatever standard method system is used, it is important that it is erected and struck in accordance with good practice, and that stability is maintained at all stages in the putting-up and taking-down.

Foundations

When designed solutions are to be used, part of the designer's responsibility will be to provide a foundation design suitable for the structure and the loads that it will carry from above. In the case of stan-dard solutions, the situation is different. There is no such thing as stan-dard ground. Each site, or even each part of a site, will have its own characteristics. What needs to be established at the start, therefore, is who will be responsible for the adequacy of the foundations of any false-work that will be erected. Too often no proper consideration is given to this point, with the result that—even if collapse does not occur—there is settlement, causing loss of line and level to the permanent structure.

The code of practice gives no guidance on this point, or indeed any views on who should be responsible. Ultimate responsibility in terms of safety rests with the main contractor under the Health and Safety at Work etc. Act.[5] It is for him to allocate the responsibility. A useful prece-dent in this respect arises in the case of scaffolding. No scaffolding con-tractor would normally accept responsibility for the foundations to the scaffold that he is required to erect. As noted in chapter 6, the Building Employers Confederation have a standard format for scaffolding quota-tions: among other matters, it requires the quoting scaffold contractor to

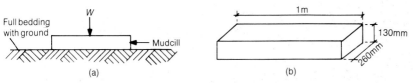

Fig. 9.7. *Standard solution foundations—worst case design approach: (a) vertical load per support $\not> 1.5\ t$; if $> 1.5\ t$ do not use assessed foundations; (b) minimum mudcill dimensions for W $\not> 1.5\ t$ per vertical support; based on proportion of mudcill to each vertical, using standard railway sleepers*

indicate the loads brought down by the scaffold in each standard, so that the main contractor can arrange for a suitable foundation to be prepared. For standard solution falsework a similar system can be applied, or one of the following alternatives.

The first is that a worst-case design can be adopted. Figure 9.7 illustrates a standard solution of this kind for a ground bearing capacity of 60 kN/m^2, suitable for most site applications. (BS 5975 quotes 100 kN/m^2 for standard solutions.) With the arrangement shown, this has the effect of limiting the vertical load carried by any standard to 1.5 t, which is considered more realistic than the code figure. With this approach, the subcontractor would be required to work to this limiting load in pricing his quotation.

Secondly, the HSE guidance booklet on falsework gives help in determining a safe foundation for standard solution situations.

Thirdly, if really bad ground conditions exist, the help of a person qualified in soil mechanics is essential for the safety of all involved.

Whichever route is used, a clear statement and understanding on responsibility for foundations must be established at the start of operations.

DESIGNED SOLUTIONS

All designed solutions need to be prepared by suitably experienced persons and in accordance with BS 5975. The responsibility of the falsework designer is no different from that of the permanent works designer.

As much of this design work will be carried out away from the site, a first essential is the preparation of a comprehensive design brief for the designer to work to. The format of such a brief is laid down in the code.

Design brief

Whoever is responsible for preparing the design brief must ensure that the designer is provided with *all* relevant facts. Sending the working drawings to the designer and asking for a scheme is quite inadequate. The designer not only needs to know the structure loads, but information on all the following matters (see also formwork loads, chapter 10):

(a) the sequence of construction planned (i.e. the order of loading the falsework)

(b) any plant loads the formwork and falsework may have to accept (e.g. if a radial-arm distributor is to be used on the end of a concrete pump line)

(c) the method of placing loads on to the falsework (e.g. any likelihood of shock loading or surge loads)

(d) if any concrete poured in situ will require prestressing when mature (what will be a uniformly distributed load initially will become simply supported at the ends when prestressing takes place).

Any loads or situations that are not obvious must be established and included in the design brief.

Falsework for designed solutions

As in the case of the support of excavations, designed solutions can be divided into two categories: situations where 'normal' falsework methods are used; and situations where normal methods are not possible or are too expensive, and alternative solutions are needed (e.g. in a suspension bridge, the use of the permanent cables as the support for the equipment to lift the deck units into place).

'NORMAL' FALSEWORK DESIGNS

The equipment most used in connection with 'normal' falsework designs—where the supported height is in excess of the range of standard props—is some form of scaffolding. Such scaffolding will usually be one of three basic types: tube and fitting, proprietary scaffolding, or frame scaffolding.

In most cases the design and supply is sublet to scaffolding companies who specialise in this type of work. Where this is the case, a number of matters require special attention.

First, the falsework designer must be supplied with the proposed layout of the formwork above, and figured dimensions of where the loads to be supported will be situated, together with their magnitude. Such loadings, in turn, will be derived from the design brief by whoever is to be responsible for the design of the formwork.

Secondly, the falsework designer in turn must supply to those responsible for the overall falsework design the loads that will be brought down by the falsework and for which suitable foundations have to be prepared. (Specialist falsework suppliers will not be prepared to provide foundations, in the normal run of things.)

Thirdly, the design of foundations must be carried out by persons competent to do so. They will need to be provided with all available borehole data and any other relevant information which may affect the foundation design.

What type of scaffolding is actually used would normally be at the specialist firm's choice, to allow competitive bids from competing firms by maximising on the characteristics of their particular equipment. Some companies have heavy duty equipment which minimises the number of components that have to be erected. Others with frame systems may be able to show reductions in labour cost by having fewer components to be assembled.

Whoever is ultimately responsible for the falsework overall, and its cost, needs to be assured that the scheme chosen not only complies with the code, but also is the best value for money.

Where very heavy loads have to be supported, a scaffolding solution may not be sensible. The centres of the standards may become very close, the number of fittings very large, the resulting erection difficult in a congested environment, and time and cost much higher than with normal falsework situations. Where such conditions arise, alternative methods of support should be considered, in respect of both sufficiency for purpose and cost-saving potential. In particular, the use of structural

Fig. 9.8. Cantilever structure at first floor of a 28-storey building (George Wimpey plc)

Fig. 9.9 (below). Falsework for the cantilever in Fig. 9.8 (George Wimpey plc)

steel is an obvious alternative. The advantages of structural steel, in the right circumstances, are

(a) speedy erection (saving of time overall)
(b) very heavy support capability with the minimum number of vertical members
(c) lateral stiffness in both axes easy to achieve
(d) number of connections relatively small and very positive in action
(e) likely saving in cost over scaffolding.

Where structural steel is seen as a competitive solution, further economies are possible if the sections used are related to other use potential afterwards. This approach is particularly important if the falsework requirement is for one use only.

Figure 9.8 illustrates the cantilever structure at the first floor of a 28-storey office building. The shapes to be formed were complex geometrically, and the total weight of concrete to be supported at this level was some 2500 t, 14 m above basement level. Studies of the falsework requirement indicated that the use of structural steel would be much cheaper than a scaffolding solution, especially if universal column sections were used for the vertical supports. On completion of the one-off use, all the vertical members could be used as part of the company's H-pile stock for the support of major excavations (as discussed in chapter 7), or for heavy falsework at a later date. The final design, as erected, is shown in Fig. 9.9.

The importance of cost factors in falsework is illustrated by the breakdown of the final (as completed) cost of the cantilever structure described above. Of the total cost of concrete, reinforcement, formwork and falsework, the latter two items accounted for 62% of the total. And that was with the considerable saving of a large credit for the steel on completion.

For falsework, as in the case of earthworks support, the high cost leads automatically to a consideration of ways by which the permanent works can be designed to reduce the cost of temporary works. Such solutions can only come about by the designer and the contractor coming together to achieve the desired result. Each needs to understand the other's point of view in relation to the structural needs on the one hand and the requirements for efficient construction on the other. The following case studies illustrate the point in relation to both concrete and steel bridge construction.

Case study: motorway bridges

The great bulk of bridges constructed today relate to motorways. While most may not be all that spectacular, the falsework still represents a large percentage of the bridge's cost. Of equal or greater significance is the impact of such falsework on other activities elsewhere. All motorway construction depends on access along the road being maintained as continuously as possible: the sequence of construction operations involves access, to a great extent, over previous work; or, in the case of over bridges, the need for vehicular traffic to pass underneath.

Fig. 9.10. M25–M40 interchange: bridge deck details (Eastern Region, Department of the Environment and Transport; Sir William Halcrow & Partners; Tarmac Construction National Contracts)

Fig. 9.11. M25–M40 interchange; falsework in place, showing formwork to in situ areas over columns, and recently placed precast U-beams in background (Eastern Region, Department of the Environment and Transport; Sir William Halcrow & Partners; Tarmac Construction National Contracts)

The bridges described in this case study, from the M25–M40 inter-change, are an excellent example of bridge design which recognises the need to reduce the cost of falsework, and, at the same time, to give the contractor considerable scope to maximise his access on a complex inter-change.

Figure 9.10 shows the basis of the deck design. Precast U-section pre-stressed members span between in situ areas over the column lines. These U-section units are filled with polystyrene void-formers to reduce weight. Because of the design approach, falsework is only needed at the column lines and at the abutments. While a much heavier support is necessary, large areas under the bridge are now left open. In Fig. 9.11 the formwork to the in situ areas over the columns is being installed; while, in the background, a number of the precast U-beams have been landed, but without their void-forming filling. Figure 9.12 graphically illustrates the great freedom for road traffic to pass under the falsework without any hindrance either to traffic or to the bridge construction.

There is no doubt that the bridge design reduced falsework cost and greatly improved the access capability in a complex interchange; with further cost savings elsewhere on the contract.

Case study: suspension bridge construction

Suspension bridge construction has only reached the tremendous spans of today by a combination of factors. The first of these is the ability to make steel wire of the necessary strength to carry the loads

Fig. 9.12. M25–M40 interchange: view of one bridge showing the large free area for access under the structure (Eastern Region, Department of the Environment and Transport; Sir William Halcrow & Partners; Tarmac Construction National Contracts)

involved at the spans involved. Without this characteristic, the suspension bridge would be a non-runner. However, even if the strength of materials is available, the design is still not a runner if the structure cannot be erected. The second factor, therefore, is the development of the technique for spinning the main cables (Fig. 1.8). In this operation the equipment used is temporary works pure and simple. (Once the main cable is complete, the rest of the equipment is dismantled and removed.)

The main cable having been established in position, the erection of the deck calls for a different approach. To raise deck sections and connect them to their hangers, use has to be made of the main cable structure (Fig. 9.13). The analogy with the support of excavations by using permanent works as temporary works will be obvious immediately. The lifting gear for the deck sections is mounted on the main cables and holds the deck unit in place until the hangers are positioned by secondary lifting gear.

It will be only too clear from the foregoing that suspension bridge construction, and its development, is an all-in combined effort by the materials manufacturer, the structural designer and the bridge erector. As such, a suspension bridge is the outstanding example of temporary works in both pure temporary works and the use of permanent works to aid erection. In either case the role is that of falsework.

Case study: box girder bridge

A further example of falsework in relation to steel bridges is the construction of the box girder bridge over the River Foyle, Londonderry (Fig. 9.14). In this case, the bulk of the centre span was prefabricated elsewhere, and floated down the river on a barge, supported on suitable falsework. Once in position, the unit was lifted from the two cantilever sections into its final location. Once the unit was off the barge falsework, the lifting equipment was legitimately falsework until the unit was secured into the main bridge structure. While the lifting gear itself is naturally part of the temporary works, the cantilever spans can be seen as permanent works acting as temporary works (i.e. helping to support the centre section until it is self-supporting).

A point of interest in this example and the previous one is that the falsework acts from above rather than in the normal manner of supporting from below.

SPECIAL FALSEWORK SITUATIONS

It can be argued that the special falsework situation of today is the commonplace falsework of tomorrow. Certainly, nobody would call the method of constructing a suspension bridge 'special' any more, even though it still remains a superb example of the engineer's art.

From time to time, though, the bridge designer and those experienced in temporary works get the opportunity to develop a totally out of the ordinary solution to a falsework problem, which by conventional means would be time-consuming and expensive. The following is just such a case.

Fig. 9.13. Humber Bridge: raising the first deck section (photo Donald I. Innes; consulting engineer Freeman Fox Ltd)

Fig. 9.14 (below). Foyle Bridge: erection of centre span (Freeman Fox Ltd; RDL–Graham Joint Venture)

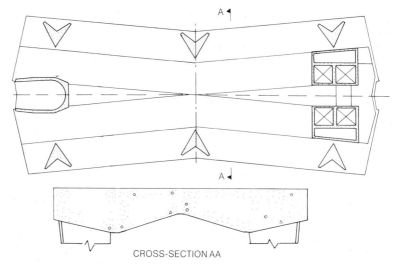

Fig. 9.15. Configuration of first floor slab

Case study: a building in London

This case study relates to a building in London, constructed close to the Thames, where the ground conditions necessitated piling of considerable depth (24.5 m). As the architectural concept required that the ground floor should be an open area, six major columns supported on pile caps provided the support for the building above, by way of a very heavy slab at first floor level, containing 1124 m^3 of concrete. With this structural arrangement, no raft slab was available for the support of falsework.

With no raft slab available, any conventional approach to the falsework would have necessitated the installation of bored piles of considerable depth, bearing in mind that the ground conditions had necessitated the structural piles being 24.5 m long. These, together with the pile caps, would have been very expensive, and of no value once the first-floor slab had been completed.

The actual configuration of the first-floor slab is shown in Fig. 9.15. As the building was not rectangular and the slab thickness varied, the requirement for formwork and its supporting falsework was far from straightforward.

In view of the difficulties and the considerable cost involved, it was decided to re-examine the situation and consider what alternative methods might be possible and less costly. It turned out that both the contractor and the permanent works designer had been thinking about the possibility of using a steel space frame mounted on the six columns, designed to be within the boundaries of the final concrete slab, and from which the soffit formwork could be hung. Joint draft proposals were drawn up, and the probable cost of such a scheme was compared with that of deep piles supporting a structural steel falsework system. These indicated that a potential saving of as much as 25% could be possible with the space frame method.

Resulting from this analysis, a top level decision was made to proceed with the space frame idea and abandon all other proposals.

Responsibilities

As both the structural engineer and the contractor were necessarily involved—the structural engineer especially, as the space frame would become part of the permanent structure—a clear division of responsibilities was needed. It was therefore agreed that

- (a) the structural engineer would be responsible for the space-frame design and detailing
- (b) the contractor would design the soffit formwork, and the method of its installation and support from the space frame.

As the work of both parties had to come together into a completed whole before the concrete was poured, a joint working party was set up to ensure that each side was fully conversant with what the other was doing.

Space-frame design and execution

The structural engineer's design for the space frame was carried out by computer as a two-way spanning lattice, with varying inertias, and specified that the formwork should be supported at the node points of the frame. Figure 9.16 illustrates the details adopted in the final design.

For erection, sections of the space frame were assembled as beams spanning from one column to another in the longitudinal direction, and lifted into place on bearings provided. The rest of the lattice was then erected in situ.

The original design concept had intended using the framework within the permissible design stresses during the wet concreting, and exceeding these stresses when the frame was surrounded by lower stressed rod

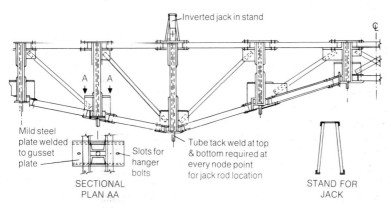

Fig. 9.16. Details of space frame design

reinforcement in the hardened stage of the concrete. In the event, the local authority would not permit this approach, and little saving in rod reinforcement over a conventional approach was possible.

Formwork design and execution

The problems concerning the formwork divided into two phases: the design of the actual forms; and how such forms were to be assembled and positioned to the frame.

As the structural engineer required that all formwork loads had to be supported at the frame node points, it was necessary for the formwork to be able to span the dimensions involved. It became apparent very early on that, with the heavy concrete load to be carried, the forms would have to be extremely rigid, and to achieve the spans needed would have to use structural steel for the main members. The result would be very heavy and unwieldy. A more economic solution was clearly desirable. In association with the structural engineer, it was eventually decided to pour initially only the first 450 mm of the concrete over the whole area of the soffit. By modifying the bottom reinforcement, the structural engineer adequately tied the 450 mm of concrete to the space frame, with the objective of using this depth of concrete as the actual formwork for the remaining head of concrete. By this means, the suspended forms had only to be designed to cope with the 450 mm head. As a result, an acceptable design in timber was possible, with a manageable weight and savings in cost.

An economic solution to the formwork having been reached, serious consideration was given to the method of erecting the formwork, as it was clear that this would play a significant part in the final design of the forms.

Erection of the forms piecemeal under the space frame would have needed elaborate scaffolding; the operation would have been costly, time-consuming and difficult. All the advantages of the space frame would have been nullified. It was, therefore, decided to consider assembling large sections on the ground floor slab and hoisting these

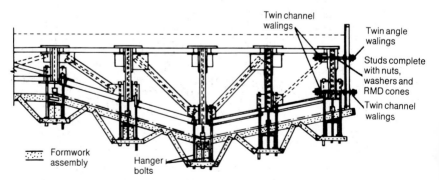

Fig. 9.17. Cross-sectional details of formwork and method of fixing to space frame

Fig. 9.18. Stoolings assembled for soffit form erection; space frame overhead
(George Wimpey plc)

Fig. 9.19. Formwork assembly complete and reinforcement fixed on centre and one
outer section; jack rods in place on centre section and connected to space frame
above (George Wimpey plc)

into position under the space frame, where they could be hung off the frame by high tensile bolts located at the node points.

To achieve these desirable objectives, a method of hoisting that was both economical and reliable was needed. After examining possible methods, the final solution was based on the use of slipform jacks. It was established that if mounted upside-down in a suitable frame bolted to the space frame, the jack could be made to pull the jack rod through the jack, rather than the reverse as in slipforming. The rods could pass down to the forms at ground-floor level, and through them to lifting yokes suitably positioned underneath. These yokes also fulfilled a double function: they provided the means of transferring the loads from the jack rods to the space frame in the final position, by carrying the she-bolt half of the high tensile bolts for the final fixing. The overall arrangement adopted is shown in Fig. 9.17.

To simplify the lifting as much as possible, it was decided to split the soffit into three sections: a centre section over the central columns; and a much larger lift, about 18 m × 15 m, on either side. Each section was assembled on purpose-made stoolings to give the exact shape of the soffit and to provide a template (Fig. 9.18). Once the forms were complete, the required reinforcement was assembled on them and the jack rods were

Table 9.1. Jacking details

Section	Area of shuttering, yd^2	Weight of reinforcement, tons	Number of jacks	Height of lift	Maximum speed of lifting	Time of lifting, hours
Centre	87	14.28	31	20′6″	1 inch in $2\frac{1}{2}$–3 min	9
North	324	28.50	82	21′9″	1 inch in 2 min	11
South	240	22.74	63	21′9″	1 inch in 2 min	$11\frac{1}{2}$

Table 9.2. Pouring sequence and concrete quantities (total 1470 yd^3)

Pour	Mix	Location	Level	Quantity, yd^3	Remarks
1	6000	Centre	Full depth	250	With plasticiser
2	4500	North	Bottom 18″	160	With plasticiser
3	4500	South	Bottom 18″	145	With plasticiser
4	4500	North-west	Top	110	
5	4500	North-east	Top	110	
6	4500	South-west	Top	94	
7	4500	South-east	Top	65	
8	4500	North central	Top	140	
9	4500	South central	Top	135	
10	4500	North central	Top	125	
11	4500	South central	Top	126	
12	4500	South-east	Stairs	18	
13	4500	South-east	Stairs	30	

Fig. 9.20. View on top of space frame before lifting, showing upside-down jacks in special stools

installed. To facilitate freedom of movement and overlapping of reinforcement on the centre section, the centre form was assembled at a higher level than the other two (Fig. 9.19).

The jacking of all three sections went without any serious problems. The only real problem was that of equalising the jack lifts, as the loading varied over the area of the forms. The performances achieved in the lifting are given in Table 9.1, together with data on the number of jacks used; the concrete involved is given in Table 9.2. Figure 9.20 shows the formwork in place and the method of connection to the frame.

Costs

An analysis of the actual costs on completion showed that space frame and formwork was 66% of the total cost, concrete was 19%, and reinforcement was 15%. In addition, the method showed a saving of 6% over a conventional falsework approach—without accounting for the cost of a piled foundation on which it would have had to sit.

Comment

This case study serves to reiterate the various points already made in relation to temporary works in which the designer becomes involved:

(a)   as construction becomes more complex, designer–contractor co-operation becomes more necessary in the cost-effective solution of temporary works problems

(b)   where joint action takes place, the contractor must establish clear areas of responsibility with the designer, or vice versa

(c)   co-ordination between the parties is crucial.

While the example above is an old one, and contains ideas that are not regularly used in falsework, the methods used are as valid now as they were at the time, and may well stimulate an answer to a problem in the future. The partial pour to minimise the cost of the soffit formwork, in particular, has been used by the author on a number of occasions since.

Changes in concrete bridge design

Other items which come under the heading of special falsework situations arise from new developments in concrete bridge design methods. The concept of precast segmental prestressed construction of bridges was a radical departure from what had gone before. As originally conceived, it still depended on falsework being available to support the units until stressed. Figure 9.21 shows both the falsework and the unit handling equipment in action on the elevated section of the A40(M) in London.

The units to be handled are of considerable weight; and, because of the deck shape, the falsework is concentrated and has to be of very heavy construction. It has to carry the handling equipment in addition to the weight of the precast unit.

Fig. 9.21. Prestressed segmental bridge construction: falsework and unit handling equipment (John Laing Construction Ltd)

More recently, segmental construction has developed much further, to the point where falsework has been done away with—at least, as generally understood. Two methods in particular have made their mark: balanced cantilever in situ concrete, and glued prestressed segmental cantilever construction. Both methods have drastically reduced the falsework element, and very much changed its character.

The in situ concrete cantilever method largely does away with falsework—the formwork being designed to move forward progressively when the previous cast has matured enough. Some vertical support initially to provide greater stability to the root cantilevers is usually all the true falsework needed. With this technique, bridges of considerable span over water or other difficult terrain become possible, and the method has been used extensively in many parts of the world.

Glued segmental prestressed cantilever construction is much more in its infancy. In this form of construction, precast sections are progressively joined together by epoxy resin, and at the appropriate moment the sections are stressed together. Two recent articles have described actual contracts where this method has been used.[6, 7] No true falsework is needed, as the units, in the order of between 70 t and 101 t each, require heavy lifting gear to position them, and this equipment is mounted on a launching gantry, itself weighing anything up to 300 t (Fig. 9.22). It is perhaps stretching the point to call the launching gantry falsework. More logically, it is part of the handling plant, but if the purist wishes to insist, it could well be described as upside-down falsework, as it is above the item to be supported.

The future for this method of construction should be interesting. For one of the contracts mentioned,[6] it has recently been reported[8] that the launching gantry has been abandoned as being too slow. Apparently, the precast units are now being handled by a large crane. In contrast, the other bridge launching gantry is reported as working well, in achieving a river estuary crossing of considerable width. Certainly, the design of the gantries requires considerable skill, and is yet another example of how extensions in bridge design are dependent on plant and temporary works equipment to enable the erection to be achieved.

SAFETY IN FALSEWORK

Falsework, by its very nature, is vulnerable to accidents. Serious accidents were the reason for the production of the *Code of practice on falsework*. In order to maintain the highest standards of safety, it is desirable that specific attention is always paid to this subject.

With the trend to breaking down construction activities into more and more subcontracted items—especially true in falsework—a desirable feature, as part of the procedural co-ordination of falsework, is the preparation of a statement of falsework policy by the main or management contractor. Such a statement can then readily be brought to the attention of subcontractors as a requirement for the acceptance of their quotation.

Such a statement is given in Table 9.3.

Fig. 9.22. Launching gantry for segmental construction (Stelmo Ltd)

FACADE RETENTION AND STRUCTURAL RENOVATION

A greater public conscience about destroying old buildings has led to the increasing growth of work where the existing facade of a building has to be preserved, and any new development built behind it. Changes to the structure of buildings due to change in type of use are also now common in areas designated for preservation. As a result of this, a new area of temporary works has opened up which can be defined as falsework in reverse: 'Falsework in reverse is any temporary structure erected to support a permanent structure before it is made non-self-supporting'! More seriously, it is the support necessary to maintain structural safety and stability while a new structure is built behind an existing facade, or radical structural alterations are carried out inside an existing building. Only recently has reliable guidance been available to those who may be involved in such work. A report from CIRIA is full of useful information.[9] Informed articles have also been written,[10, 11] and a number of specialised firms have started up in consultancy and execution of facade retention and structural alteration.

Table 9.3. Statement of safety policy: falsework

1. All personnel are required to co-operate with Company (the Main or Managing Contractor) measures to assure the safety of falsework structures.
2. Falsework is to be designed, erected, used and dismantled in accordance with BS 5975 : 1982, *Code of practice for falsework.*
3. Site managements are responsible for the safety of falsework carried out under their control, and they should follow the guidance on procedures and responsibilities in section 2 of BS 5975. On larger sites, this will include the appointment of a Falsework Co-ordinator. Subsidiary and subcontractor managements must review the arrangements made and satisfy themselves that tasks are clearly defined and that nominated staff are technically qualified to perform their duties.
4. The approval of falsework proposals by a Resident Engineer or Architect does not relieve site management of any of its responsibilities.
5. When the Company is acting as Main or Managing Contractor, site management will observe their responsibilities under section 4 of the Health and Safety at Work etc. Act and ensure that methods of work used by subcontractors are safe and sufficient. All subcontracts for falsework must require that the subcontractor complies with BS 5975.
6. Specialist advice and design services for all falsework matters are available from .... (to suit individual company practice).
7. Company Health and Safety Officers will advise management of the requirements of the Health and Safety at Work etc. Act and any related legislation applicable to falsework.
8. Additional guidance can be obtained from the following documents:
   (a) BS 5975, *Code of practice for falsework*
   (b) BS 5531, *Code of practice for safety in the erection of structural frames*
   (c) the Building Employers Confederation manual *Construction safety,* chapter 21.

Both BS 5975 and the BEC manual (chapter 21) contain comprehensive checklists for use when inspecting falsework.

Any temporary works organisations who may become involved in this area of work need to be aware of the problems that lie ahead.

Facade retention, in particular, is always very much a one-off situation. The building developer must recognise that before any work is done, a thorough and detailed survey of the existing structure needs to be carried out. Such a survey will need adequate money spent on it. Failure to spend enough on the survey will usually cost a great deal more later on. In one case known to the author, where the survey was inadequate, a building facade was shored for 18 months while the new structure was built inside. When the time came to connect new with old, it was found that all the old windows had wooden lintels which were full of dry rot! In consequence the whole facade had to be demolished and an exact copy built in new materials. The delay to the building completion was considerable, and the loss of rent was an additional cost over the original estimate.

Methods of support

The ways of supporting a facade are numerous, and the method chosen will depend on the structure itself and its location in relation to the public highway. Five basic methods can be listed: a solution used may involve a combination of more than one of them. The basic methods are as follows.

Fig. 9.23. Retained facade of a building after demolition of the remainder (George Wimpey plc)

(a)   External support only—provides completely clear interior.

(b)   Internal support utilising existing internal walls as buttresses, with some internal horizontal bracing.

(c)   Internal support from temporary works only.

(d)   Introducing a new steel-framed structure within the existing building before any significant demolition is carried out.

(e)   External–internal temporary works astride the facade.

Which method or combination of methods to use can only be decided in the light of the particular structure to be dealt with. The eventual choice will require close collaboration with the structural engineer and the local building inspector responsible for building safety. Decisions will also be affected by the possibility, or not, of being able to use the pavement area and/or a part of the highway for external support.

Figure 9.23 shows the retained facade of a building after demolition of the remainder. Parts of the party walls have been retained to provide a buttress effect, with the addition of horizontal bracing to provide lateral stability and to protect the party wall on the left of the picture. The new structure is designed to miss the buttresses left for stability. They will only be removed when the facade is tied into the new frame.

By contrast, Fig. 9.24 shows the inside of a major building where all the internal walls have been removed. On most elevations, steel towers,

Fig. 9.24. Structural steel support to facade (Trollope & Colls Ltd)

sited over the pavement, provided the main support and linked in to the beam system on the left hand side of the photo. The internal steel tower is supporting the central elevation through the horizontal steel lattice beams. In this case the street was too narrow for the tower to be outside.

From these two examples, the need for total integration between the designer and contractor will be only too apparent. In particular, the method of connection between the facade and the new frame is critical. The article referred to already[11] has useful advice to give in this respect.

10

Formwork

In BS 4340, *Glossary of formwork terms*,[1] formwork is defined as, 'A structure, usually temporary, but in some cases wholly or partly permanent, used to contain poured concrete to mould it to the required dimensions and support it until it is able to support itself. It consists, primarily, of the face contact material and the bearers that directly support the face material.'

While this definition is clear, and provides a separation from falsework, certain situations arise where such a sharp separation is inconvenient. Many of the proprietary systems which come within the category of standard solutions, as described in the previous chapter, come as a complete entity: the forms and the support to them are a complete package. The 'table forms' or 'flying forms' are falsework and formwork combined, and their efficiency depends on handling and use in the combined state. (Even the simple standard solution of props, bearers, joists and a plywood deck is best dealt with as a whole.) Because of this situation, proprietary soffit forms and flying forms are dealt with wholly in this chapter. Such an approach is very much in line with that adopted in the USA, where 'shoring' always includes the deck forms on top.

Similar problems do not arise when dealing with wall and beam forms. Beams, in particular, tend to bring clearly defined loads on to falsework, and separation of the two is straightforward. With walls, the situation is usually precise. Walls tend to be constructed on previously constructed work; outside the actual forms, additional temporary works usually involve only the provision of lateral stability, and the working platforms necessary for the reinforcement assembly, the erection of the forms and the pouring of the concrete.

LEGAL REQUIREMENTS
The following have a direct bearing on formwork:

(a) The Health and Safety at Work etc. Act 1974
(b) The Construction (Working Places) Regulations 1966
(c) The Construction (Lifting) Regulations 1961
(d) the contract conditions.

While the above list covers the main legislative items in relation to formwork, it is by no means complete. It is the responsibility of the individual concerned to make sure that any relevant legal requirements have been complied with.

When formwork is being carried out over water, the Construction (General Provisions) Regulations 1961 also apply.[2]

CONTRACTUAL RESPONSIBILITIES

Although, contractually, the contractor is responsible for formwork—as part of the more general temporary works—it should be necessarily part of the contract that the temporary works designer is made aware of any matters in relation to the design of the permanent works which are not readily apparent from the drawings or specification. A Health and Safety Executive guidance note fully supports this view.[3] It is desirable, therefore, to consult the designer of the permanent structure, before any temporary works design is started, regarding any matters that may not be apparent from the drawings which would affect the conduct of the temporary works. The guidance note mentioned above, for example, makes the point that designers must endeavour to avoid instabilities during erection in their design. If this is not possible, it must be made quite clear that the contractor will need to provide suitable temporary works for a defined situation.

A typical example of what can happen if the contractor is not adequately briefed is given below.

Case study

A six-storey office building was designed as a composite steel and concrete frame. The steel frame required casing in concrete, while concrete floors provided the lateral stiffness. In tendering, the contractor understood that the steel frame allowed all casing formwork to be hung off the steel beams, and that it would be able to carry the in situ floor loads as well, including the weight of the formwork. In the event, the situation turned out to be quite different.

As, at the time in question, all steel frames in buildings were required to be cased in concrete, the designer decided to save on his steel frame by making the casing part of the structure by reinforcing the concrete. This decision made the steelwork so flimsy that only the first four floors could be erected as a first stage, and then only when provided with temporary wire diagonal guys.

When the contractor submitted his formwork details, hung off the steelwork, he was belatedly told that the steel beams were too light to accept the formwork and wet concrete loads. The beam casings would have to be propped from the ground in the first case, and from the floor below for the following floors and beams.

Table 10.1. Cost breakdown for a concrete bridge structure 14 m above ground level, with only one use possible for the falsework and formwork	Falsework and formwork	62%
	Reinforcement	20%
	Concrete	18%
		100%

Only after the four floors were complete were the steel erectors able to return and erect the last two lifts. It requires no imagination to see that the overall result was anything but economic—yet the original concept was to use the composite design to save the client money!

This case study from the early days of composite construction serves two purposes: to emphasise that design to save money must also make sure that the execution is also going to save money; and to illustrate the need for the contractor to be adequately briefed on matters that were far from apparent from the drawings or specification.

ECONOMIC FACTORS

Formwork efficiency depends, above all, on an adequate understanding of the cost factors involved. For this to happen, certain matters in relation to the concrete process need to be recognised.

First, the cost of the concrete is a fixed sum, no matter how many times the particular pour is repeated.

Secondly, the same applies in relation to the reinforcement needed.

Thirdly, the cost of the formwork is divided into two: the provision of the forms, and their erection and dismantling. Erection and dismantling will be a fixed sum per use, but the actual material cost, as measured, will be dependent on the number of uses that can be achieved. The greater the repetition the designer can contrive, the cheaper the formwork to produce the design will be.

It is a useful exercise for those involved in concrete construction to take a priced bill of quantities, for the type of work in which they are involved, and break down all the items—formwork, falsework, reinforcement and the concrete—in cost terms, and then to convert such figures into percentages of the total cost for the finished concrete. By such means a clear understanding of where the money lies can be established. The answers achieved can be surprising to even experienced concrete engineers.

Tables 10.1 and 10.2 give examples of such breakdowns for a bridge type structure and a traditional six-storey building. It must be borne in mind that these figures apply only to the particular situations described.

Table 10.2. Cost breakdown for the reinforced concrete frame of a fairly typical office building, six storeys in height; the figures include cost of materials and are expressed as a percentage of total cost

	Columns	Beams	Slabs	Walls	Overall
Formwork	4.5 +	8.5 +	18.5 +	8 =	39.5
	(24.4)	(33.0)	(47.7)	(53.1)	
Reinforcement	12 +	14.5 +	3 +	3.5 =	33.0
	(60.9)	(56.3)	(7.1)	(23.8)	
Concrete	3 +	3 +	18 +	3.5 =	27.5
	(14.7)	(10.7)	(45.2)	(23.1)	
	(100.0)	(100.0)	(100.0)	(100.0)	(100.0)

Fig. 10.1 (above). Steel formwork for circular tank in a sewage works (Rapid Metal Developments Ltd)

Fig. 10.2. Slipforming the main piers to the Humber Bridge (photo Donald I. Innes, consulting engineers Freeman Fox Ltd)

To be of value for management purposes on a contract, figures need to be prepared for the particular contract.

A further aspect of formwork economics arises where concrete construction is called upon to achieve considerable accuracy. Probably the most significant area, in this respect, is in the formwork for sewage works. Often circular tanks will contain operating equipment which is required to rotate on a central pedestal, either spraying fluid on to filter beds or scraping surface scum during the purification process. For the systems to be efficient, the circularity of the tanks is of great importance. Specifications for such tanks call for very tight tolerances, and the accuracy of the formwork becomes important. To achieve these tolerances, it is usually necessary to have the formwork made very accurately in structural steel (Fig. 10.1). While the initial cost may be high, good repetition is normally possible to allow reduction of the unit cost, while obtaining the accuracy desired. (Failure to achieve the accuracy specified can result in remedial measures and delays that can far exceed the additional cost of the steel forms.)

In a different context, the slipforming of the towers of the Humber Bridge provided a considerable accuracy problem (Fig. 10.2).

It should be clear, therefore, that careful analysis of the requirements for the forms needs to be carried out to establish the method which will provide the best and most economic answer to the specific problem.

GUIDE TO GOOD PRACTICE

In the UK, the definitive document in relation to formwork is *Formwork: a guide to good practice.*[4] A comprehensive volume, it deals with all aspects of formwork in building and civil engineering construction, from simple timber and plywood examples to highly sophisticated tunnel and bridge forms in steel. Design and practice are covered in detail. The guide has been carefully written to be fully compatible with the *Code of practice for falsework*. It clearly is a must for all who may become involved at any stage with formwork, whether in design, detailing or execution. It will undoubtedly become the unofficial code of practice for formwork.

Probably the only comparable work in existence at the present time is the American publication, *Formwork for concrete.*[5]

Because of the detail covered by *Formwork: a guide to good practice*, this chapter concentrates on the commercial aspects of formwork, and those areas that do not seem ever to be covered elsewhere.

CATEGORIES OF FORMWORK

As with falsework, in the previous chapter, formwork can be divided into two categories: standard solution methods and designed formwork. As far as horizontal slabs are concerned, the division between the categories can be taken on the same basis as in the case of falsework. However, formwork extends beyond horizontal slabs, and involves the forming of walls; the lining of tunnels; curved shapes in domes etc.; very deep beams or beams of complex shape; shafts, chimneys and towers for

Fig. 10.3. Proprietary formwork panels used for forming walls (Scaffolding (Great Britain) Ltd)

various purposes, often of considerable height; and such items as the face formwork for the construction of dams.

Because of the wide range of use involved, the division between standard and designed solutions needs to be stated in more detailed terms than that for falsework. The following delineation is suggested.

(a) Standard solutions may be used for the formation of the soffit surfaces of suspended slabs where the loading is within the range of normal industrial and commercial structures; for the formation of walls up to 7 m in height; and providing the vertical sides of beams not exceeding 1 m in height.

(b) All other cases should be designed by persons competent to do such work (in particular, tunnel and dam forms, very long and deep beams, chimney and shaft formwork, and all complex shapes, whether folded plates, domes or other solid geometrical figures).

STANDARD SOLUTIONS

As in the case of falsework, standard solutions can fall into a number of distinct groups. The first consists of standard designs provided in-house for tabulated loading conditions. These would cover walls, beams and slabs, within the limitations stated above.

The second group consists of standard proprietary forming methods marketed by specialist suppliers for use within the limitations of

Fig. 10.4. Proprietary panels, of the type shown in Fig. 10.3, in use forming soffit slabs (Scaffolding (Great Britain) Ltd)

Fig. 10.5. Use of mixed equipment: heavy duty beams bring high point loads on to bearers; bearer capacity and stability must match these loads (photo A. J. Goldsmith)

published design tables. Proprietary panel systems usually are designed to function in walls and slabs, and sometimes beams as well (Figs 10.3 and 10.4). Tables are provided to suit the particular application.

The third group of standard solutions consists of standard tables provided in codes, textbooks, Health and Safety Executive guidance notes, and other recognised authoritative sources.

When using proprietary equipment from more than one manufacturer (e.g. form panels from one supplier supported by falsework from another), it is most important that compatibility is properly checked; in particular, that maximum load capability is of the correct order for safe transference from one system to the other (Fig. 10.5).

One particular value of standard equipment is that method study can establish labour values for the erection and dismantling stages, from which more competitive pricing can be applied at the tender stage.

Also, with proprietary formwork, hiring can give known rates per use, per unit time. That the cost will go up if the site programme falls behind provides a management spur to maintain or improve on the projected turnround of the forms.

DESIGNED SOLUTIONS

Once one gets away from the straightforward, standard solution situation, the need for purpose design is only too apparent—or should be. It

Fig. 10.6. Table form equipment with Portaform extractor (Scaffolding (Great Britain) Ltd)

is not just a case of designing a solution that will resist often very high concrete pressures. The efficiency of the fix–strike cycle, the minimising of labour content and the maintenance of the required accuracy are all, in the end, cost factors of considerable importance. Such needs increase considerably where very high use life is possible; for example, in tunnel and dam formwork. Money spent to achieve long life can be a key decision in the overall economy.

In circular work, such as sewage works tanks, money spent on rigid forms and accurate design will usually save large sums of money in remedial work at a later stage (Fig. 10.1).

TABLE AND FLYING FORMS

As mentioned in the introduction to this chapter, table and flying forms are dealt with wholly within this chapter.

A table form can be defined as an area of soffit formwork with its attendant supporting structure built as an integrated whole, and, in operation, struck, moved and re-erected in one piece. Figure 10.6 is a typical example. To function safely, such a unit needs to carry at least an external handrail system. Most, in practice, also provide a working platform.

The advent of aluminium sections and lightweight pressed steel members has made possible the use of much larger tables, for which the American term 'flying forms' has been accepted and used in the leading authoritative publication in the UK.[4]

Further developments in this field have introduced hydraulics into the fix–strike sequence. As a result, soffits containing waffle or trough sections can now be struck in one unit, with or without the assistance of compressed air.

Economics

The economics of using table and flying forms depends on the number of uses that can be achieved. However, in assessing the cost of provision, it is first necessary to recognise where the cost lies.

In general terms, the 'table top' will be the most expensive item within the whole. The reason, of course, is that it may carry waffle or trough formers, and changes in section to accommodate beams; and, even if the soffit is entirely flat, it will be suffering from wear and tear after a significant number of uses. The support structure (falsework element), by contrast, is usually composed of standard equipment, which can be taken into store and reused many times over.

In the early days of table forms, it used to be argued that a minimum of twelve uses was necessary to make a table form pay against traditional methods. Now, with the cost of labour and the cost of employing labour what it is, a much lower number of uses will usually be economic; six to eight is often quoted. The figure can be even lower if a contractor obtains a second contract, at the right time, to allow a follow-on use with little alteration of the previous contract's equipment.

The most usual use of table and flying forms relates to multi-storey residential or commercial application. In such a case, when external

Fig. 10.7. Hydraulic table form, with trough units above, and carrying beam side forms (photo A. J. Goldsmith)

Fig. 10.8. End view of hydraulic table form shown in Fig. 10.7; table travels progressively forward, filling in slab (photo A. J. Goldsmith)

Fig. 10.9. Danish proprietary soffit forms: no falsework needed for spans up to 7 m; wall forms in position above (Scanform, Denmark)

handrail and toeboard protection is provided, and possibly an external walkway as well, no external scaffold is needed in the structural phase, giving a marked saving in overall cost. The only additional protection that will be necessary is the edge barrier when the forms have been removed. Whether or not a scaffold will be needed for the cladding will depend on the cladding system and its method of erection (see also chapters 6 and 11).

In spite of the generally vertical application, there are situations where the same approach can provide sound economic advantage when used horizontally. An example shown in Figs 10.7 and 10.8. The circumstances relate to a large shopping mall, where a large area slab is supported by columns and beams. The overall concept is as follows: the beam bottoms are supported on frame scaffold units and the steel is fixed; the slab in between, which is troughed in section, is supported on a hydraulic table support system; the beam side forms are also carried on the tables, and hinged to the soffit forms. With the arrangement illustrated, a section of the floor slab can be poured, together with the adjacent beam. Once the slab reaches an adequate strength, the hydraulic table system (and the related beam side form) can be struck, moved to the next location, cleaned and re-set, the slab reinforcement fixed, and so on. The beam bottom form is not disturbed in any way until the whole bay is complete and mature.

Many proprietary table forms exist, in many countries around the world. With competition, it is not surprising that the method of support has often been whittled away, to the point where the soffit formwork has been made so strong that no true falsework is needed at all. Figure 10.9 illustrates a Danish method where the floor forms can span some 7 m without any other support. The steel form is carried on roller brackets bolted to walls or columns. These can lower the form 50 mm on striking, and the form can be rolled out.

INFLUENCE OF REINFORCEMENT

The designer of formwork usually works off the Engineer's dimensioned outline drawings. What must not be neglected, but often is, is to relate the proposed formwork scheme to the arrangement of the reinforcement. The way in which reinforcement is detailed can often have a significant effect on formwork cost.

Case study: a culvert

Figure 10.10 shows the reinforcement to a culvert. The culvert is not long enough for the use of a travelling form to be considered.

A study of possible options suggests that the most economic will be to pour the walls with crane-handled full height panels, and follow on with the roof separately. It is not until the reinforcement details are studied carefully that it is apparent that this solution is not possible. The way the

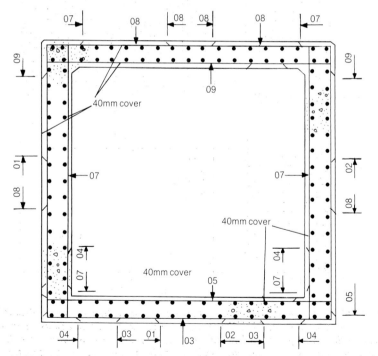

Fig. 10.10. Culvert reinforcement; location of bar mark 08 is critical

reinforcement is detailed means that virtually all the reinforcement has to be fixed before the walls can be poured. A study of the reinforcing bar marked 08 provides the clue. It will be clear, therefore, that crane-handled large panels cannot be used.

The only solution, in the end, was to erect and dismantle all the formwork to the walls piecemeal, at greater cost.

It is worth adding that this example and the one that follows are taken from real life contract details.

Case study: a staircase

A staircase is detailed climbing up between two walls (Fig. 10.11). The stairs are detailed to have the tread reinforcement spanning horizontally from one wall to the other. To construct as detailed, the walls have to be poured to the soffit of the stair treads, the stairs formed and poured and, finally, the remainder of each wall. It takes little thought to realise that this is not the most economical way of doing things.

The solution is really quite simple and involves the revision of the stair detailing. If starter bars are provided in each wall, the walls can be

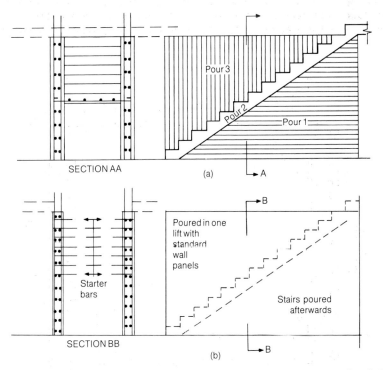

Fig. 10.11. Staircase reinforcement—effect on formwork: (a) staircase as detailed: to meet demands of reinforcement as detailed, stairs have to be poured as integral part of walls; three pours needed, and specially shaped panels for pours 1 and 3; (b) revised detailing: starter bars only; wall poured in one lift, stairs later; a better solution is to detail stairs spanning top to bottom

poured in one lift, with the staircase also poured in one lift afterwards. Better still, the design can be modified to span top to bottom, when the stairs do not need to connect with the walls at all.

In either solution, the formwork cost is greatly reduced, and time is saved, too.

UNFORESEEN LOADS

The *Code of practice for falsework* emphasises the importance of the design brief, of which part is the estimation of loads to be supported. What needs to be recognised here is that the loads to be supported by the falsework first have to be supported by the formwork! Only then are they transmitted to the falsework below.

The code lists the following:

(a) weight of the permanent structure
(b) the effect of loading sequence (i.e. the sequence in which the pours will be carried out)
(c) loading from the plant and methods to be used
(d) weight of the formwork.

When assessing the loads that any plant will bring on to the formwork, it is important to bear in mind the location in which the work will be carried out and any special features that arise, even though the method

Fig. 10.12. Part of Elf structure in basin (Sir Robert McAlpine & Sons Ltd)

Fig. 10.13. Compressor and generator on Cormorant slipform (Sir Robert McAlpine & Sons Ltd)

Fig. 10.14. General view of Cormorant, showing the cranes, concrete distribution equipment, mess huts, offices, toilets etc., all carried on the slipform assembly (Sir Robert McAlpine & Sons Ltd)

being used may be well known. These points are illustrated by an example in relation to slipform construction.

Case study

At Ardyne Point, a national contractor was constructing gravity platforms for the North Sea oilfield. The base sections were formed by slipforming the very large cellular structure. In Fig. 10.12, part of the Elf Field structure is seen. The slipform equipment is carrying tower cranes, concrete-placing booms, offices and mess huts. Four tower cranes and four placing booms in all were carried on the slipform. With the planning done properly, as in this case, these were not unforeseen loads, but they were far from usual.

The extent of the plant and equipment which had to be carried on the slipforms in constructing such vast structures is further illustrated by the compressor and generator shown in Fig. 10.13. The Cormorant Field structure slipform is carrying all the loads already illustrated, with an additional two concrete-placing booms (Fig. 10.14).

Sources of unforeseen loads

Assessment of construction loadings, however carefully done, fails to draw attention to unforeseen loads from other sources.

The most likely unforeseen loads will be in relation to the way in which the reinforcement spacers are situated. What is usually completely forgotten is that spacers, of whatever type, bring point loads on to the formwork. Where such point loads come is in the lap of the gods. Unless the positions are actually specified, no one will know until the steelfixer has made a decision as to where he will put them. In locating such spacers, it is human nature to minimise the task. It follows that the stiffer the reinforcement used (i.e. the bigger the bars or the more rigid the prefabricated reinforcement cage) the fewer spacers will be seen to be necessary to maintain the required cover.

Not only are high point loads brought on to the form lining material by the sheer weight of reinforcement, but additional loads can occur when the concrete is poured. Close spacing of bars will cause the concrete to hang on the lower reinforcement until vibration takes place— with the result that more loading comes on to the spacer. The consequential possibilities are are illustrated in Fig. 10.15.

The author personally knows of a motorway bridge which has a soffit covered with projecting circular pimples. All are attributable to the excess loading on the plywood formwork from the sparsely located spacers, and were proved to be so. It is not a long jump to wonder how many falsework failures were triggered by excessive point loads on elements of the formwork above, which, in the end, triggered progressive collapse in falsework inadequately braced to resist the unexpected loads.

Another source for unforeseen loads arises during the erection stage. It is not unknown for soffit forms to be erected over part of the area, and such a space to be used for stockpiling materials for the next area of formwork, or for placing heavy parcels of reinforcement. It is an open

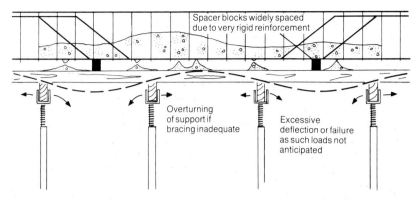

Fig. 10.15. Unforeseen loads due to wide spacing of spacer blocks: high point loads introduced from weight of reinforcement, and hang-up of concrete on reinforcement prior to vibration

question as to how many soffit forms and their attendant falsework have collapsed as a direct result, or, alternatively, have been subjected to high deflections. The *Code of practice for falsework* calls for careful checking that the loads are as stated in the design brief. It is equally important that the same principles are applied to the formwork as well.

AVOIDING FORMWORK

Occasions arise where what is detailed in in situ concrete is difficult to achieve to the quality or accuracy required. In such cases, serious consideration should be given to solutions using precast rather than in situ concrete. An example of such action is given in chapter 11. It is one of several examples in the author's experience where the change produced a better result in both time and quality terms. Success needs the co-operation of the structural engineer, of course, but the more both sides come together to give the client the best value for his money the better.

STOP END COSTS AND THEIR EVALUATION

Unless the location of stop ends has been specified on the drawings, and become a measured item, the contractor is responsible for assessing the quantity needed and allowing for their cost in his tender submission. As an item of work it is probably the one that receives least attention when a suspended slab is being priced. The number of times 'something to cover for stop ends' is added must be legion, because taking off all the stop ends needed is tedious. Both the estimators and planners prefer to spend their time on more expensive items.

In fact, the cost of stop ends, and the scabbling of the surface before new concrete is placed against it, is far greater than most people realise. In suspended slab construction where bays are specified based on the middle third rule, the stop end cost becomes a significant percentage of the overall cost of the slab in question. To overcome this problem, it is possible to develop a relatively simple system for stop end cost evaluation at the tender planning stage.

It is important to note that the method put forward depends for its accuracy on the bay size being determined by the mid-third rule for the division of suspended slabs. Given this, site trials have shown that variations from a 'standard' bay are largely self-correcting. Why this should be so is demonstrated in Figs 10.16 and 10.17.

Since the original development of the method, factual checks have been made on site, in which it was found that the graphs give values that are 95–98% of the actual costs in the field.

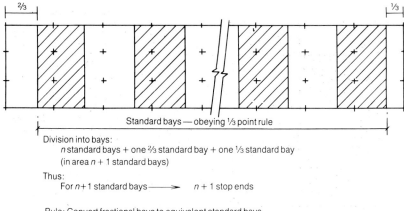

Standard bays — obeying ⅓ point rule

Division into bays:
    n standard bays + one ⅔ standard bay + one ⅓ standard bay
    (in area n + 1 standard bays)

Thus:
    For n + 1 standard bays ⟶ n + 1 stop ends

Rule: Convert fractional bays to equivalent standard bays.
Then number of stop ends will equal number of bays.

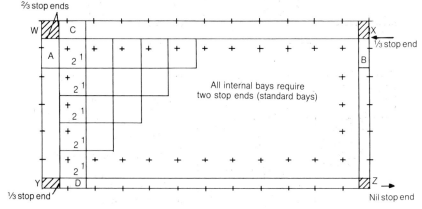

Consider external bays — bearing in mind ⅓ point rule:

    A + B = one standard bay. Summation of stop ends for A + B is same as for standard bay.
    C + D = one standard bay. Summation of stop ends for C + D is same as for one standard bay.
    W + X + Y + Z = one standard bay. Summation of stop ends for W + X + Y + Z is same as for
                 standard bay.
Thus:
    All standard bays have two stop ends, and length of stop end is constant.

Fig. 10.16. Stop ends across full width of building

Stop end types

Using the mid-third rule, the division of suspended concrete slabs for pouring involves either a single stop end across the width of the slab, or division of the slab into rectilinear bays less than the slab width. The first case is straightforward. Surprisingly, analysis of possible bay configurations in the second case shows that, irrespective of whether the bays are poured hit and miss or as a continuous progression, the average number of stop ends required is, in fact, only on two sides of any given bay (Figs 10.16 and 10.17).

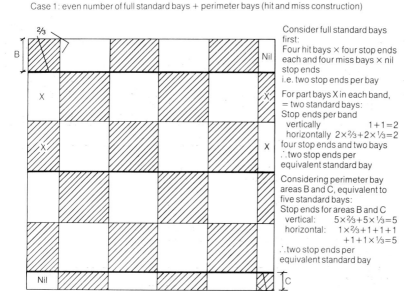

Case 1: even number of full standard bays + perimeter bays (hit and miss construction)

Consider full standard bays first:
Four hit bays × four stop ends each and four miss bays × nil stop ends
i.e. two stop ends per bay

For part bays X in each band, = two standard bays:
Stop ends per band
vertically $\qquad$ $1+1=2$
horizontally $2\times\frac{2}{3}+2\times\frac{1}{3}=2$
four stop ends and two bays
∴ two stop ends per equivalent standard bay

Considering perimeter bay areas B and C, equivalent to five standard bays:
Stop ends for areas B and C
vertical: $\qquad$ $5\times\frac{2}{3}+5\times\frac{1}{3}=5$
horizontal: $\quad 1\times\frac{2}{3}+1+1+1$
$\qquad +1+1\times\frac{1}{3}=5$
∴ two stop ends per equivalent standard bay

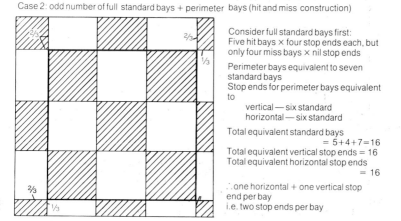

Case 2: odd number of full standard bays + perimeter bays (hit and miss construction)

Consider full standard bays first:
Five hit bays × four stop ends each, but only four miss bays × nil stop ends

Perimeter bays equivalent to seven standard bays
Stop ends for perimeter bays equivalent to
vertical — six standard
horizontal — six standard

Total equivalent standard bays
$= 5+4+7=16$
Total equivalent vertical stop ends = 16
Total equivalent horizontal stop ends
$= 16$

∴ one horizontal + one vertical stop end per bay
i.e. two stop ends per bay

Fig. 10.17. Stop ends with rectilinear bays

It can be said, therefore, that in the situation specified, only two types of stop end condition exist: single stop ends across the full width of the slab; and two-sided stop ends, where the bays are less than the slab width. As a result, it is possible to create graphs, one for each case quoted above. Provided that the bay area is known and the length of the major stop end is established, the unit cost of stop ends as an extra over (e.o.) per square metre of formwork can be read off directly. The unit cost

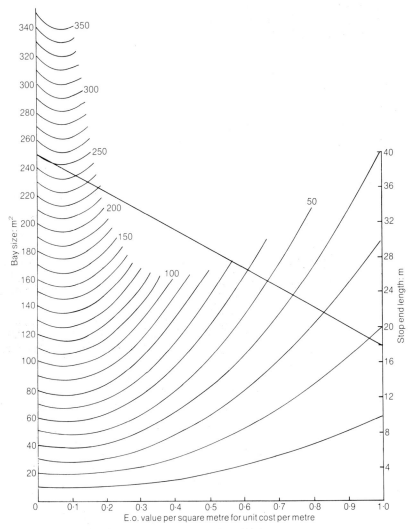

Fig. 10.18. Stop end cost: bays having one stop end (example shown: 250 m² bays with 18 m stop end; where line crosses 250 m² graph, extra over (e.o.) value per square metre for unit cost per metre is 0.065; therefore if stop end cost is £2 per metre, e.o. per square metre of decking is £0.13)

from the graphs enables many types of stop end to be accurately priced, provided the cost per metre of a particular type of stop end is known.

Method of calculation for costing graphs
  Using the notation

y   cost of stop end per unit area of soffit formwork, £/m²
C   stop end cost per unit length, £/m
A   bay area, m²
L   major stop end length, m
l   minor stop end length, m

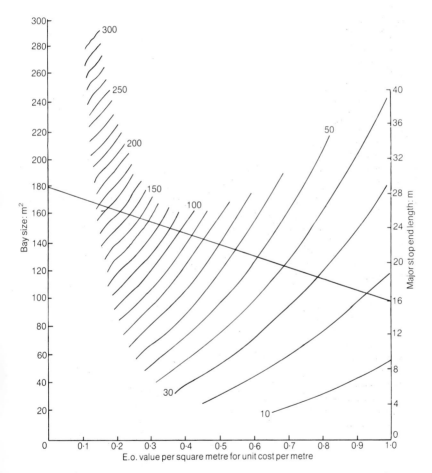

Fig. 10.19. Stop end cost: bays having two stop ends (example shown: 180 m² bays with a 16 m major stop end length; where line crosses 180 m² graph, extra over (e.o.) value per square metre for unit cost per metre is 0.15; therefore if stop end cost is £2 per metre, e.o. per square metre of decking is £0.30)

the relationship between these elements is given by

$$y = C(L + l)/A \qquad (1)$$

for all cases. But where a single stop end across the width of the slab is used, $l = 0$ and thus

$$y = CL/A \qquad (2)$$

The two graphs (Figs 10.18 and 10.19) are plotted on the basis of equations (2) and (1) respectively, but with C values taken as unity (£1 per metre).

How to use the graphs

In order to determine the values of stop end costs per square metre of soffit formwork, adopt the following procedure.

(a) Assess which type of stop end is operative.

(b) Establish bay area—from specified requirement or by planning need. (It is only necessary to fix the general bay size. Odd bays at start and finish of the slab area (i.e. perimeter bays) are accounted for in the graphs (see Figs 10.16 and 10.17).)

(c) Determine either
   (i) single stop end length or
   (ii) major stop end length for a standard bay (if the bay is square, any side).

(d) Lay ruler on graph: on left hand side to bay area, on right hand side to single or major stop end length.

(e) Mark point where rule crosses curve for required bay area.

(f) From that point read down vertically to x axis. Value obtained is e.o. cost per square metre of soffit formwork for a stop end of unit value (£1 per metre).

(g) Correct by multiplying the answer by the actual rate per metre for the stop end in question.

FORMATION OF MECHANICAL KEYS TO CONCRETE

The use of mosaics and tiles as finishes to concrete elements is often specified by architects and, in the past, many examples have occurred where the mosaics or tiling have parted company with the structure after a relatively short time. In many cases the failure has been due to inadequate adhesion with the concrete. The method described below was successfully tried and used as standard on a civic building in the south of England. Its use was continued on a further contract requiring the fixing of tiling to the walls of a swimming pool.

Possible methods

The methods possible for the formation of keys, to the surface of concrete, are numerous. They include bush hammering or similar; using retarders applied to the form surface; using proprietary liners to the form, which can be peeled off, leaving a keyed surface; high pressure water-jetting; using adhesives without a key; and using expanded metal lathing. Each of the methods listed has characteristics which give cause for doubt about its use. As the civic building quoted had some 11 250 m^2 of mosaic to be applied, the method finally adopted had to satisfy both effective adhesion and a competitive cost.

Each of the above methods was examined for pros and cons and the results are summarised below.

In the case of bush hammering, the cost quoted by the specialist was considered too high. It did not cover for attendances, scaffolding or shielding against dust. In the centre of a major city, dust would cause considerable complaint at the least, if not prohibition by the local authority.

Retarding of the concrete surface was rejected by the structural engineers as unsuitable. Retarders are notoriously unreliable, as they start to harden immediately the forms are struck. Unless all areas of the forms are scrubbed together, some areas will be satisfactory, while others will hardly show any surface removal at all.

Proprietary liners to the forms are commonly used to form keyed surfaces. The rubber and the plastic liners are initially expensive; economy depends on obtaining a large number of uses. As the wall shapes on the contract in question were complex, high wastage of the material in cutting would have been inevitable. Although perhaps the initial first choice, it was not going to be cost-effective.

In the case of high pressure water-jetting, examination suggested that the cost would be very high, and there was no guarantee of the result being suitable for mosaic adhesion. The mess created by the water was eventually the ruling-out factor, as the building was immediately adjacent to the public highway.

The use of adhesives without a mechanical key was not regarded as a suitable method by the specialist subcontractor. Concrete tolerances to the structural elements could not be guaranteed to be accurate enough, especially as some of the walls to be clad rose the full height of the building, which was some 30 m.

In the case of expanded metal lathing, the idea was to lightly tack the expanded metal to the forms, so that, when the forms were struck, the expanded metal would be left behind to give a rough surface for the backing coat to bond to. The suggestion was rejected by the consulting engineer because of the risk of possible corrosion and staining of the mosaic surface, with final failure.

Method used

The method eventually used was suggested by site management, approved by the consultants and happily accepted by the mosaic subcontractor, as the degree of surface exposure achieved satisfied BS 212 for the keying of concrete to mosaic.

Light gauge galvanised steel mesh, 25 mm × 12 mm, 16 g, was fixed to the forms by air-driven divergent staples at 50 mm centres (Fig. 10.20). The forms were coated with a chemical release agent before each use.

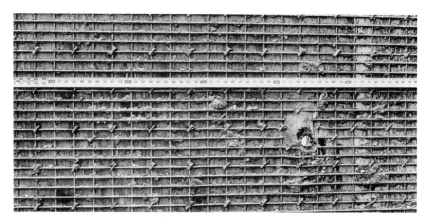

Fig. 10.20. Welded mesh fabric fixed to form

Fig. 10.21. Wall detail as struck

Fig. 10.22. Beam detail as struck

Fig. 10.23. Tile-fixing to column

When the forms were struck an excellent key was produced (Figs 10.21 and 10.22).

With this method, it will be clear that the striking time is a crucial element for success. Before general use, trials were carried out and the striking times to be adopted were agreed with the Engineer. Under normal conditions, with temperatures in the range, say, 10–18°C, 5 hours was agreed (on the hottest summer days $3\frac{1}{2}$ hours). Only under winter conditions was the striking time increased to a maximum of 16 hours.

Failure to comply with the striking times established can be expensive. The mesh can lock into the concrete, and the forms then have to be forcibly removed, leaving the mesh behind. This in turn, literally has to be dug out. The following remedial work is difficult and expensive. It is also a key point that pour sizes have to be limited so that the concrete is of a similar age when striking.

After each strike the forms were beaten to remove loose cement that was trapped behind the mesh. Some staples also needed replacing. Ten uses were achieved without excessive maintenance costs.

Figure 10.23 illustrates the mosaic tile fixing. Tiles were bedded in 1 : 3 cement : sand mix. The overall thickness of the backing, the levelling coat and the mosaic was 25 mm.

11

Erection of structural frames

In this chapter, structural frames are taken to encompass the following types: precast concrete; steelwork; space frames; timber structures; aluminium; and plastic. The most common are precast concrete and structural steel. The wide scope has been deliberately chosen to be the same as that covered in BS 5531, *Code of practice for safety in erecting structural frames*.[1] In addition, it also fits in well with the HSE Guidance Note GS 28,[2] *Safe erection of structures.*

In view of the current fierce competition between concrete and steel as structural and cladding methods, bringing the two together in a chapter of this kind may seem rather odd, to say the least. In fact, a study of the documents referred to above will show that, in safety terms, there is a great similarity between the two.

Structural frame systems are designed to minimise temporary works in erection. However, the desire to avoid temporary works can, in fact, create other problems, because of the nature of the preformed component concept.

LEGISLATION AND THE REQUIREMENTS OF SAFETY

The principal legislation relevant to the erection of structural frames is

Health and Safety at Work etc. Act 1974
Factories Act 1961
The Construction (General Provisions) Regulations 1961
The Construction (Lifting Operations) Regulations 1961
The Construction (Working Places) Regulations 1966.

Anyone working in this field should check the current legislation situation, as changes may have been made in the interim.

To comply with such legislation, the contractor will need to provide a safe means of access to the place of work; a safe place of work, in relation both to adequate working space and to protection from falls; and protection from the activities of others (falls of materials, tools etc. from above). To do so, scaffolding, fans, screens and safety nets may be required. When erection takes place over water, a boat in the charge of a competent boatman, trained in rescue methods, has to be manned and in position at all times when work is taking place. In addition, life-jackets have to be worn by all personnel working over the water.[3]

Within the same general context, both BS 5531 and GS 28 draw attention to the need for adequate consideration to be given—both at the design stage and while erection is taking place—to the risks that may arise from lack of stability in the frame at any stage of its erection, together with any weakness in the structure when erection is incomplete. Types of support and their sphere of application have been detailed and tabulated in GS 28 part 2 at some length. The importance of handling trusses and other frameworks in a way that does not cause reverse stresses to those designed for is also covered, together with the types of lifting bridles than can be provided to overcome such problems.

Anyone involved in the design of structural frames should be familiar with both the code and the HSE GS 28 and, as far as is reasonably possible, ensure that the design detailing minimises any temporary instability. If such instability is unavoidable, the drawings should adequately portray the needs for support and how they are to be effected; for example, the use of push/pull props, temporary staging etc. and the loads that have to be stabilised.

OPERATIONAL TEMPORARY WORKS

Both BS 5531 and GS 28 are concerned with safety and the temporary works needed for this purpose. What must be recognised, however, is that the adoption of structural frames, in the context stated at the start of this chapter, has the effect of introducing temporary works elsewhere. Such items will be needed for efficient handling of structural elements on site; proper storage until required; accuracy in offering to the fixing location; and general operational efficiency. As such, they play a significant part in the efficiency of the erection of the structure as a whole. At times such temporary works can be surprisingly extensive.

Access

The components of structural frames, as delivered to site, usually require the use of heavy articulated vehicles. It becomes important, therefore, that adequate provision in respect of site access is made for such vehicles and the weights that they are likely to be carrying; in all weather conditions. Guidance in relation to the provision of such temporary roads is referred to in chapter 4.

If mobile cranes are to be used in the erection, there will be a requirement for hard surfaces at and between lifting points, suitable for the weight of the crane and its operating loads, as well as adequate support for the crane's outriggers. Where tower cranes are used, foundations suitable for the crane type in question must be provided. (In either case, see chapter 5.)

Storage areas

Hardstandings for the storage of structural components should be designed with as much care as the main access roads. While the loadings may well vary, depending on the type of structural frame involved, very heavy loading conditions can arise. It is important that the site planning gives adequate consideration to the method and height of stacking, the loadings determined and the hardstandings designed to suit.

A further aspect of storage relates to the temporary support of the elements when unloaded. As different methods are likely for different types of structural framework, this aspect is considered separately later in the chapter.

Cranage

To be efficient in erection, any method of structural framing wherever possible needs to be designed so that the individual weights of components are within a reasonably narrow band, and all within the capability of one crane type. Failure in this respect by the designer can lead to greatly increased costs for the structure.

Case study

A barrack complex was being constructed for a NATO country after the Second World War. For speed it was decided to use precast concrete structural elements.

All columns, individual beams, stair units etc. were designed to be within a weight range of 1.5–3 t. So far so good. Unfortunately, someone had the great idea of precasting the individual barrack unit floors in one piece. Constructed in special steel moulds on site—coffered in section—each element weighted 25 t. To extract the floor unit from the mould, a special gantry crane was needed. The unit then had to be loaded on to a special low-loader, driven over the site to the erection location, and lifted into position by a very heavy mobile crane specially brought into the site on each occasion that a unit had to be lifted.

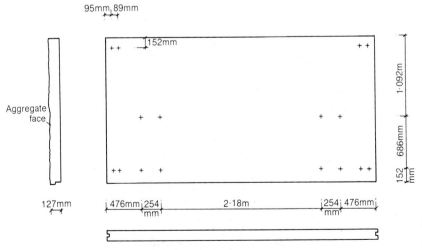

Fig. 11.1. Detail of socket fixings: drawing covering permanent and temporary inserts

It requires little imagination to see how the cost of both the operation and the associated temporary works could have been greatly reduced. Suffice it to say, if ever there was a case where in situ concrete for the floors was a runner, this must have been it. The gantry crane and the cost of track, the low loader and the strengthened roads, and the heavy mobile crane would all have been eliminated.

TEMPORARY WORKS RELATED TO PRECAST CONCRETE

The use of precast concrete for a structural frame, for the cladding of a structure, or where the precast elements provide both the frame and the cladding in one unit, requires the provision of temporary works of a variety of kinds. Those associated with safety have already been mentioned: safe access to the work place, safe work place, and so on. These apart, the following items need to be determined and allowed for at the tender stage.

Methods of handling, storage and casting

Key questions are the following. First, how will the unit be cast, and in what type of mould; and in what position (attitude) will it be on the delivery lorry?

Fig. 11.2. A-frame for back-to-back temporary support of precast elements when off-loaded; note edge-protection members

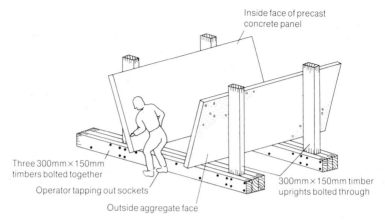

Fig. 11.3. Support method for large panel precast units

Secondly (leading on from the first item), agreement on the location of fixings and any additional lifting inserts is essential. While the requirements for the permanent fixings will be specified by the Engineer, the contractor will be responsible for any additional inserts or fixings necessary for temporary support; for anchoring any push/pull props needed; and for any additional lifting, if the unit has to be altered in attitude from that on the delivery vehicle, to achieve the right hanging position for lifting and fixing in the structure. To avoid any misunderstandings, all lifting and handling inserts should be incorporated on one drawing for the firm who will manufacture the units, showing the dimensional locations, and the type of fixing and/or insert (Fig. 11.1). If additional reinforcement is needed to stop a unit cracking, where turning is necessary, this should be clearly marked on the reinforcement drawing.

Thirdly, to minimise space requirements and to allow all units to be in the correct position for direct lifting into place, some form of racking needs to be provided (Fig. 11.2).

Fourthly, such racking also needs to be suitable for inserts in the units to be cleaned out, and lifting eyes etc. to be screwed in. Figure 11.3 illustrates a simple form of support for use with large panel units. Polyurethane strips, or similar, should be provided to avoid damage to edges or surface treatment.

Fifthly, agreement should be reached on the weight of all units that have to be handled and lifted.

Of the above items, the need to change the attitude of an element can be the most awkward. There are questions that need answering by the Engineer: Is the reinforcement adequate for the bending that will occur when a unit is up-ended? If not, what additional steel is needed?

Where elements already have their final finish, any alteration of attitude can cause damage and arrangements need to be made to prevent such damage. Figure 11.4 illustrates how the problem can be overcome in a simple way.

Erection of units

At the pre-tender stage a careful examination should have been made of all the units that have to be lifted. Weight is obviously crucial, but shape should not be neglected. Centres of gravity that are in unusual locations can make lifting very awkward and the final locating into position difficult. In such instances, special lifting beams may be necessary to keep the unit hanging in the right position for installation. Such a beam is illustrated in Fig. 11.5.

In this example, the lifting point has been designed to allow the unit to remain level, in spite of the return section of the unit. The lower beams of the lifting unit, that actually connect to the precast element, have been designed to be adjustable in relation to the main beam. With this arrangement, final adjustments can be made on site, to ensure that the unit hangs truly level or vertical as the case may be.

Fixing procedures

The permanant fixings for precast structural elements will be specified by the structural engineer. The contractor, on the other hand, is concerned with getting any lift off the crane hook as quickly as possible, so that the crane can be earning money by lifting other units. For this to be possible, the contractor has to make arrangements for the temporary support of column, wall or beam sections. That this is a cost-saving necessity is an advantage to all parties. All structural frames, of whatever type, need to be erected accurately, in terms of line and level. Failure to do so can cause endless problems: buildings get out of square, floors cease to be level, and, perhaps worst of all, any subsequent cladding will not fit.

Temporary supporting of structural members provides the time to make sure that line and level are being accurately achieved, and all overall dimensions maintained.

In most cases, push/pull props provide the most straightforward answer (Fig. 11.6). Any such arrangement (with the additional fixing locations required) needs to be established at the pre-contract stage,

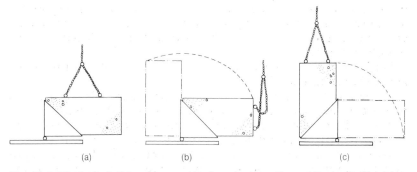

| (a) | (b) | (c) |

Fig. 11.4. Method of tilting precast units from horizontal to vertical attitude: (a) place precast concrete panel in swivel frame; (b) change lifting chains (brothers) to end position; (c) hoist panel to vertical position, then hoist clear of swivel frame

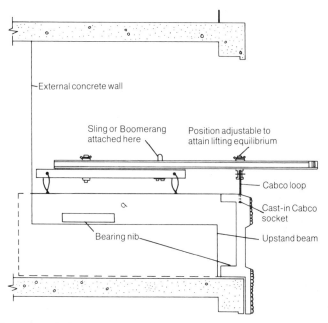

Fig. 11.5. Design of lifting gear for unsymmetrical units: corner profile panel cladding method; sectional elevation of corner panel and lifting brace (each 'leg' of a corner panel was 2.15 m long)

Fig. 11.6. Push/pull props supporting precast units: templates for setting out units (see Fig. 11.9) visible on right hand side

Fig. 11.7. Hopper forms at columns for connection concreting

before any orders are placed for the manufacture of units. It must be established with the structural engineer, however, that the anchorage points for such props are safe for the forces likely to arise.

With the temporary holding members in position, the final lining and levelling can take place without any pressure to take chances.

Whatever the final fixing method—grouting, welding and casing in in situ concrete, bolting or any other method—it is good practice to try out the jointing at ground level. What may look satisfactory on a drawing may be found in practice to be very awkward to execute accurately. Trials will prove the viability, one way or another. A method developed from early trials for the concreting of a structural connection is shown in Fig. 11.7. The hopper-like formwork is designed to give, with vibration, a positive head, to ensure full filling of the space between the floor and the unit connecting to it.

TEMPORARY WORKS RELATED TO STEEL ERECTION

In the erection of structural steel frames, the common factors already covered in relation to safety, access etc. apply just as much as with precast concrete. Safety, however, is more difficult to achieve. Steel erectors have a tradition of 'daring' and tend to resist scaffolding or other safety measures. Indeed, it is often said that too much scaffolding would make steel uneconomic, as the scaffold is only needed for very short periods in any location. The introduction of troughed steel permanent

*Fig. 11.8. Steel frame
with profiled steel
decking: overseas photo;
in the UK it would be
illegal not to have edge
protection*

formwork for the concrete floor, normally used as a horizontal stiffener to the structure, has made a big difference to safety, as the decking provides a catchment for anyone who may fall from above (Fig. 11.8).

Today, much of the structural steel erected can satisfy fire regulations without the steel being encased in concrete (by use of dry claddings or fire-resistant spray coatings). It is only where such concrete cladding is called for that temporary works arise in any complexity or quantity. Without doubt, such casing is costly and time-consuming; the provision of safe access for its execution is difficult and costly, and it is obstructive to all follow-on activities.

Everything involved is in small quantities: the amount of concrete per metre, the area of formwork and the weight of reinforcement. At the same time, the labour intensity is very high for the measured work done. Anyone who has ever been associated with a contract with large quantities of such activity will testify to the frustrating and, usually, loss-making character of casing work.

Provided that adequate time is available at the pre-contract stage, much can be done to eliminate this particular problem. The simple answer is to pre-case the steel sections before erection.

To adopt such a method requires adequate planning and discussion with the structural engineer and the steelwork contractor. When organised properly, it can provide a first-class and economical result.

In any pre-case analysis, a number of key points need to be examined.

(*a*) Pre-casing is to the members, but excludes splice areas (in situ).

(*b*) What will be the weight increase in lifting cased elements?

(c) Who will do the casing?
(d) Where will it be carried out?

Experience suggests that casing is best carried out on site. Much less weight has to be hauled to the site. If this is adopted, additional time will be needed between delivery of the steelwork and its erection. Equally, adequate storage facilities must be available on site: the items being cased will have to be laid out individually. Only when mature can they be stacked on top of each other—in the order required for the final erection sequence. With the above in mind, it is clearly best if the main contractor is made responsible for the actual casing operation.

In planning the temporary works needed for pre-casing, trouble should be taken to establish the most convenient attitude for any member to be cased. For example, it will be much easier and will use less formwork if a column unit is cased lying on its side. Such an analysis needs doing for all the elements that may be involved. Once established, the type of stooling and formwork needed can be detailed (Fig. 11.9).

It will be clear from the illustration that the casing procedure resembles a precasting operation, with the capability of using the mould many times in a short period of time. The biggest advantage, of course, is that all operations are carried out on or near the ground. Little scaffolding is needed, and considerable savings result. The examples shown in Fig. 11.9 are taken from actual use in the pre-casing of steel for a grandstand at a racecourse; hence the raking members to support pre-cast decking.

In the case quoted above, steel was delivered to site before the actual contract started and was stored in a course car park. The area for casing was adjacent. By the time steel erection started, all casing was complete. This particular procedure had to be adopted as the time available for demolition of existing stands and the erection of the new was extremely

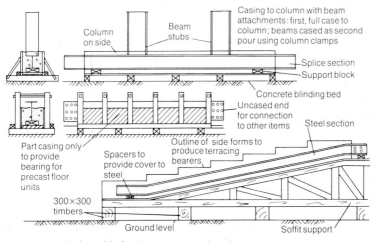

Fig. 11.9. Detail of moulds for pre-casing steelwork

*Fig. 11.10 (above).
Tubular steel roof with
lift core tower and safety
netting*

*Fig. 11.11. Tubular steel
subsidiary roof with
initial falsework support*

limited. In other circumstances, if the available programme time permits, the casing programme can be less onerous.

ERECTION OF MAJOR ROOFS IN STEEL

The enclosure of large areas with steel roof structures may necessitate various types of temporary works. The examples shown in Figs 11.10 and 11.11 illustrate the enclosure of a shopping centre to provide an environmentally controlled complex. The complex was already operating, and considerable thought had to be given to the sequence of work to allow the shops to continue in business, while at the same time protecting the public from danger.

A great deal of temporary support in the erection of the roof was avoided by having the structural steel tower seen in the left centre of Fig. 11.10. This structure is to contain lifts and a staircase to connect the shopping mall with various levels of an adjacent multi-storey car park. The tower was erected first, and designed to be of adequate stiffness and stability to provide the initial temporary support to the roof members. These had to be limited in size and weight because of the limited access and crane capacity in such a confined area. Seen in the background of Fig. 11.11, the roof covers a large area and stability in erection was a crucial factor. This is an excellent example of the use of permanent works as temporary works in the initial phase. Outside the main roof area, a

Fig. 11.12. Cantilever fixing platform for curtain wall fixings installation

number of side aisles are being covered in by a roof at a lower level. Figure 11.11 illustrates the erection of these smaller roofs and shows the centre-line support scaffolding. The individual tubular half-trusses are rested on this support for connection together. Lateral and longitudinal stability of such temporary supports is crucial, and a careful study of the photo will show the diagonal bracing provided in both directions.

On a large sloping roof of this type, safe working is less easy to achieve than with vertical or horizontal structures. Figure 11.10 shows the use of safety netting under the roof framework to catch anyone on the roof who might fall. This netting also supports a fine mesh net to stop any bits and pieces falling on to the public or workers below.

ERECTION OF CURTAIN WALLING

Aluminium or other metal-framed curtain walling could be considered a structural frame. It is often carried out on in situ concrete structures that have been built without the use of scaffolding. The casting-in of mullion fixings as the pour proceeds is notoriously inaccurate and leads to recriminations with the curtain walling specialist. With modern drilling equipment it is far better to drill and fix when the structure is well in advance of the curtain walling. Any inaccuracies can be ironed out in the process. The problem with this method is providing access to install the fixings when no scaffolding is available.

Figure 11.12 shows one contractor's solution to this problem. On the fourth floor, in the centre of the picture is what looks like a staircase unit projecting outside the building. Closer study will reveal that it is a fixing platform projecting outside the building, for the curtain wall fixings. It jacks against the floor and ceiling for stability and has the stair access incorporated within it: a small but effective piece of temporary works.

PRECAST CONCRETE AS A CLADDING: AIDS TO ERECTION

It is a prerequisite of successful precast concrete cladding of any structure that the structure is in itself accurate to the tolerances specified. A great deal of time and money can be lost on a contract if the frame is inaccurately constructed. Endless time and money is lost 'adjusting' the frame dimensions to fit. Hacking away at the frame does not endear the contractor to the structural engineer, either!

Assuming that all is well dimensionally, adequate consideration needs to be given to the handling, placing, and lining and levelling of the cladding units. It is on the competence of the erectors at this stage that the final appearance of the structure will depend.

Procedures should be established in relation to the sequence of erection, and how the lining and levelling are to be carried out prior to the final fixing. The importance of these operations is related to the need to release the cladding unit from the crane hook as quickly as one can, to maintain the momentum of lifting units as much as possible. To achieve this situation, it will be immediately apparent that aids to lining and levelling and temporary support systems are needed. A number of such methods are described and illustrated below.

Unbalanced elements

Reference has already been made to temporary lifting beams to offset unsymmetrical units, so that when raised to their final location they hang in the correct position for fixing. Such lifting beams usually need to be made by the contractor to suit special conditions for the site in question. Also, this probably will be cheaper than going to a specialised manufacturer.

Whoever makes a lifting beam, it is a legal requirement that it must be proof-tested and have the safe working load clearly marked on it.

Overhang obstructions to handling

Other situations arise when cladding units have to be positioned in locations where there is some kind of overhang above, which prevents the hoist rope of the crane remaining in line with the unit below. The problem is resolved quite readily by the use of a piece of equipment known as a 'boomerang' (Fig. 11.13). The principle of operation is quite simple. The load hangs from the lower leg and the lifting point is at the outer corner of the top leg. The upper leg has to be made longer than the obstruction to the hoist rope, and is fitted with rollers at its extremity. In lowering the load, the crane allows the upper leg of the boomerang to make contact with the floor above the placing location. As lowering continues, the upper leg will move inwards on its rollers; and the unit, while moving downwards, will also move inwards of the crane hoist rope line.

Once the principle is understood, a good structural designer will have no difficulty in designing such a unit for any particular special circumstances. Figure 11.14, for example, illustrates a modification of the standard boomerang. In this case, the boomerang is designed with two top

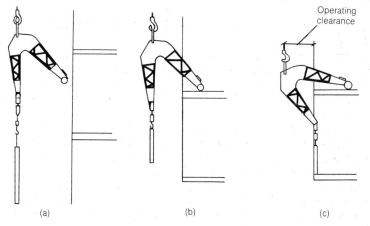

(a) (b) (c)

Fig. 11.13. Boomerang lifting unit: (a) the boomerang and its load are lowered until the roller at the end of the upper arm is at the required level; (b) after location, the lowering continues and the lower arm and its load begin to pivot inwards about the roller located on the floor above; (c) the load is located in the building at the required level and is ready to be secured (Scaffolding (Great Britain) Ltd)

Fig. 11.14. Split-leg boomerang unit for column cladding: sectional elevation shows boomerang (simplified) placing column cladding; horizontal section shows typical top fixing A' and side fixing B' (weight of typical panel 1 t; weight of boomerang 1 t; total weight 2 t)

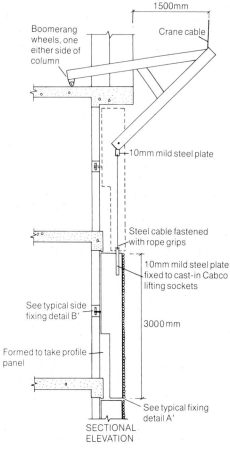

Fig. 11.15 (below). Temporary fixing of precast panels: (a) plan; (b) detail of profile panel anchor point

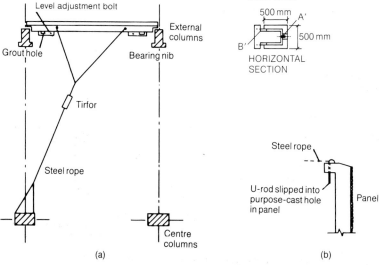

legs in order to simplify the erection of precast column casing units. This creates a balanced support (with the column casing hanging vertically), and results in an easier fixing situation. Having to push and strain to locate cladding elements is a recipe for damage to the units.

Temporary fixing of panels

However well the precast panels are made and however accurate the structure is, it is always advantageous to have the ability to release the units from the crane, both to allow the crane to get on with the lifting and to create the opportunity to ensure that the panels along the line of the structure are 'eye-sweet'. With the best will in the world, some distortion in the precast units is likely to take place. It is therefore desirable to set out the line and level of the panels; provide a temporary fixing system; and, once a long length has been erected, adjust to give the desirable eye-sweet appearance. This is particularly necessary where the cladding units butt together along the whole facade. If the panels are within a column line, and cannot be lined up, the temporary fixing only needs to be provided to release the crane as quickly as possible. A method of doing this is illustrated in Fig. 11.15. A Tirfor is anchored to a column by means of a steel rope, and to the top of a cladding panel by a U-rod slipped into a hole, purpose-cast when the panel was made. It should be a guiding rule that precast panels are always pulled into final alignment, as this is so much easier to do than push.

Precast cladding to structural steel

More and more structures in steel are being clad in precast concrete panels. In many cases the steelwork will be dry-cased (or sprayed), and the precast units have to be adequately connected to the steel structure. Some ideas in relation to both temporary and permanent fixings are given in Figs 11.16–11.18. In the first two, temporary fixings are shown, while the last figure shows in detail the final erection sequence.

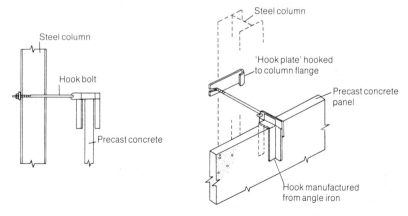

Fig. 11.16. Temporary fixing of precast panels to structural steel

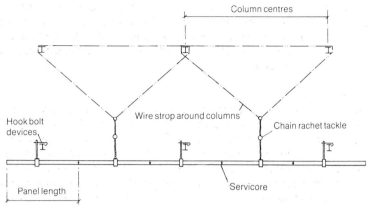

Fig. 11.17. Temporary fixing of precast panels to structural steel to achieve 'eye-sweet' line: plan showing tie-in devices in operation

1. Measure and mark centre-line on top edge of precast concrete panel (PCCP).

2. Measure and mark half column section to either side of centre-line.

3. Place straight edge (spirit level) across column flange.

4. Adjust PCCP to align marks (achieved by tightening down adjacent PCCP, then 'pulling' the PCCP in question to position by bottlescrew device).

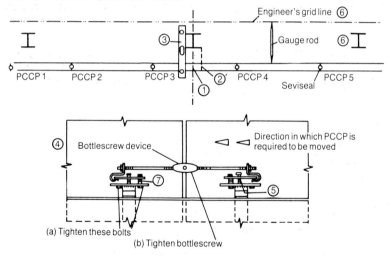

5. Level PCCP to datum mark (previously marked on columns by engineer), achieved by adjusting set screw.

6. Adjust PCCP to line (chalk grid line previously put on slab by engineer), achieved by 'easing out' or 'pulling in' PCCP to gauge rod.

7. 'Washer-up' gap and tighten securing bolts.

8. Plumb PCCP on inside face (plumb rule) and tighten bottom securing bolts.

9. Once the PCCPs adjacent the columns have been finally erected the intermediate PCCP (numbered 2–4) can be aligned to them.

Fig. 11.18. Final arrangements for fixing precast units to steel structure

Where precast cladding is directly fixed to structural steel, it has to be remembered that, until the usually in situ floor slab has been cast, there may well be torque forces in the steel beams for which its strength is inadequate. It is wise to discuss this matter with the structural engineer before any problems arise.

Accuracy in erection

Many structures cause problems in the cladding stage because insufficient care is given to maintaining the plan area of the building to a sufficiently accurate set of dimensions. The same equally applies to the height of the structure: creeping errors in height can cause chaos when the cladding, of whatever type, is applied. A simple aid to make sure that the height is correct is based on the principle of drain rods. A set of rods, each rod the exact height of a floor, has been shown to be highly effective in maintaining the building height without creeping errors. A rod is added at each floor and all levels for that floor taken from the top of it.

Position in plan can also be dealt with fairly simply by the use of templates. Figure 11.19 illustrates such a template for a contract where the precast structure also provided the finished elevation. Eye-sweetness is clearly important, and was made more difficult by the building elevation being curved. The final result turned out to be very satisfactory: the templates at each floor were matched to two base lines brought up the building by Auto Plumb equipment. Push/pull props were used to

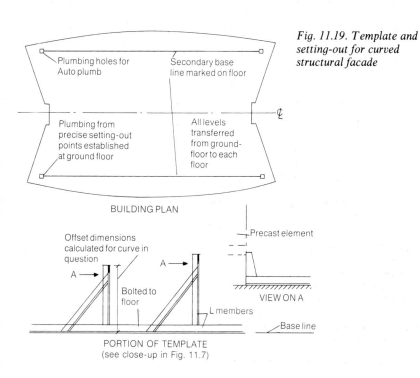

Fig. 11.19. Template and setting-out for curved structural facade

locate the members initially and while eye-sweetness was achieved. It was only then that the structural units were grouted.

USE OF PRECAST CONCRETE TO IMPROVE QUALITY AND MINIMISE ON TEMPORARY WORKS

There are occasions in concrete construction when the shapes called for in in situ concrete would be difficult to achieve in reasonable time and cost. Complex formwork may be needed, or the section specified would be difficult to pour and consolidate, yet strike cleanly. The following examples illustrate the point.

Example: cooling tower base legs

A major cooling tower was designed with unusual base legs (Fig. 11.20). To pour in situ would have been time-consuming: the first lift could only be poured to the cross of the legs; thence a second pour would have been required, to include the circular beam from which the shell section would spring. Maintenance of the line and slope of the legs would have been awkward, unless the supporting falsework was very rigid and accurate to line.

As seen in the figure, the eventual decision was to precast each cruciform section, lift it into place, and support by the relatively small amount of raking shore scaffolding. The bulk of the scaffolding was of very light construction, to provide access to the top of the rakers for fixing to the precast units.

Fig. 11.20. Precast X-legs to cooling tower (ICI Petrochemicals Ltd)

The solution adopted saved time, improved quality and reduced the formwork and falsework costs, as all the cruciform units could be cast outside any critical path, using the minimum number of moulds.

Example: building fenestration

In this example, the building in question was designed to have a projecting fenestration. Because of this, the window frames came back to the beams and columns at an angle. The effect of this design was to require beams at floor levels of a very complex shape, which included various grooves. At the same time, the distance between floors at these beams had to be very accurate to ensure a snug fit of the window units.

The contractor was very concerned about the ability to erect the beam forms to the required line and level, and, more especially, the ability to strike the awkward shape without damaging the features necessary to ensure that the windows fitted accurately. It was put to the Engineer that a more accurate result, coupled with guaranteed quality, would be achieved if these beams were precast, with in situ connections at the columns. The shape that had to be achieved is shown in Fig. 11.21.

The Engineer agreed to this suggestion, and the construction was carried out in the way put forward. The quality achieved was better than anyone had hoped for, with the result that the window-fixing went without a hitch. The actual construction is illustrated in Fig. 11.22. It should be noted that, with the precast beams, long sections of the edge of the floor could be set out with great accuracy and positioned exactly above those on the floor below.

Quantity surveyors would probably say that precast concrete costs more money than in situ concrete. In direct terms that may be so, but

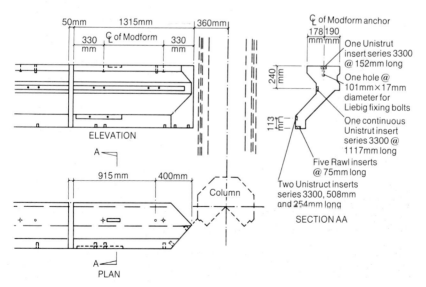

Fig. 11.21. Use of precast beam for greater quality

Fig. 11.22. Precast beams from Fig. 11.21 in place in the structure (George Wimpey plc)

taking all factors into account, the final result was cheaper: time was saved; formwork costs were reduced, as the precast units gave many uses from specially made moulds; and no striking time was needed. Perhaps more importantly, the quality was as desired—an achievement which would have been very much in doubt if the in situ method had been used.

Comment

From the examples given, it has to be recognised that the temporary works engineer has a role to play both in reducing cost whenever possible, and in aiding the achievement of good quality in situations where it might otherwise be difficult to accomplish.

12

Miscellaneous temporary works

The great majority of temporary works conveniently fall into clearly defined categories, and these are described in the previous chapters. However, contractors will also need to solve problems of a less conventional kind. Some situations may be unique, others may require an inventive mind and others a flash of inspiration!

This chapter deals with temporary works which do not readily fit into defined categories. Each example given is in the form of an actual case study covering the solution of a particular type of problem, and demonstrates the way in which those involved in temporary works can effectively solve unusual problems.

CONSTRUCTION OF A DEEP DROP MANHOLE

The situation facing a site is illustrated in Fig. 12.1. The foul sewer from a housing estate has to be connected to a deep sewer on the opposite side of a busy main road. The client specifies that the drop manhole is to be constructed in a shaft. From there, a heading is to be dug under the road and connected into an existing manhole on the trunk sewer. The drop manhole is approximately 7 m deep.

In considering the method to be adopted, it was clear that the shaft construction would be slow and would involve a complex timbering system; and, more importantly, would cost more than had been allowed in the tender. Such situations concentrate the minds of site agents wonderfully, and expert advice was sought.

The eventual solution was at once imaginative and totally safe, and enabled a profit to be made on the bill of quantities rates.

The key idea was to employ a piling firm to install a large-diameter liner, to the required depth of the manhole, and then auger it out as if making a pile. In a matter of a few hours the shaft was complete. The liner was left in place and the piling equipment was removed from the site (Fig. 12.2).

Somewhat surprisingly, the piling firm was agreeable to the cross-section of the heading being burnt out of the side of the liner, provided only that the contractor adequately welded the cut-out back into place once the work was completed. Thus, a secure shaft with an entry for the heading was achieved on the first day.

The heading construction was carried out in the traditional manner, and Fig. 12.3 shows the arrival at the trunk sewer manhole. After the

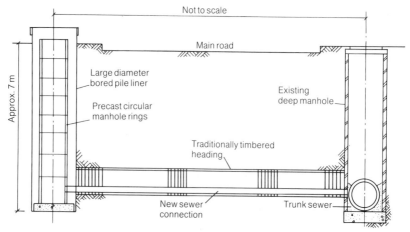

Fig. 12.1. Deep manhole construction: cross-section

horizontal pipe was laid and connected into the existing manhole, precast circular manhole sections were positioned (Fig. 12.4) and the liner was slowly withdrawn, while concrete filled the gap between the concrete rings and the earth face. The final item was the drop pipe itself.

The overall cost was less than allowed in the bill of quantities. Time was saved as the operation took much less time than the alternative

Fig. 12.2. Bored pile liner in position and excavated

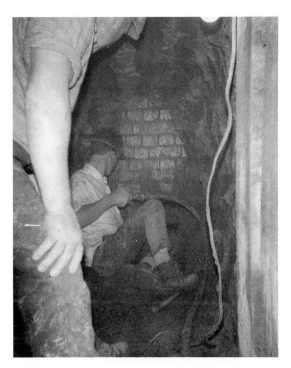

Fig. 12.3. Arrival at existing brick manhole

Fig. 12.4 (below). Precast manhole rings in course of installation inside liner

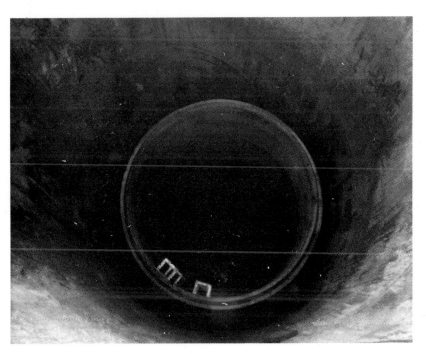

approach, and as a welcome bonus, greater safety in the shaft was realised.

It is, however, fair to say that the work was done at a time when piling firms were short of work. Liners are initially expensive, and in normal times it may well have been uneconomic to leave a liner in one location for so long.

When this method was mentioned later to other company employees, it was generally agreed that the site were very lucky to have been allowed to cut a hole in the liner tube. In fact, this was not absolutely necessary. The tube could have been driven to a level above the heading

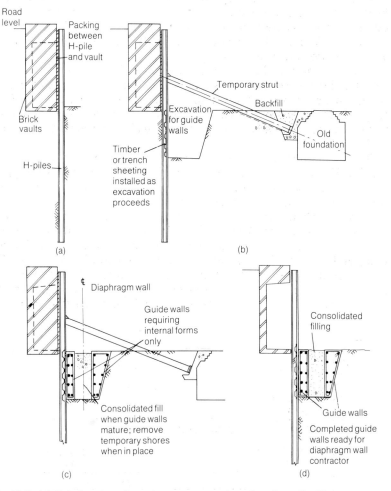

Fig. 12.5. (a) Existing situation prior to construction of guide walls; (b) propping to H-piles and sheeting to guide wall excavation; (c) guide walls concreted and space between backfilled; (d) strutting removed and site ready for diaphragm wall contractor

entry, and the remaining depth could have been timbered in a conventional way or used a proprietary strutting system (see chapter 7).

As a method, it remains a splendid example of opportunist temporary works.

GUIDE TRENCHES FOR DIAPHRAGM WALLS

All diaphragm wall installations require the provision of 'guide' trenches (Fig. 12.5). Such trenches are normally the responsibility of the main contractor, for installation and, it should be remembered, the removal of the internal wall before excavation gets properly under way.

When considering how they should be constructed, it should be borne in mind that they are frequently at the boundary of the site and may impinge on the stability of the boundary support. Overall stability and safety, therefore, are important factors. A typical situation of this type and its solution are given below.

The situation that had to be dealt with is shown in part (a) of Fig. 12.5. Old brick pavement vaults were already supported by H-piling, and the guide trench outer leaf had to be immediately behind these H-pile supports. How this was done, with the stability of the H-piling and the vaults maintained, is shown in the operational sequence (b) to (d) of Fig. 12.5.

Before any excavation was attempted, temporary raking shores to the existing H-piles were positioned, using old foundations as their support. This was necessary as, when excavated, the H-pile unsupported length was too great for the stability required.

Once the shores were installed, the initial excavation of the guide trench was carried out. The H-piling already in place made the support to the excavation on the vault side very simple. Trench sheeting was used, and was installed as the excavation proceeded (part (b) of Fig. 12.5). The internal side of the wall was excavated to a slope, to avoid the need for any support. Concrete was given away, but the only formwork needed was for the two internal faces—overall, the cheapest solution.

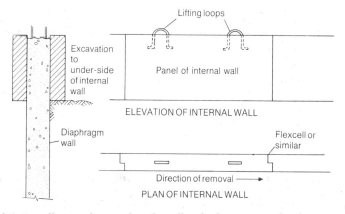

Fig. 12.6. Installation of internal guide wall to facilitate removal at least cost

With the walls complete, the space between them was filled with well consolidated fill and the temporary shores were removed (parts (c) and (d) of Fig. 12.5). Everything was then ready for the diaphragm wall construction. While this was under way, the stability was maintained by the trench being full of bentonite or the concrete itself, and the fact that such walls are constructed on a one hit and three miss basis.

One final matter needs consideration in these situations. Once the site excavation starts, there comes a moment when the internal guide wall will have to be removed. The good planner should have already foreseen this requirement and planned the design accordingly (Fig. 12.6). The inner guide trench wall, instead of being concreted as a continuous pour, is broken up into convenient lengths by Flexcell, or similar, with lifting loops cast into the top of each length as shown. Instead of a tedious breaking-up of the wall, it is possible to lift it out in sections and load directly on to a vehicle for taking off site: a considerable economy, and similar to that shown in chapter 5 for tower crane tracks in suitable circumstances.

USE OF STRAINING WIRES TO STABILISE LOADS

Occasions often arise when it is necessary to raise or lower loads up or down the sides of completed structures. Dismantling a climbing tower crane or renewing plant room equipment are typical examples. The key problem is how to avoid the load hitting the structure and causing damage to the cladding when gusty conditions occur, perhaps unexpectedly.

In chapter 5, a temporary rig for lowering tower crane mast sections is described. This rig required that the lowering operation took place down the side of the building, some 100 m in height, the finish to which was high quality precast concrete. Damage to the cladding would have been a disaster, as the cladding was the structural element as well.

A great deal of thought was given to the problem and specialist advice was sought. In fact, the solution was very simple. Two wire ropes were stretched from top to bottom of the building, with a built-in tension of about 3 t in each. A clipping system—a scaffold coupler—was attached to the load to be lowered, and the whole was lowered one floor. Here the load was clipped to each straining wire, and lowering to the ground was completed. Even in windy conditions the movement of the load was very small, and at no time was there any cause for anxiety. Figure 12.7 shows a crane mast section being lowered down the building side: one of the straining wires can be seen clearly, while the other can be picked out on the extreme left of the structure outline.

Figure 12.8 illustrates the principle in reverse. A chiller unit is being lifted to the top of a 29-storey building. It was after the building was complete and occupied that a decision was made to install additional air conditioning for a computer suite. The straining wires are readily seen. The two outside wires are the hoist ropes from the winches used, while the two inner ropes are the tensioned guides. Note also the roof rig cantilevering out from the building, which has to be adequately anchored to

Fig. 12.7 (above). Crane section being lowered down the side of tall building: straining wire stabilising load is in centre of picture (George Wimpey plc)

Fig. 12.8. Chiller unit well up the building face: hoist and straining wires clearly visible (photo J. Mustajew)

the roof of the structure. It goes without saying that the suspension points on the roof must be discussed with and agreed by the structural designer.

The simplest way to provide the tension in the guide wires is with concrete blocks of the required weight, freely suspended and suitably damped.

What may surprise many people is the relatively small tension required to provide the anti-movement stability. The expertise in the cases quoted was provided by British Ropes Ltd.

STRENGTHENING WEAK BRICKWORK BEFORE SHORING

Situations frequently arise where old lime-mortar brickwork has to be shored up, either to allow new construction to proceed alongside or as part of a refurbishment programme for a building. Such brickwork needs careful examination prior to any shoring taking place, to establish its integrity and ability to resist the shore loads without pulling apart.

Where the brickwork is dubious or the lime mortar has clearly lost its strength, the following strengthening method has been successfully used for strengthening the brickwork prior to shoring (Fig. 12.9).

The first stage was to rake out all joints to a depth of at least 25 mm. On completion, the required number of needles were installed through the wall, each passing through a continuous timber, 225 mm × 100 mm in section (Fig. 12.9 (a)). In front of the brickwork, a light fabric mesh was fixed some 35 mm from the brick face. A 75 mm coating of gunite was then sprayed over the entire wall face and around the horizontal support timber as well (Fig. 12.9 (b)). Once hardened, the raking sup-

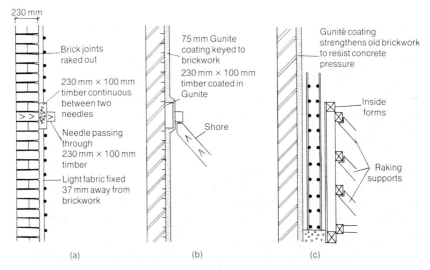

Fig. 12.9. Gunite support to assist shoring of weak brick walls: (a) preparation of wall; (b) gunite complete and shores placed; (c) gunite assists brickwork to resist concrete pressure

Fig. 12.10. Use of roller conveyor to speed up the filling and hoisting of concrete skips (George Wimpey plc)

ports were installed. It will be clear that the support loads are now transferred over a wide area of the brickwork, through the needles, the horizontal timbers and the gunite into the brick joints as well.

In the case quoted above, the method also solved a further problem. A concrete wall of the new structure adjacent had to be poured against the brickwork, and there was some concern as to whether the brickwork, in its weak condition, would be able to resist the pressure. The gunite skin materially strengthened the brickwork against concrete pressure, and allowed 3.3 m lifts to be poured without any trouble (Fig. 12.9 (c)).

IMPROVING SKIP FEEDING EFFICIENCY

Where concrete is being placed by crane, ready-mixed concrete vehicles are usually seen waiting to fill the next skip for the whole crane lift, pour and return cycle. The waiting time can be greatly reduced by a simple piece of temporary works.

Figure 12.10 illustrates the method. All that is required is a length of roller conveyor upon which concrete skips can stand. Plywood sheets make their movement on the rollers easy. In the illustration, the right hand skip is empty and being rolled under the concrete delivery vehicle discharge chute. The left hand skip has just been filled and is being lifted

Fig. 12.11. Turntable for three 1 m³ concrete skips

Fig. 12.12. Use of jubilee track and bogies to load skips, while a helicopter lifts already loaded one (British Insulated Callenders Cables Ltd)

away by the crane. (For the observant, the concrete in question is not badly graded, but no-fines.) The saving in time is quite significant.

In this case, an additional temporary ramp was needed for the concrete vehicle to give an adequate discharge height into the skips. If ready-mixed concrete vehicles were in use it would not be necessary.

A more sophisticated situation is shown in Fig. 12.11. Here, it is really a piece of plant, but the setting-up is temporary works. The turntable holds three 1 m³ skips filled in turn from a 3 m³ capacity concrete transporter. Thus the vehicle can empty its load directly and return to the site mixing plant, while the three skips are handled by the crane.

A third example of this type is shown in Fig. 12.12. Concrete is being taken by helicopter to remote power line bases in the adjoining hills. To create maximum safety, the skips are filled from the ready-mix trucks and rolled to the pick-up position on a short length of jubilee track. In this way, lifting and filling can proceed at the same time, as illustrated.

LOCATING HOLDING-DOWN BOLTS IN LARGE-VOLUME POURS

The growth in the use of high-volume pours in concrete has created the problem of how holding-down bolts can be positioned accurately in a large and deep mass of concrete. This is especially true when several groups of bolts have to be dealt with, with group interrelationship needing to be accurate. How this problem can be resolved effectively, yet economically, is illustrated in some detail in Fig. 12.13.

In this example, a circular template holding 48 bolts had to be accurately supported over a concrete base pour of approximately 700 m³. In addition, ten groups of four bolts each had to be located accurately in relation to the main circular template. The bottoms of the main template bolts also required positioning in a similar template, to make sure that, once concreting was complete, they were truly plumb. The depth of the base was 2 m.

As will be seen from Fig. 12.13, the support system was based on the use of scaffold tubes, to be concreted in with the pour, with the exception of the top layer holding the top template. The cost of the lost tube was surprisingly small, and, as second-hand material was used, a lot cheaper than making a heavy support rig from steel sections. The method was proposed to the Engineer and no objection was raised, provided that the vertical tubes were filled with grout on completion.

The actual detailed method of use and installation was as follows. The base was carried on piles and each was drilled to accept a short length of scaffold tube, 600 mm long. These tubes were grouted into place so that their top level was set at 400 mm above blinding level. Once the grout had set, longer tubes were coupled to the stubs using internal tube couplers. The length of these tubes was such that they fixed the final top of concrete level (see section BB and the elevation of standards in Fig. 12.13). A further joint pin was inserted, together with a short length of tube to provide the right height of support for the bolt templates.

The whole assembly was laced and braced together as shown. Once the horizontal support tubes had been levelled accurately, the main tem-

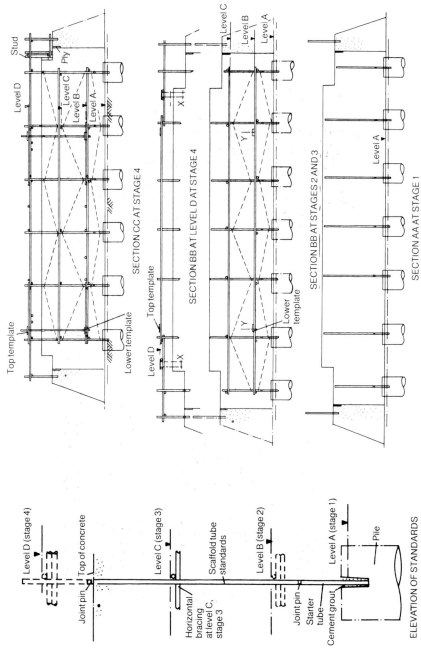

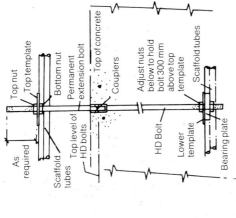

DETAIL X FOR HANGING
HOLDING-DOWN BOLTS FROM
SCAFFOLD

Tack-weld
Top
template
Top nut
Tack-weld
Scaffold tubes
Bottom
nut
Temporary
extension bolts
Couplers
HD bolts
Tack-weld
Top level of
HD bolts
Top of
concrete

As
required
Top nut
Top template
Scaffold
tubes
Top level of
HD bolts
Bottom nut
Permanent
extension bolt
Top of concrete
Couplers
Adjust nuts
below to hold
bolt 300 mm
above top
template
Scaffold tubes
HD Bolt
Lower
template
Bearing plate
DETAIL AT Y
(see notes on method of fixing bolts in
position)

Method of fixing bolts in position
Attach coupler and extension to each bolt; hang the bolts on
templates placed on scaffold tubes; check for position and
level; tack-weld templates to scaffold tubes and tighten
bottom nuts for rigidity.

*Fig. 12.13 (facing page and above). Scaffold support arrangement for the positioning of holding-down bolts in high
volume pour (for plan see Fig. 12.14) (George Wimpey plc)*

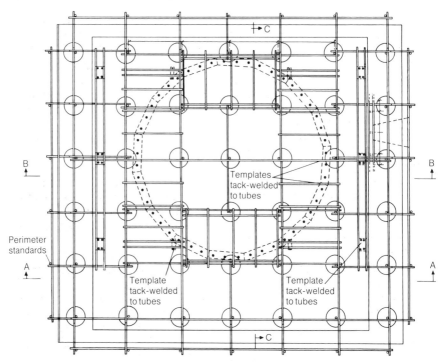

Fig. 12.14. Plan of support arrangement, showing the location of bolt clusters
(George Wimpey plc)

Fig. 12.15. Actual pour in progress with clear view of main template (ICI
Agricultural Division)

plate was positioned, checked for position and level, and tack-welded to the support tubes. The same procedure was followed for the bottom end of the bolts and their similar template (see detail at Y in Fig. 12.13). The importance of getting the bolts exactly in the right place and to the right level is emphasised by the fact that a 600 t pressure vessel had to be lowered over the 48 bolts in the main template. Any failure to fit would have cost a very large sum of money in very heavy lifting gear standing by while the problem was resolved.

The smaller groups of bolts, of much shorter length, were dealt with somewhat differently. Detail X for hanging holding-down bolts from scaffold (Fig. 12.13) illustrates the method, and Fig. 12.14 the relative locations. A top template was provided into which the holding-down bolts, with an extension length, were supported. This method was necessary as the bolts were shorter and projected much less from the top concrete surface. The scaffold tube levels were able to be maintained at a similar grid level arrangement as shown.

The main template was approximately 7.5 m in diameter. It was made for the client by the pressure vessel manufacturer, so that an exact match was certain (Fig. 12.14).

Figure 12.15 illustrates the concreting operation in progress. The main template—and its size—is clearly visible, while two groups of four bolts can be seen on the right. The scaffold tube assembly has also been utilised to provide support for walkways and vibrator motors. It also provided a good support for platforms when the top surface of the pour was finished off.

There is one further point of note in this case study. As will be seen from Fig. 12.13, the extent of the base was defined by a weak concrete external 'wall'. This was made thick enough to take the place of any supporting sheeting and ensure an unobstructed working area for all following operations.

PREVENTION OF ROCK FALLS

The need to stabilise rock faces can arise for a number of reasons: the effects of long term erosion loosening pieces of rock, which are eventually dislodged and fall; the very work of stabilising such rock faces causing dislodgements by the vibration of drills installing rock anchors; and the need to save money on temporary excavations in rock by having as steep a face as possible. The following method, of which several examples are given, has proved to be both effective and economical. One company, which has carried out a number of major contracts, first developed the method when asked to stabilise the rock face under Edinburgh Castle.

The method of stabilisation specified was by drilling and grouting into place rock anchors. In the assessment of the detailed method, some concern was felt that the vibration of the drilling operations might dislodge significant pieces of rock. Not only would these be highly dangerous to the drillers working off scaffolding adjacent to the rock mass, but, once in motion, the pieces of rock would descend at increasing speed until they reached the main line railway into Waverley station—with consequences too frightening to imagine.

Early discussions on safety measures went as far as the idea of building concrete retaining walls heavy enough to stop the high momentum of falling rock. Not only would the design be a gamble—the size of rock fall and its momentum could only be guessed at—the cost would be prohibitive. Further consideration provided the solution, in itself very simple and cheap compared with the early ideas, and a method that avoided the momentum problem altogether. In other words—do not let the rock start moving!

The face to be stabilised by rock anchors was covered by heavy linked anti-submarine netting secured by rock bolts grouted into the rock. It was further secured by a pattern of steel wire ropes also secured by rock bolts. The effect was to provide a mesh over the face to be drilled, bolted and grouted, and any rock movement would be constrained by the netting. As a further safety measure for the drillers working on the face, a fine mesh was attached to the anti-submarine netting to stop any small pieces of rock falling on to those installing the anchors.

The initial success of this approach led to the development of the principle of providing permanent stabilisation purely by the netting.

Case study 1

In a main road in a valley, where the sides were steep and in exposed rock, rock falls had occurred from time to time, providing a serious hazard to road users. After a geological survey, the entire rock face for a length of 150 m was covered with heavy linked anti-submarine netting secured by Macalloy bar rock bolts, cement-grouted into place. The netting was further secured by a grid of vertical and horizontal wire ropes, which were also anchored to rock bolts. How this was done is illustrated in Fig. 12.16. The technique was so successful that it has been used on a number of contracts elsewhere.

Case study 2

A derivation of the system described above was used in 1974 as part of the construction of a large dry dock to allow the fabrication of a 500 000 t concrete platform for the Ninion oil field in the North Sea. A considerable rock face was created in the construction of the dock, and the contractor wanted the rock face stabilised to avoid possible hazard to workers and equipment.

After removing loose material, the stabilisation contractor covered the entire rock face with chain-link mesh overlaid with anti-submarine netting as in case study 1. (Anti-submarine netting is also often described as Torpedo netting.) Netting totalling 18 000 m² was suspended from a line of rock bolts driven vertically into the rock at the top of the excavation and anchored in the same way at the bottom. Straining wires in steel wire rope were also added, again secured by rock bolts.

The importance of the effectiveness of this protection is only too clear when a study is made of Fig. 12.17. Both types of netting are visible.

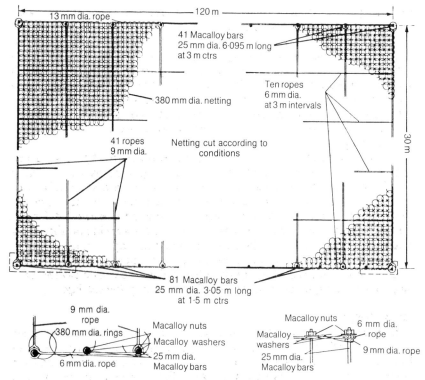

Fig. 12.16. Netting to rock face: details of anchorage system (Wimpey Laboratories Ltd)

Fig. 12.17. Detail of anti-submarine netting with chain link cover to prevent rock falls at gravity oilfield platform dry dock site (Wimpey Laboratories Ltd; Howard Doris Ltd)

Fig. 12.18. Use of grout bags for filling under viaduct structure (British Rail Eastern Division; Wimpey Laboratories Ltd)

Fig. 12.19 (below). View under the viaduct showing jack arches and 'stop end' grout bags (British Rail Eastern Division; Wimpey Laboratories Ltd)

USE OF GROUT BAGS AS FORMWORK

A railway viaduct constructed in steel with brick jack arches between cross-beams was coming to the end of its life, and the Eastern Region of British Rail were faced with a problem. The line involved was a very busy commuter route, and closure for reconstruction would create great problems. The problem was eventually solved in an unusual way and with considerable economy.

British Rail engineers decided to fill up the entire area under the viaduct with a PFA–cement mixture, leaving the original structure in place but supported on the PFA–cement filling. With this approach, no demolition would be necessary, or reconstruction either. More importantly, the whole operation could be carried out without any disruption to the railway services. The savings in such a method were considerable.

The original method proposed by British Rail was for the PFA–cement mixture to be poured in 0.5 m lifts, utilising standard single-face formwork to retain the liquid mix. The contractor eventually chosen to carry out the work could see problems with both the small lifts of formwork and the climbing of it as the level of the work rose. After studying the problem, the contractor suggested the use of grout bags as temporary formwork to provide a containment area into which the fill mixture could be pumped. British Rail accepted this method as being quicker and gave the go-ahead.

The grout bags are illustrated in Fig. 12.18. Made in fabric, and of various lengths to suit the various modules to be met, they were designed to give a height of 0.5 m when filled with the PFA–cement mix.

Operations began with the production of a well consolidated hard base foundation to support the PFA–cement filling to come. Once this was complete, the first layer of grout bags was positioned and pumped full of the PFA–cement mixture.

When the mixture had set, the area enclosed by the bags was pumped full of the PFA–cement and this was allowed to set. The next layer of grout bags was then laid in such a way as to form a batter, and filled. Again the pounded area was pumped full and the mixture was allowed to set.

The procedure continued until the space under the deck was completely filled. Figure 12.18 shows the work at an advanced stage. Figure 12.19, at the same stage as the previous figure, shows what is in effect a stop end in the length of the viaduct to be filled. On one side a brick wall provides the formwork. The jack arch brickwork in the deck is clearly visible.

The general bulk filling was 12 : 1 PFA/cement, but under the brick arches the mix was strengthened to 6 : 1. To ensure that no voids were left under the arches, bleed holes were drilled through the brickwork of the arches, and the 6 : 1 mix was pressurised to minimise any voids and to make sure that the mix was made to penetrate the bleed holes.

The results achieved were so successful that, at the time of writing, the contractor concerned has been awarded a follow-on contract to fill under another elderly viaduct on the same line.

13

The site set-up

There is little doubt that the poor relative in temporary works is the site set-up: that is, the provision of all the items needed in relation to accommodation, storage, canteens, sanitation, and drying. Indeed, many people probably do not think of such things as temporary works at all! Yet it is in this area that the wellbeing of those who work on site depends.

LEGISLATION

A number of items of legislation have to be complied with in relation to the site set-up. These are The Construction (Health and Welfare) Regulations 1966,[1] Fire Certificates (Special Premises) Regulations 1976,[2] and the Offices Shops and Railway Premises Act 1963[3] (applicable under certain circumstances).

The Construction (Health and Welfare) Regulations 1966

These construction regulations lay down the scale of equipment and accommodation in respect of the following:

(a) first aid boxes or cases and their contents
(b) requirements for training in first aid treatment
(c) if more than 25 persons are employed, additional requirements needed
(d) the conditions for larger sites, where fully equipped first aid rooms have to be provided
(e) the scale of accommodation for drying rooms and protective clothing storage and for taking meals
(f) provision of washing facilities
(g) provision of sanitary facilities
(h) provision of protective clothing
(i) safe access to the facilities provided.

Fire Certificates (Special Premises) Regulations 1976

These regulations lay down the special premises for which a fire certificate is required, and the procedure for obtaining one. The issue of such certificates is vested in the Health and Safety Executive.

In relation to the construction site, schedule 1 is the key section. The situations requiring a fire certificate are specified. They include (paragraph 15) any building or part of a building which is constructed for temporary use in connection with building operations or civil engineering construction.

However, compliance with conditions listed in part II of schedule 1 avoids the need for a certificate.

Offices, Shops and Railway Premises Act 1963

This Act states in the preamble: 'An Act to make fresh provision for securing the health, safety and welfare of persons employed to work in office or shop premises . . . .'.

Paragraph 3 (i) further states: 'This act shall not apply to any premises to which it would, apart from this subsection, apply, if the period of time worked there during each week does not normally exceed twenty-one hours.'

In a contractor's site office, there are likely to be those who work more than 21 hours and those that are outside most of the time. Clearly the accommodation for those working more than 21 hours must comply with the Act.

Scales of accommodation

In assessing the amount of accommodation to be provided on a given site, the above legislation must be understood and complied with. As far as office accommodation is concerned, the number of staff that need to be accommodated also has to be established, together with the space requirements for each.

As this situation will arise every time a contract is tendered for, it can save time and money if accommodation layout drawings are prepared, as standard details, for varying types of contract. Such drawings can, in

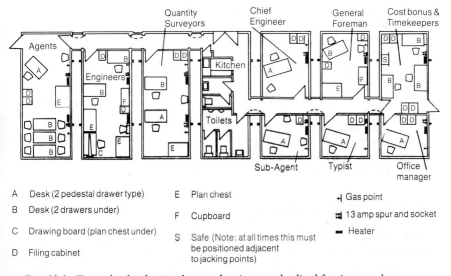

A   Desk (2 pedestal drawer type)
B   Desk (2 drawers under)
C   Drawing board (plan chest under)
D   Filing cabinet
E   Plan chest
F   Cupboard
S   Safe (Note: at all times this must be positioned adjacent to jacking points)

⊣ Gas point
⇥ 13 amp spur and socket
▬ Heater

Fig. 13.1. Typical cabin hutting layout showing standardised furniture scales

addition, allow for the inclusion of standard furnishing arrangements and room sizes for the various staff activities which will be involved. Figure 13.1 illustrates the type of format that has been found to work well in practice and create standardisation in a company.

Care in assessing the accommodation and storage requirements at the tender stage is important, both in respect of allowing enough money for their provision and establishing how much space they will need. The latter is particularly important where a site may be restricted. It is not uncommon in central redevelopment sites to have to rent accommodation outside the site boundary costing more than site hutting would (see also chapter 4 in relation to re-creation of space on restricted sites for off-loading and storage facilities). Even on sites where space is not a problem, the location of facilities is important, both for efficiency in organisation and avoiding any new works. It is not unknown for the site office to be found sitting over a new sewer line. The cost of the resultant move is only reducing profit unnecessarily and would not have happened if the planning had been properly carried out at the tender stage.

Where all accommodation has to be provided within a restricted site, the only solution may well be to move offices and stores progressively as the construction progresses. It is not unknown for four or five moves to be necessary. Proper financial allowance is clearly necessary at the tender stage to cover the cost involved.

TYPES OF ACCOMMODATION

The provision of offices, stores and welfare facilities on a site can involve significant cost, both in assembly and dismantling, together with transport and storage when not in use. It is prudent, therefore, to use systems that minimise cost in their erection, use and dismantling.

Fig. 13.2. Two-tier jack-leg hutting (S. Wernick & Sons Ltd)

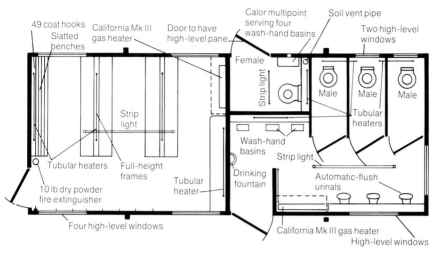

Fig. 13.3. Jack-leg toilet and drying room unit (proposal): 7.3 m by 2.75 m; height 2.1 m

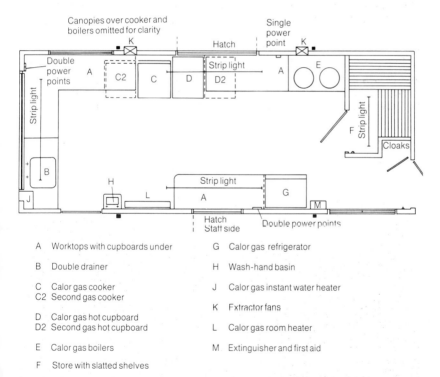

A	Worktops with cupboards under	G	Calor gas refrigerator
B	Double drainer	H	Wash-hand basin
C	Calor gas cooker	J	Calor gas instant water heater
C2	Second gas cooker		
		K	Extractor fans
D	Calor gas hot cupboard		
D2	Second gas hot cupboard	L	Calor gas room heater
E	Calor gas boilers	M	Extinguisher and first aid
F	Store with slatted shelves		

Fig. 13.4. Jack-leg kitchen unit: 24 ft 0 in by 9 ft 9 in overall; internal height 7 ft 0 in

Jack-leg cabins

The modern jack-leg cabin type of hutting provides the best answer at present for offices, welfare facilities and situations of similar use. As each unit comes as an entity, the standard of finish, insulation and electrical systems are pre-installed as a permanent part of the hut. Link units, for joining a number of huts together, allow a complex to be built up of whatever size the contract calls for. At the same time, wiring links provide electrical continuity on a simple plug-in basis. As the units are delivered as an entity, and not tipped up in any way, the furniture needed can be included in the particular hut it is required for.

The design of the jack-leg system is such that, where site conditions are limited, one cabin can be erected on top of another, to save space (Fig. 13.2). Adequate foundations are necessary and should be assessed by a competent person. Cases are not unknown where jack-leg units have been stacked three high. While the box sections of the jack legs themselves are usually strong enough for the loads of a three-tier structure, lateral stability becomes suspect. The usual practice in such circumstances is to design a steel frame of suitable strength which can link the tiers together at the ends to form lateral bracing. In three-tier situations, the stability needs must be dealt with by a person competent in structural design.

This same type of unit is readily capable of development into toilet units, drying rooms and canteen elements—kitchen sections and eating areas. Examples are given in Figs 13.3 and 13.4.

Container units

With vandalism and theft major problems on construction sites, the safeguarding of attractive stores, together with tools and tackle, has become an important aspect when considering site accommodation.

Fig. 13.5. Off-loading container secure store (Swift Plant Hire)

Probably the best solution to high security accommodation is the development of steel standard containers into secure storage for sites. Readily delivered to site and off-loaded by a vehicle-mounted crane (Fig. 13.5), they are also available as office units for use in locations where there is a high vandal risk. As with the jack-leg buildings, no erection or dismantling is needed and the simplest of foundations will suffice (Fig. 13.6). Containers of this type are readily available for either sale or hire.

Non-secure stores

Many items of material need a form of covered storage, without needing high risk protection. It is usually the policy to site such covered accommodation within a fenced compound. The materials in question are such items as timber, window and door frames, holding-down bolts and, in the case of building work, items such as plasterboard.

The form of cover provided desirably allows access for palleted or banded loads handled by fork lift, as many bulk items are now delivered in this way. An economical approach to this form of storage, which utilises old types of ship-lap hutting, is commonly called the 'half-hut' method. The basic principle is shown in Figs 13.7 and 13.8. A standard ship-lap hut is literally cut in two, in a longitudinal direction. The open face of each half is provided with columns to support the roof, while plastic curtains are hung from rings running on a scaffold tube fixed at the top and stopped from blowing apart by similar rings on a scaffold

Fig. 13.6. Container secure store in use (Swift Plant Hire)

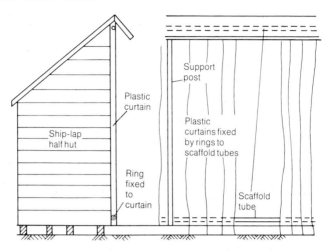

Fig. 13.7. 'Half-hut' store principle

tube at the bottom. The curtains are easily pulled open or shut. As the whole of one side is open, access for depositing pallets or banded or shrink-wrapped loads within is straightforward.

Fencing of compounds

Many materials are habitually used for the fencing of compounds on site. That most commonly used is some form of chain link, yet in practice

Fig. 13.8. 'Half-hut' store in use

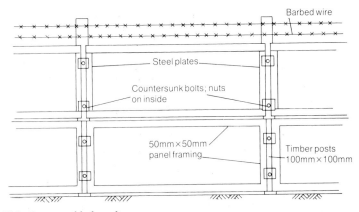

Fig. 13.9. Recoverable hoarding system

it is a method that is far from satisfactory. Although the erection is easy, by unskilled labour, and the fencing allows a clear view of what is happening inside the compound, only minimal resistance to thieves is provided. The overall disadvantages are the low security; recovery is generally poor; the fencing looks unsightly on subsequent use; it is ill-suited to sloping sites; and it is awkward to dismantle and store.

A better solution, which, while initially dearer, is cheaper in the long run, is shown in Fig. 13.9. Framed plywood panels, which can be manufactured in-house, are used in association with timber posts. The panels are attached to the posts by bolts and steel plates, as shown, with the countersunk heads of the bolts facing the outside of the hoarding or compound. Total recovery is possible without damage if the posts are wedged into concrete sockets from the inside.

While the materials used are not fireproof and the surface may lend itself to graffiti, the author's experience over some ten years has shown it to provide a secure fence, less easy to climb over than chain link. The only maintenance needed is a coat of wood preservative from time to time.

SITE SERVICES
Drainage

In the interests of site hygiene, toilet and washing facilities should, wherever possible, be connected to a mains sewerage system. In planning the site facilities complex, with this in mind, the local sewage authority will have to be contacted both to obtain approval and to find out their requirements as to the connection itself. Clearly this needs doing at the tender stage, so that all costs can be included.

Water, electricity and telephone

Water, electricity and telephone are all vital services. Water and electricity connections to mains will depend on whether available mains are within a reasonable distance from the site. If not, it may prove cheaper or be essential to bring in water by tanker, and pump to site facilities and other user terminals. In the case of electricity, the cost of laying cables over a considerable distance may be prohibitive, and the economic answer prove to be the use of a generator of suitable capacity. Such judgements must be made after a proper site visit, when all the matters affecting the contract temporary works should have been assessed and the appropriate allowances made in the tender. (The format of an *aide memoire* form for site visits is given in chapter 4.)

SAFETY PRECAUTIONS

Safety matters need to be an integral part of the overall provision of site accommodation. Not only must the general provisions of the Health and Safety at Work etc. Act be complied with, but also more specific matters.

Fire precautions

Where it is desired to avoid the need for a fire certificate, any temporary buildings must comply with part II of schedule 1 of the Fire Certificates (Special Premises) Regulations in respect of means of escape and the requirements for fire-fighting equipment.

Alternatively, if the premises have to have a certificate, as laid down in part I of schedule 1, any conditions laid down by the Health and Safety Executive as appropriate to the circumstances have to be complied with. Such conditions may affect the way in which the building is constructed.

Where the Offices, Shops and Railway Premises Act applies to site offices, the requirements laid down therein must be met and the design will need to comply with the escape requirements specified.

Use of LPG on site

Liquid petroleum gases (LPGs) are defined as commercial butane, commercial propane and any mixture of both. Their use is controlled by the Highly Flammable Liquids and LPG Regulations.[4]

Either type is frequently used for heating or cooking on construction sites. While LPGs are not toxic, they can produce a narcotic effect which can lead to asphyxiation if too much air is displaced. Adequate ventilation in areas used for heating and cooking is essential.

LPGs are heavier than air, and if a leak occurs the vapour can seep into cellars, drains and excavations. Such vapour can travel considerable distances and if, in the process, it reaches a source of ignition, a violent explosion will occur which can flash back to the source of the leak. Considerable care is therefore necessary in installation and operation to ensure that all possible safety measures are taken. The following rules should always be followed in relation to storage.

    (*a*) A suitable open-air compound should be provided for the storage of LPG cylinders, such that any cylinder is at least 1.5 m from the fence.

    (*b*) Storage must be at ground level or above—never below ground level.

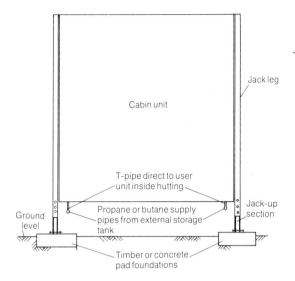

Fig. 13.10. Location of LPG pipework to hutting for safe use

(c) Storage facilities must not be sited near excavations, drains or basements.

(d) A prominent notice at the entrance of the compound stating 'LPG—Highly Flammable' is required, together with notices prohibiting smoking and naked lights.

(e) A dry-powder extinguisher must be provided at any storage area in an easily accessible position.

In use, the following matters must be complied with.

(a) Always ensure that any pipework and connections are carried out by fitters trained for this type of gas. In any case, make sure that the correct equipment is being used and that a regulator is included in the system.

(b) Site cylinders used for heating and cooking outside the building.

(c) Keep all pipework outside the building as far as possible. Only T in at the appliance location (Fig. 13.10).

(d) Provide adequate ventilation at the heater or cooker. At heaters, an air intake vent should be provided at the back of the heater and an outlet vent above near ceiling level. A similar intake vent should be provided for a cooker, while an extract vent can be incorporated with a fume extract.

If there is any doubt about the use and installation of LPG, the advice of the company supplying the gas should be sought. Failure to comply with well established rules can be disastrous.

Protection of children

Construction sites can be a magnet for children and many accidents occur to children on construction sites. In considering site set-up needs,

Table 13.1. Cost items related to an accommodation unit (type A1, senior married, two/three bed bungalow)*

Local purchase price if obtained overseas
FOB
Inland transport—UK
CIF
Customs duty
Port clearance
Inland transport—overseas
Erect and dismantle

Air conditioners/heaters (11 500 BTU)—five per bungalow
Furniture
    single beds c/w mattresses and headboards
    double beds c/w mattresses and headboards
    wardrobes
    dining table and chairs
    coffee tables
    easy chairs
    sofas
    writing tables
    reading lamps
    bedside tables
    dressers
    chests of drawers
    kitchen tables and chairs
Soft furnishings
    carpets
    curtains and rods
    bed linen and towels
Kitchen equipment
    crockery
    cooking utensils
    cutlery
    rubbish bins
    17 ft^3 fridges with freezer section
    four-burner cookers with oven and hood
    toasters
Waste-paper bins
Washing machines c/w spin dryer
Irons and ironing boards
Chubb GP powder 3 kg fire extinguishers (four per bungalow)
Other items

* Supplier's quotation is taken to include for basic fixtures such as kitchen and toilet equipment and units, extractor fans etc.
Shipping data. Weight of building 22 300 lb/1011 kg; knocked down 1596 ft^3/45.19 m^3 *plus* pre-erected 4332 ft^3/122.69 m^3.

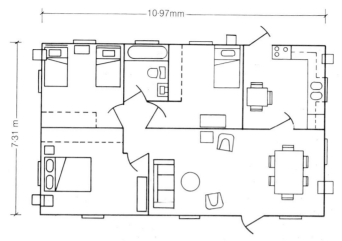

Fig. 13.11. Example of camp accommodation (not to scale): type A1, senior married, two/three-bed bungalow, area 80 m²

due regard has to be paid to protective measures necessary to prevent, so far as possible, children from having accidents on sites. A Health and Safety Executive guidance note[5] gives valuable advice in this respect.

However, with the best will in the world, sites are not easy to protect. Some contractors have found that better results arise by talking to children in local schools about the danger and offering a tangible reward to the school—to the benefit of the children—if no accidents occur to local children during the course of the contract. One prize given was a new set of football strips for the school team! And well worth the money. Such rewards can easily be tailored to a particular school's needs, by discussion with the head teacher.

CONSTRUCTION SITE CAMPS

Although in the UK construction site camps only arise where a civil engineering contract is in a remote area, the provision of high standard expatriate accommodation is frequently necessary overseas. Sometimes such camps are based on the accommodation to be provided for the staff who will operate the facility on completion. As such, they will be priced, measured and paid for as permanent works, and are no problem at the estimating stage. The real problem usually arises where the camp has to be provided by the contractor and removed on completion.

For a contractor who regularly works abroad, it pays to have standard camp details which can be put together to form a camp suitable for the number of expatriate staff required. An example of how this can be achieved is given below.

Accommodation

The scale of accommodation for the various grades of staff anticipated should be established, comprising area of accommodation, furnishings to

Table 13.2. Cost items related to a kitchen–diner unit (type K1)*

Local purchase price if obtained overseas
FOB
Inland transport—UK
CIF
Customs duty
Port clearance
Inland transport—overseas
Erect and dismantle

Air conditioners/heaters (11 500 BTU)
Steel folding chairs with padded seats
1800 × 900 dining tables with plastic laminate tops
Six-burner ranges with grill and oven
2400 × 1200 range hoods
1200 × 600 stainless steel work tables
80 gallon water heaters
Coffee urns
Freezer panels
Meat racks and meat blocks
Fridge panel
400 dia. wall-mounted extractor fans
Dishwashing units
Stainless steel double-drainer sink units
Deep-fat fryers
Drinking fountains
Kitchen, dining utensils
Food mixers
Meat slicers
Hand sinks
Cold food tables
Steam tables
Toasters
Ice machines
Chubb GP powder 6 kg fire extinguishers (one for K1; two for K2)
Chubb 6 ft square fire blankets (one for K1 or K2)

* Supplier's quotation is taken to include for basic fixtures such as floor and wall units etc.
Shipping data. Weight of building 15 000 lb/6800 kg; knocked down 1120 ft^3/31.71 m^3 *plus* pre-erected 6720 ft^3/190.29 m^3.

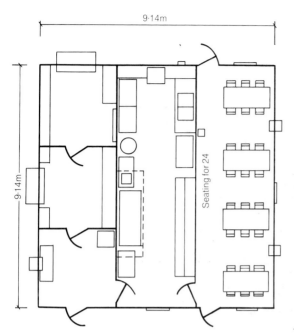

9·14m

9·14m

Seating for 24

Fig. 13.12. Example of kitchen–dining unit (not to scale): type K1, for up to 36 staff, area 83.54 m²

Fig. 13.13 (below). Typical layout of camp for 70 men

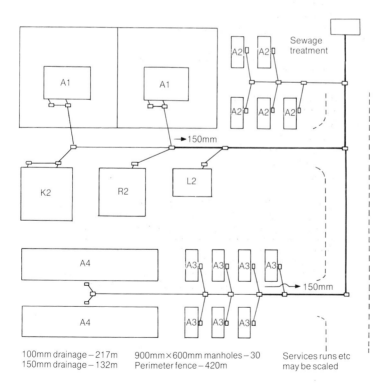

Sewage treatment

A2 A2

A1 A1

A2 A2 A2

→150mm

K2 R2 L2

A4 A3 A3 A3 A3

→ 150mm

A4 A3 A3 A3

100mm drainage – 217m   900mm × 600mm manholes – 30   Services runs etc
150mm drainage – 132m   Perimeter fence – 420m   may be scaled

Fig. 13.14. Site facilities: Ardyne Point gravity platform production facility (Sir Robert McAlpine & Sons Ltd)

be provided, equipment and any other facilities. Figure 13.11 shows typical accommodation in plan, giving area and indicating the furniture provided. A tabulation of all cost items related to a specific accommodation unit (Table 13.1) allows the estimator, at the tender stage, to put a cost to all the elements listed on the form, for the location in question.

At the bottom of the sheet, the relevant data for the shipping company is worked out and recorded. Too often such information becomes a last-minute scramble because no one has thought about such things!

An example of a kitchen–diner unit is given in Fig. 13.12 and Table 13.2. Other facilities that will need examination are recreation units and laundry facilities.

In addition to the actual accommodation units, it is also a good idea, for estimating purposes, to include typical site layouts from which drainage and other service needs can be taken off (Fig. 13.13).

The method put forward makes life a great deal easier for both the planner and the estimator, and enables a much more accurate assessment of cost. While many contractors would perhaps not admit it, the pricing of the camp is often a last-minute scramble because no ready data exists to help. Having a standard set of components allows greater accuracy in pricing what, after all, is often a major cost item; and, perhaps more importantly, makes feedback of cost data specific to known scales of space and equipment.

OTHER FACILITIES

Apart from the general requirements dealt with above, large civil engineering contracts (such as those for the construction of gravity platforms for the North Sea oilfields) may involve extensive covered facilities for the repair and maintenance of plant, protection of vehicles and so on. Indeed, in the more remote areas, provision may be necessary for the generation of the site's own electricity. All such aspects will need to be examined, and proper allowance made at the tender stage.

To the above must be added the temporary works associated with plant (chapter 5), and those induced by the influence of the site and its boundaries (chapter 4).

The potential extent of all these requirements is nicely summed up in Fig. 13.14, showing the Ardyne Point gravity platform production facility. The area occupied is extensive, yet the principles put forward in this chapter still had to be applied.

References and further reading

CHAPTER 1. INTRODUCTION
Reference
1. HEALTH AND SAFETY EXECUTIVE. *Safe erection of structures*. Guidance Note GS 28. Her Majesty's Stationery Office, London. Part 1, *Initial planning and design*, 1984; Part 2, *Site management and procedures*, 1985; Part 3, *Working places and access*, 1986; Part 4, *Legislation and training*, 1986.

CHAPTER 2. CONTRACTUAL, LEGAL AND CODE REQUIREMENTS
Reference
1. HEALTH AND SAFETY EXECUTIVE. *Safe erection of structures*. Guidance Note GS 28. Her Majesty's Stationery Office, London. Part 1, *Initial planning and design*, 1984; Part 2, *Site management and procedures*, 1985; Part 3, *Working places and access*, 1986; Part 4, *Legislation and training*, 1986.
Further reading
FREETH E. & DAVEY P. (eds). *AJ legal handbook*. Architectural Press, London, 1979, 2nd edn. A mine of information on the law as related to building, contract and the duties and responsibilities of architects.
PITT P. H. *Building control in inner London 1987*. Architectural Press, London, 1987.
PITT P. H. *Building control by local act 1987*. Architectural Press, London, 1987.

CHAPTER 4. THE EFFECT OF THE SITE AND ITS BOUNDARIES
References
1. *The Construction (General Provisions) Regulations 1961*. SI 1961 No. 1580. Her Majesty's Stationery Office, London.
2. HEALTH AND SAFETY EXECUTIVE. *Avoidance of danger from overhead electric lines*. Guidance Note GS 6. Her Majesty's Stationery Office, London, 1977.
3. Woolerton and Wilson vs Richard Costain (Midlands) Ltd. 1970. 1. *All England law reports*, p. 483.
4. BRITISH RAILWAYS. *Notes for guidance of developers and others responsible for construction work adjacent to the Board's operational railway*. Civil Engineering Department Handbook 36. BR, 1978.
5. LONDON REGIONAL TRANSPORT, DEPARTMENT OF CIVIL ENGINEERING. *Notes and special conditions for work affecting London Regional Transport*. LRT, London, 1984.
6. *Health and Safety at Work etc. Act 1974*. Her Majesty's Stationery Office, London.
7. *Control of Pollution Act 1974*. Her Majesty's Stationery Office, London.

8. BRITISH STANDARDS INSTITUTION. *Code of practice for noise control on construction and demolition sites.* BS 5228: 1975. BSI, London.
9. BUILDING EMPLOYERS CONFEDERATION. *Construction safety.* Building Advisory Service, London; updated regularly.

CHAPTER 5. PLANT-ASSOCIATED TEMPORARY WORKS

Reference
1. BRITISH STANDARDS INSTITUTION. *Safe use of cranes (mobile cranes, tower cranes and derrick cranes).* CP 3010 : 1972. BSI, London. This code gives comprehensive guidance on all aspects of crane operation. It lists all other codes which are relevant in relation to ancillary equipment. It also contains a list of regulations, more extensive than that given below.

Regulations
Published by Her Majesty's Stationery Office, London:
The Construction (Lifting Operations) Regulations 1961. SI 1961 No. 1581.
The Construction (Working Places) Regulations 1966. SI 1966 No. 94.
The Construction (General Provisions) Regulations 1961. SI 1961 No. 1580.
Any working place associated with any of the plant operations covered in this chapter must comply with the Health and Safety at Work etc. Act 1974.

CHAPTER 6. SCAFFOLDING

References
1. BRITISH STANDARDS INSTITUTION. *Code of practice for access and working scaffolds and special structures in steel.* BS 5973 : 1981. BSI, London. (Supersedes CP 97 parts 1 and 3.)
2. BRITISH STANDARDS INSTITUTION. *Code of practice for temporarily installed suspended scaffolds and access equipment.* BS 5974 : 1982. BSI, London.
3. WILSHERE C. J. *Access scaffolding.* ICE Works Construction Guide. Thomas Telford Ltd, London, 1981.
4. BRAND R. E. *Falsework and access scaffolds in tubular steel.* McGraw-Hill, 1975.
5. BUILDING EMPLOYERS CONFEDERATION and NATIONAL ASSOCIATION OF SCAFFOLDING CONTRACTORS. *Model form of quotation for the hire, erection and dismantling of scaffolding.* BEC, London, 1986.
6. BUILDING EMPLOYERS CONFEDERATION and NATIONAL ASSOCIATION OF SCAFFOLDING CONTRACTORS. *Model conditions of contract for the hire, erection and dismantling of scaffolding.* BEC, London, 1986.
7. *Health and Safety at Work etc. Act 1974.* Her Majesty's Stationery Office, London.
8. BRITISH STANDARDS INSTITUTION. *Specification for industrial safety nets.* BS 3913 : 1982. BSI, London.
9. BRITISH STANDARDS INSTITUTION. *The use of safety nets on constructional works.* CP 93 : 1972. BSI, London.

Guidance note
HEALTH AND SAFETY EXECUTIVE. *Suspended access equipment.* Guidance Note PM 30. Her Majesty's Stationery Office, London, 1983.

CHAPTER 7. SUPPORT OF EXCAVATIONS

References
1. *Health and Safety at Work etc. Act. 1974.* Her Majesty's Stationery Office, London.

2. *The Construction (General Provisions) Regulations 1961.* SI 1961 No. 1580. Her Majesty's Stationery Office, London.
3. MANSON K. Rights of support. *Building,* 1974, 31 May, 91 and 92.
4. MANSON K. Damage to services. *Building,* 1974, 8 Oct., 132 and 137.
5. *Control of Pollution Act 1974.* Her Majesty's Stationery Office, London, sections 60 and 61.
6. *City of London (St Paul's Cathedral Preservation) Act 1935.* Her Majesty's Stationery Office, London.
7. IRVINE D. J. and SMITH R. J. H. *Trenching practice.* Construction Industry Research and Information Association, London, 1983, report 97.
8. TIMBER RESEARCH AND DEVELOPMENT ASSOCIATION. *Timber in excavations.* TRADA, High Wycombe, 1981.
9. BUILDING EMPLOYERS CONFEDERATION. *Construction safety.* Building Advisory Service, London; updated regularly.
10. MACKAY E. B. *Proprietary trench support systems.* Construction Industry Research and Information Association, London, 1982, report 95, 2nd edn.
11. TIMBER RESEARCH AND DEVELOPMENT ASSOCIATION. *Simplified rules for the inspection of second hand timber for loadbearing use.* Folding pocket document. TRADA, High Wycombe, 1981.

Relevant codes and standards

BRITISH STANDARDS INSTITUTION. *Foundations.* CP 2004 : 1974. BSI, London.
BRITISH STANDARDS INSTITUTION. *Code of practice for earthworks.* BS 6031 : 1981. BSI, London.
BRITISH STANDARDS INSTITUTION. *Code of practice for noise control on construction and demolition sites.* BS 5228 : 1975. BSI, London.

CHAPTER 8.   USE OF PERMANENT WORKS AS TEMPORARY SUPPORT OF EXCAVATIONS

References

1. Deep foundations for the British Library. *Ground Engineering,* 1984, Apr., 20–26.
2. First 'Stent Wall' installed at Kingston-upon-Thames. *Ground Engineering,* 1985, Oct., 27, 28, 30 and 31.
3. MUNDY J. K. The Piccadilly Line extension. *Fork lift trucks in construction: proceedings of seminar.* Polytechnic of Central London, 1973.

Further reading

CORBETT B. O. *et al.* A loadbearing wall at Kensington and Chelsea Town Hall, London. *Diaphragm walls and anchorages.* Institution of Civil Engineers, London, 1975, 57–62.
FLEMING W. G. K. and SLIWINSKI Z. J. *The use and influence of bentonite in bored pile construction.* Construction Industry Research and Information Association, London, 1977, report P.G3.
FRISCHMANN W. W. and WILSON J. Top down construction of deep basements. *Concrete,* 1984, Nov., 7–10.
GODDEN H. W. Application of bentonite trenches in foundations. *Concrete in the ground: proceedings of conference.* Concrete Society, 1984.
Ground Engineering. Magazine published bi-monthly.
INSTITUTION OF STRUCTURAL ENGINEERS. *Design and construction of deep basements.* ISE, London, 1975.
NEAL D. The effects of concrete mix on secant piling. *Concrete in the ground: proceedings of conference.* Concrete Society, 1984.

Codes of practice

BRITISH STANDARDS INSTITUTION. *Code of practice for safety precautions in the construction of large diameter boreholes for piling and other purposes.* BS 5573 : 1978. BSI, London.

BRITISH STANDARDS INSTITUTION. *Code of practice for earthworks.* BS 6031 : 1981. BSI, London.

BRITISH STANDARDS INSTITUTION. *Foundations.* CP 2004 : 1974. BSI, London.

CHAPTER 9.   FALSEWORK

References

1. BRITISH STANDARDS INSTITUTION. *Code of practice for falsework.* BS 5975 : 1982. BSI, London.
2. *Interim report of the Advisory Committee on Falsework.* Her Majesty's Stationery Office, London, 1974.
3. *Final report of the Advisory Committee on Falsework.* Her Majesty's Stationery Office, London, 1976.
4. HEALTH AND SAFETY EXECUTIVE. *Safety of falsework for in situ beams and slabs.* Guidance booklet HSG 32. Her Majesty's Stationery Office, London, 1987.
5. *Health and Safety at Work etc. Act 1974.* Her Majesty's Stationery Office, London.
6. Cardiff debut for UK's largest launching girder. *Concrete*, 1986, Mar., 8–10.
7. Nuttall glues up Torridge Bridge. *Construction News*, 1986, 22 May.
8. Grangetown Viaduct. *Concrete*, 1986, Aug., 29.
9. CONSTRUCTION INDUSTRY RESEARCH AND INFORMATION ASSOCIATION. *Structural renovation of traditional structures.* CIRIA, 1986, report 111.
10. RELPH-KNIGHT L. The facade can be a nightmare. *Civil Engineering*, 1984, Mar., 29–32.
11. HIGHFIELD D. Building behind historic facades. *Building Technology and Management* (Chartered Institute of Building), 1984, Jan., 18–25.

Further reading

BRAND R. E. *Falsework and access scaffolds in tubular steel.* McGraw Hill, 1975.

THE CONCRETE SOCIETY and THE INSTITUTION OF STRUCTURAL ENGINEERS. *Falsework.* Report of a joint committee; technical report TRCS 4. Concrete Society, London, 1971.

GRANT M. *Scaffold falsework design.* Viewpoint Publications, Slough, 1978.

CHAPTER 10.   FORMWORK

References

1. BRITISH STANDARDS INSTITUTION. *Glossary of formwork terms.* BS 4340 : 1968. BSI, London.
2. *The Construction (General Provisions) Regulations 1961.* SI 1961 No. 1580. Her Majesty's Stationery Office, London, Part VIII.
3. HEALTH AND SAFETY EXECUTIVE. *Safe erection of structures.* Guidance Note GS 28. Her Majesty's Stationery Office, London. Part 1, *Initial planning and design*, 1984; Part 2, *Site management and procedures*, 1985; Part 3, *Working places and access*, 1986; Part 4, *Legislation and training*, 1986.
4. THE CONCRETE SOCIETY and THE INSTITUTION OF STRUCTURAL ENGINEERS. *Formwork: a guide to good practice.* Concrete Society, London, 1986.
5. HURD M. K. *Formwork for concrete.* American Concrete Institute, Detroit, 1979, 4th edn.

Further reading

The reader is referred to the large number of references quoted in *Formwork: a guide to good practice.*[4]

TIMBER RESEARCH AND DEVELOPMENT ASSOCIATION. *Timber in temporary works: a guide to available literature.* (Section on formwork.) TRADA, High Wycombe, 1981.

CHAPTER 11. ERECTION OF STRUCTURAL FRAMES

References

1. BRITISH STANDARDS INSTITUTION. *Code of practice for safety in erecting structural frames.* BS 5531 : 1978. BSI, London.
2. HEALTH AND SAFETY EXECUTIVE. *Safe erection of structures.* Guidance Note GS 28. Her Majesty's Stationery Office, London. Part 1, *Initial planning and design,* 1984; Part 2, *Site management and procedures,* 1985; Part 3, *Working places and access,* 1986; Part 4, *Legislation and training,* 1986.
3. *The Construction (General Provisions) Regulations 1961.* SI 1961 No. 1580. Her Majesty's Stationery Office, London, Part VIII.

Further reading

BRITISH STANDARDS INSTITUTION. *Code of practice for the design of joints and jointing in building construction.* BS 6093 : 1981. BSI, London.

CONCRETE SOCIETY. *Cladding: the provision of compression joints in the cladding of a reinforced concrete building.* Concrete Society, London, 1970, Data Sheet CSI 1.

CONCRETE SOCIETY *et al. Guide to precast concrete cladding.* Concrete Society, London, 1977, Technical Report 14.

CONCRETE SOCIETY *et al. Precast concrete cladding: proceedings of symposium.* Concrete Society, London, 1978.

CHAPTER 13. THE SITE SET-UP

References

1. *The Construction (Health and Welfare) Regulations 1966.* SI 1966 No. 95. Her Majesty's Stationery Office, London.
2. *Fire Certificates (Special Premises) Regulations 1976.* SI 1976 No. 2003. Her Majesty's Stationery Office, London.
3. *Offices, Shops and Railway Premises Act 1963.* Her Majesty's Stationery Office, London, chapter 41.
4. *Highly Flammable Liquids and LPG Regulations 1972.* SI 1972 No. 917. Her Majesty's Stationery Office, London.
5. HEALTH AND SAFETY EXECUTIVE. *Accidents to children on construction sites.* Guidance Note GS 7. Her Majesty's Stationery Office, London, 1977.

Further reading

BUILDING EMPLOYERS CONFEDERATION. *Construction safety.* Building Advisory Service, London; updated regularly. The most comprehensive manual on the legal requirements for construction safety on site. It is practical and easy to read. It should be on all sites.

NATIONAL JOINT COUNCIL FOR THE BUILDING INDUSTRY. *Site safe and you.* NJCBI, London, 1986. A pocket-book designed for lower-level supervision, covering in checklist form all aspects of construction activity that may come under gangers, charge hands and foremen. The law is not detailed at all. If the checklists are complied with, the legal requirements will be satisfied.

Index

Access, off site, problems, 27–30
Access, on site, 30–31
 ground-level obstructions, 31
 overhead obstructions, 30
 underground obstructions, 31–32
Acts of Parliament
 Ancient Monuments and
  Archaeological Areas Act 1979, 17
 Building Act 1984, 16, 38, 104, 105
 City of London (St Paul's Cathedral
  Preservation) Act 1935, 16, 106
 Control of Pollution Act 1974,
  13–14, 41
 Factories Act 1961, 165, see also
  Regulations made under the
  Factories Acts
 GLC General Powers Act 1966, 16,
  104
 Health and Safety at Work etc. Act
  1974, 13, 41, 70, 77, 103, 165
 Highways Acts, 16
 London Buildings Acts
  (Amendment) Act 1939, 16, 104
 London Government Act 1963, 16,
  105
 Offices, Shops and Railway
  Premises Act 1963, 261
 Roads (Scotland) Act 1970, 17
Advisory Committee on Falsework,
 166–167
 report of, 167

Balanced cantilever bridge
 construction, 189
Berlin Wall method, see H-piling
Boundary conditions
 adjacent buildings, 37–38
 adjacent railway property, 38–41
 adjacent trees, 38
 adjoining owners' rights, 37

Box and plate support methods, 114
Bragg committee, reports, 167
British Rail handbook 36, 38, 39
British Standards and codes of
 practice
 BS 3913, Specification for industrial
  safety nets, 93
 BS 4340, Glossary of formwork terms,
  195
 BS 5531, Code of practice for safety
  in erecting sttructural frames, 220
 BS 5973, Code of practice for access
  and working scaffolds..., 77
 BS 5974, Code of practice for
  temporarily installed suspended
  scaffolds..., 77
 BS 5975, Code of practice for
  falsework, 77, 165, 167–169, 174,
  199
 CP 93, The use of safety nets on
  constructional works, 93
 CP 3010, Safe use of cranes, 55
Buildings to be retained on site
 influence on plant and method, 32
 protective measures, 32

Camps, construction site, 271–274
 scales of accommodation, 271
 scales of equipment and furnishings,
  271–274
 tabulations for pricing, 274
 typical layouts, 273
Cantilever scaffolds, 101
Case studies, permanent works used as
 temporary works, 147–164
 Barton anchorage, Humber Bridge,
  152
 contractor and Engineer liaison, 151
 M25–M40 interchange, 158–161
 Piccadilly line extension, 156–158

Case studies—*continued*
redevelopment on sloping site,
161–164
redevelopment site with three
basements, 147–151
redevelopment with five basements,
152–156
Checking of scaffolds, 97
checklist for, 97
statutory requirements, 97
Chemical stabilisation, 136
Cladding, *see* Precast concrete
cladding
Codes of practice, *see* British
Standards and codes of practice
Compounds, provision of, 266–267
perimeter fencing, 266–267
recovery after use, 267
Concrete-placing booms, 63–66
loads on permanent works, 64
rail-mounted types, 64
Construction regulations, *see*
Regulations
Container units, 264–265
anti-vandal, 264
for attractive stores and equipment,
264
Contiguous piling, 139–141, 158
to make watertight, 141
restrictions on use, 141
Control of noise
Control of Pollution Act 1974, 41
influence on method, 41
noise limits, 41
protection against noise: others, 41;
workforce, 41
Cost of temporary works
assessment, 23
excavation example, 23–24
minimising cost, 25
trench support example, 23
Curtain walling, erection of, 232
access for installation when no
external scaffolding, 232

Deep manhole, construction of,
241–245
use of pile liner tube, 241
Designer, temporary works
avoidance of fragmentation of
construction, 26
knowledge of plant and methods, 26
originality of thought, 26

Diaphragm walling, 137–139
advantages, 139
guide walls, 138
principles, 137
Diaphragm walls, guide trenches, *see*
Guide trenches for diaphragm
walls
Drag boxes, 113

Equipment for temporary works
benefits of standardisation, 19
falsework, 22
formwork, 22
H-piling, 20
scaffolding, 20
steel sections, 20–22
Excavation to safe batter, 136
Excavations
adjoining owners' rights, 104
agreements with adjoining owners,
104
damage to existing services, 105–106
legislation, 103–104
support of, 103–136: designed
solutions, 110–111, 117–135;
standard solutions, 110–111;
types of support, 107–108;
without physical structural
additions, 136

Facade retention, 191–194
falsework in new role, 191
guidance, 191
methods of support, 192–194
surveys of existing property, 192
Falsework, 165–194
case studies, 177–188
cost factors, 177, 187
definitions, 165
designed solutions, 169, 174–175:
design brief, 174; design checking,
11, 168
legislation, 165–166
'normal' falsework design, 175–177
procedures, 167–169
special situations, 180–189:
balanced cantilever bridges, 188;
glued segmental prestressed
concrete construction, 188; space
frames, 182, 183–184
standard solutions, 169–174:
compatibility of components, 171;
foundations, 173–174; guidance,
171

Falsework—*continued*
statement of safety policy, 189
Falsework co-ordinator, 165, 168
Forms of contract in the UK, 10
form GC/Works/1, 11–12
ICE form of contract, 10–11
modification to ICE form by
Department of Transport, 11
standard form of building contract,
10
Form of contract overseas, 12
FIDIC (for civil engineering), 12–13
Formwork, 195–219
avoidance, 211: use of precast
elements to improve accuracy and
quality, 211
contractual responsibilities,
196–197: case study, 196–197;
designer role in providing
information, 196
definition, 195
designed solutions, 199, 202–203:
cost factors, 203; high accuracy
needs, 203
economic factors, 197–199: cost of
high accuracy, 199; understanding
where cost lies, 197
flying forms, *see* table forms
guide to good practice, 199
legislation, 195–196
over water, 196
standard solutions, 199, 200–202:
groups of, 200
table forms, 203–206: economics,
203–206
unforeseen loads on, 208–211:
creation by reinforcement spacers,
210; in slipform construction,
210; stacking of material, 210

Glued segmental prestressed concrete
bridge construction, 189
Ground freezing, 136
Grout bags, use as formwork for filling
under viaduct, 259
Guide trenches for diaphragm walls,
245–246
minimising removal cost, 246
sequence of construction, 245

H-piling, scope of use, 118–132
basic method of use, 118–120
examples of use, 124–131
flexibility, 121–123

H-piling—*continued*
value of steel faces, 124
Health and Safety Executive
Guidance Note GS 6, *Avoidance of
danger from overhead electrical
lines*, 30
Guidance Note GS 28, *Safe erection
of structures*, 8, 17, 220
Hoists, 69–76
access from hoist to building, 74–76:
drawbridges, 74; scaffold towers,
74
anchorages to building, 69, 71–74
foundations, 70–71
free-standing conditions, 71
loads taken by ties, 71
Holding-down bolts, location and
positioning, 251–255
assembly, 255
support system, 251
templates, 251
Hydraulic struts, 112–113

Jackleg hutting, 264
foundations, 264
lateral stability in three-tier cases,
264

Libore, *see* Secant piling
London Regional Transport notes for
guidance, 38

Mechanical keys in concrete,
formation of, 216–219
recommended method, 217–219
Mobile cranes, 66–67
foundations for outriggers, 67
provision of stable areas, 66
Mobile work platforms, 97

Noise regulations, 106

Old basements
influence on access, 33
influence on planning, 33

Permanent works used as temporary
works, 137–164
case studies, 147–164
contractual boundaries, 137
contractual relationships, 145–147:
consultant specifying support,
145–146; divisions of
responsibility, 145, 147; examples
in practice, 145–147; when
contractor proposes use, 147

Plant and transport, facilities for
repair and maintenance, 275
Precast concrete, 223–227
erection of units, 225: lifting beams
to provide even lifting, 225;
temporary support while lining
up, 225–227
fixings for temporary support, 224
methods of handling, 223–224
methods of support in store,
223–224
Precast concrete cladding, erection of,
232–238
aids to lining and levelling, 232
'boomerang' lifting device, 233
overhang obstructions to handling,
233–235
procedures, 232
providing for eye-sweet adjustment,
235
temporary lifting beams, 233
Precast concrete cladding to structural
steel, 235–237
accuracy in erection, 237
creeping errors in height, 237
temporary and permanent fixings,
235
torque forces, 237
Precast elements as substitutes for in
situ elements to improve quality
and to minimise temporary
works, 238–240

Re-creation of space on site, 34–36,
149, 153
Regulations, Highly Flammable
Liquids and LPG Regulations,
268
Regulations made under the Factories
Acts
Construction (General Provisions)
Regulations 1961, 14, 30, 70, 77,
103, 166, 196
Construction (Health and Welfare)
Regulations 1966, 15, 166, 260
Construction (Lifting Operations)
Regulations 1961, 15, 70, 106–107,
166
Construction (Working Places)
Regulations 1966, 14–15, 70, 77,
166
Fire Certificates (Special Premises)
Regulations 1976, 15, 260

Reinforcement, influence on formwork,
206–208
case studies, 206–208
detailing, 206
Rock falls, prevention of, 255–256
anti-submarine netting, 256
examples, 256
method, 255
Roofs, space frame, erection of,
231–232
safety netting, 232
temporary supports, stability of,
232
use of permanent work as
temporary support, 231

Safety in falsework, 189
Safety nets, 91–97
British Standards for, 93
use on tall buildings, 93–97
with slipform construction, 91
Safety of buildings in London, 104
Safety of the public
legal requirements, 41
protective measures, 41
Safety on site, 17–18, 268–271
fire precautions, 268
protection of children, 269–270:
liaison with schools, 270; rewards,
270
use of liquid petroleum gases,
268–269
Scaffolding, 77–102
code of practice, 77
design checks by hirer, 88
introductory literature, 77
legislation, 77
method statements, 78–79
model form of contract, 83
model form of quotation, 79
planning for, 78
protection of the public, 83–87
safety conditions, 79–87
standard details, 88
statutory inspections, 88
Scaffold ties, 82–89
for handling plant, 90–91
through windows, 88
to outside structure, 89
Secant piling, 142–145
Libore system, 142–143, 156, 158
Stent Wall method, 143–145
Shields, 113

Short-term scaffolds, 97–99
  form of cost comparison, 98
  v. mobile work platforms, 97
Site amenities, 260–275
  accommodation, 261–267
  legislation, 260–261
  re-creation of space, 262
  storage requirements, 262
Site batching plants, 67–69
  bin walls, 68
  cost of setting up, 68
  temporary works, 68
Site inspections, suitable form for, 27
Site safety, *see* Safety on site
Site services, 267–268
  drainage, 267
  water, electricity, telephone, 267
Skip feeding, improving efficiency,
    249–251
  use of Jubilee track, 251
  use of roller conveyors, 249
  use of turntables, 251
Soldier piling, *see* H-piling
Special situations, 99–102
Steel sheet piling, scope of use,
    132–135
  driving and permissible noise levels,
    135
  modern driving hammers, 135
Steel structures, 227–231
  formwork for casing, 228
  pre-casing methods, 228: cost
    savings, 229; reduction of
    scaffolding, 229
Stent Wall, *see* Secant piling
Stop end forms
  cost of, evaluation of, 211–216
  types, 213–215
Stores, non-secure, 265–266
  form of cover, 265
  items in category, 265
Straining wires to stabilise loads,
    246–248
Strengthening weak brickwork,
    248–249

Structural frames, erection of, 220–240
  legislation, 220–221
  risks to be avoided: temporary
    instability, 221; weaknesses at
    incomplete stages, 221
  temporary works in, 220–223
Structural renovation, *see* Façade
    retention
Support of excavations, *see*
    Excavations

Templates to improve accuracy in
    erection, 237
Temporary works
  definition, 1
  design–construct situation, 6
  education and training, 8–9
  integration with permanent works, 7
  scope of activities, 1
  significance, 6
Tower cranes, temporary works for,
    44–63
  anchorage to structures, 61–63
  climbing types, 55–61: climbing
    collars, 55; cost factors, 57–61;
    dismantling, 57–61; dismantling
    derricks, 59; loads on permanent
    works, 56; mobile rotary tower
    cranes, 57–59; special rigs, 59–61;
    static base design, 56
  rail-mounted types: design of track
    for, 45; track systems, 45–51
  static-base types, 51–55: design of
    base, 51; minimising cost, 53;
    setting up, 55
Trees on site
  effect on method and plant, 32
  protection, 32
Trespass, 42–43
  above and below ground, 42
  legal precedent, 42

Watercourses, 36–37
  need for bridging (temporary), 36
  need for diversions, 36
Well-pointing, 136